AUTHENTIC ASSESSMENT
FOR ENGLISH LANGUAGE LEARNERS

. . . .

PRACTICAL APPROACHES
FOR TEACHERS

. . . .

J. MICHAEL O'MALLEY
LORRAINE VALDEZ PIERCE

Longman

A Publication of the World Language Division

*Vice President and
Director of Product Development:*
Judith M. Bittinger
Executive Editor:
Elinor Chamas
Editorial:
Clare Siska
Cover Design, Interior Design, and Production:
Will Winslow, Graphic Associates
Photography:
Kathy Berry, Polly Colwell, Carmen Danies,
Ellen Egan, Ben Swecker
Production and Manufacturing:
James W. Gibbons

We would like to thank the following teachers
for agreeing to appear in photographs or for
agreeing to let us take pictures in their class-
rooms. In Arlington County Public Schools, the
teachers are Barbara Fagan, Kate Kane, Robin
Liten-Tejada, Laura McDermott, and Elizabeth
Varela; in Fairfax County Public Schools, the
teacher is Kay Huston; in Prince William County
Public Schools, the teachers are Merrille Bittle,
Ginette Cain, Kate Dail, Vincent DiPaolo, Alice
Dzanis, Jennifer Foust, Beverly Hartung, Paul
Jacobs, Becky Patonetz, John Robinson, and
Maria Yackshaw.

We would also like to express our appreciation
to the parents of students in the following
Virginia schools for permitting a photograph of
their children to appear in the book: Gunston
Middle School, Wakefield High School, and
Williamsburg Middle School (Arlington County
Public Schools); Rolling Valley Elementary
School (Fairfax County Public Schools); and
Beville Middle School, Fred Lynn Middle
School, Henderson Elementary School,
McAuliffe Elementary School, and Woodbridge
High School (Prince William County Public
Schools).

See the Index of Figures and Reproducibles,
page viii, for a list of pages that may be repro-
duced for classroom use.

FOREWORD

. . . .

During the past 15 years, two themes have dominated public discourse on education in North America: (1) the perceived need for public schools to demonstrate more accountability to the societies that fund them, and (2) ways in which schools should accommodate to the rapid growth in cultural and linguistic diversity in urban centers and, specifically, ways of addressing the persistent educational underachievement of many students from culturally diverse backgrounds.

Debates on these issues have been volatile and frequently confused. (See Cummins and Sayers, 1995,[1] for a review). Not surprisingly, policy initiatives have often been contradictory. For example, in some states calls for greater accountability have been translated into increased use of standardized tests, while in others authentic assessment approaches have been vigorously pursued. Similarly, in some contexts we find examples of innovative and visionary approaches to the instruction of English language learners (ELLs) at the same time as policy-makers in other contexts are reverting to discredited "sink-or-swim" programs in response to the renewed xenophobic rhetoric against all forms of diversity.

Issues of diversity and assessment have intersected frequently throughout this century. In the early decades, standardized IQ tests were mobilized by eugenics advocates in order to weed out and repatriate what they called "feeble-minded aliens." Standardized tests, together with ineffective educational programs, were also responsible for the massive over-representation of culturally diverse students in special education programs which came to public attention during the 1960s and 1970s. More recently, the concern has been that because it usually requires at least five years for ELL stu-

---

1. Cummins, J., and D. Sayers. 1995. *Brave New Schools: Challenging Cultural Illiteracy through Global Learning Networks*. New York: St. Martin's Press.

dents to catch up academically in English, standardized achievement tests are likely to underestimate students' academic progress and potential to a very significant extent. This form of inappropriate assessment can distort both program placement and teachers' academic expectations for ELL students.

When these specific concerns about the uses of standardized tests with culturally diverse students are added to the more general concerns that such tests focus primarily on lower-level cognitive skills and tend to squeeze higher-order thinking and creative writing out of the curriculum, the rationale for exploring alternatives is compelling indeed. Teachers have welcomed the possibility of assessment strategies that permit students to demonstrate the entire scope of what they have learned and that provide guidance to both teachers and students about effective directions for continued learning. However, they have also been concerned and sometimes frustrated by the fact that authentic assessment procedures have appeared time-consuming and cumbersome and in some cases overly subjective.

This volume, I believe, is the answer to the prayers of many teachers and administrators. J. Michael O'Malley and Lorraine Valdez Pierce have synthesized in a lucid, practical, and theoretically sophisticated way the major strategies for implementing authentic assessment in the classroom and the school as a whole. Procedures for ensuring reliability and validity are clearly outlined in language and content areas across the curriculum, thereby addressing concerns that authentic assessment entails sacrificing objectivity. In fact, it is very clear from the procedures and examples discussed throughout this volume that it is only through authentic assessment that real validity can be attained. This is particularly the case for ELL students. Authentic assessment is tied directly to the curriculum that students have experienced within the classroom, thereby permitting students to demonstrate the linguistic and academic progress that they have made and the extent to which they have attained curricular goals that are realistic for the time period they have been learning English. By contrast, most standardized tests assess knowledge and skills that are not specific to the curriculum of any classroom and certainly not to the learning histories of ELL students.

What many teachers and administrators have not realized up to this point is that authentic assessment is highly cost-effective both from a time perspective and from the perspective of maximizing the impact of instruction. As the authors point out, assessment and instruction are two interlocking and interdependent components of any educational program. Thus, the assessment procedures described in this volume are not external to the instructional process; they are an integral part of it. They formalize and organize the monitoring of student progress that many teachers do intuitively and in a non-systematic way. This permits teachers to discover much more about their students' prior knowledge, language needs, and learning progress and greatly increases the effectiveness of feedback they give to students. By contrast, most standardized assessment is an "add-on" process that takes time away from and frequently contributes very little to instruction apart from a score whose accuracy for ELL students is questionable.

An additional way in which the authentic assessment approach advocated by the authors contributes to instruction is through the creative involvement of students in all phases of the process. Students are respected as partners in a learning relationship. They are active constructors of their own knowledge and do not have to be coerced into learning. Establishment of this kind of collaborative relationship between teacher and student is fundamental to generating a sense of trust and belonging among all students, but especially so among ELL students. Many ELL students are trying to find their way in the borderlands between cultures and the collaborative teacher-student relationship established in the context of authentic assessment generates a sense of confidence, trust, and power that fuels students' classroom participation.

As we move towards the next millennium in an age of information explosion, it is common to hear educators, business leaders, and policy-makers stress the need for life-long learning. Schools should be producing students who know how to set their own learning goals and who are capable and motivated to pursue these goals efficiently. The authors of this timely volume have provided a blueprint for how educators can guide ELL students to take control of their own learning and become independent thinkers and users of language. They have also shown how schools can respond to calls for accountability in ways that augment and enhance the learning process rather than subtract from it.

Jim Cummins
Professor, Curriculum Department
Ontario Institute for Studies in Education
December 1995

TABLE OF CONTENTS

• • • • • • • • • • • • • • •

INDEX OF FIGURES
AND REPRODUCIBLES

• • • • • • • • • • • • • • • •

Those figures designated by a ♦ may be repro-
duced for classroom use.

PREFACE

· · · · · · · · · · · · · · · · · ·

We have written this book to provide teachers of English language learners (ELLs)[1] with approaches for using authentic assessment and for applying the results of assessment to instruction. The book emerged out of numerous requests from teachers of ELL students who identified the need for informative assessment procedures that are sensitive to the needs of students and reflect current approaches to instruction. These teachers wanted to have access to observation procedures and ways of assessing student work that would strengthen their ability to provide effective instruction and prepare ELL students for grade-level classrooms. This book is an effort to address the need these teachers identified and to provide you, the teacher, with a broad range of interesting and useful assessment techniques. Our intent is to offer an array from which you can select authentic assessment approaches that are most suitable in your own classroom.

The book is written on behalf of ELL students. We believe that the educational strengths and needs of these students can be identified most effectively through multiple forms of assessment. The use of authentic, multiple assessments should provide these students with varied opportunities to demonstrate what they know and can do. ELL students are often asked to demonstrate their knowledge and skills in a limited variety of ways that do not enable them to communicate successfully with their teachers. By offering an extended menu of authentic assessment techniques, we hope to enable students to become more effective in assessing and conveying their own knowledge, skills, and strategies. This should support self-directed learning, increased motivation, and learner autonomy.

Assessment is authentic when it corresponds to and mirrors good classroom instruction. When students participate in authentic assessment, neither they nor an observer in the classroom should be able to tell any difference between the assessment and other interesting and engaging instructional activities. A key element in authentic assessment is informed teacher judgment, or judgment in which your professional evaluation of the results is valued and respected. The assessment is also authentic when the results can be used to improve instruction based on accurate knowledge of student progress. This is essential in making assessment authentic because both you and your students should find assessment to be important for improving teaching and learning. *Authentic* implies that tasks used in assessment are valued in the real world by students.

In responding to a need for improved assessment procedures, we have attempted to link the assessments to major changes occurring in research and practice. We did not feel that it was enough to present you with a book of forms or observation procedures for rating student performance without also describing their connection to innovative instructional approaches. We have found that teachers see more ways to use authentic assessment in their classrooms and to apply assessments in meaningful ways when they have a larger picture of how the assessments relate to major innovations in curriculum and instruction. Because we were selective in what we presented as context, this book gives us an opportunity to show teachers what we think is important in instruction as well as in assessment. In this regard, we have presented a series of vignettes in the last chapter to illustrate the close connection between assessment and instruction and to illustrate what we believe to be good assessment practices. Some teachers may wish to read these vignettes before reading the rest of the book to get a picture of authentic assessment in action. We have also provided a series of suggested application activities at the end of other chapters that give continued opportunities to try out some of the procedures.

The assessment techniques in this book originated from a series of workshops and presentations

---

1. We use the term *English language learners* or *English language learning (ELL)* students instead of the more customary *limited English proficient (LEP)* because we prefer the more positive emphasis.

on authentic assessment we have conducted over a period of years for teachers of ELL students. The topics of these presentations included assessment in all four language skills—listening, speaking, reading, writing—and covered integrated assessment of language and content in mathematics, science, and social studies. We gave these presentations and workshops at conferences and special sessions on assessment held for teachers and administrators in English as a Second Language (ESL) and bilingual programs. These activities were conducted as part of the Georgetown University Evaluation Assistance Center (EAC)-East, a technical assistance center funded by the U.S. Department of Education under Title VII of the Elementary and Secondary Education Act. Through the EAC-East, we were able to meet with and provide technical assistance to administrators and teachers in programs for ELL students in numerous states in the eastern half of the country as well as at meetings and conferences across the states.

We appreciate the time taken by Jim Cummins and Joan Herman, whose writings we greatly respect, to read the manuscript and provide us with their comments. Cummins's views on education and assessment for ELL students are reflected in the foreword to this book. Herman's comments add a perspective from research on authentic assessment, policy, and practice with native speakers of English.

We are grateful to the many teachers who provided us with feedback on the assessment approaches we introduced in the presentations and workshops we have conducted. We are especially grateful to teachers and teacher supervisors who commented on drafts of the manuscript, and wish to give a special note of appreciation to the following: Margo Gottlieb of the Illinois Resource Center for her detailed reading of the full manuscript, Sandra Fradd of the University of Miami and Toni Ogimachi of CTB/McGraw Hill for also reading the draft manuscript. We thank Mary Helman of Fairfax County Public Schools, Virginia and Mary Ellen Quinn, Visiting Professor of Mathematics at Our Lady of the Lake University, San Antonio, Texas for their careful reading and many helpful suggestions with the chapter on assessment in the content areas. We are also grateful to teachers and staff developers from Virginia's public schools who read and commented on various chapters. In Arlington Public Schools, Virginia, these included Barbara Fagan and Lee Gough. In Fairfax County Public Schools, Virginia, the teachers were Carol Beck, Fran Dixon, Mary Lou Kulsick, Becky Miskill, Diana Poodiak, and Claire Waller. In Prince William County Public Schools, teachers who read selected chapters were Kate Dail, Kristen Misencik, and Rhonda Shaw. Varya Trueheart, from Montgomery County Public Schools, Maryland, also served as a reviewer.

Despite all the excellent assistance we received on the initial drafts of this book, the possibility remains for errors of omission or commission, which are solely the responsibility of the authors.

We would also like to thank the teachers who, as graduate students in Dr. Valdez Pierce's assessment and curriculum development courses, developed sample formats for their ELL students and allowed us to use them. These teachers include: Steve Copley, Jennifer Eury, Donna O'Neill, Lisa Morse, Mark Crossman, Karen Harrison, and Claire Waller. A special thank you to Nancy Romeo of Rolling Valley Elementary School, Fairfax County Public Schools, Virginia, for providing us with her student's portfolio.

We would also like to acknowledge a number of others who contributed to this project in various ways, most especially our families and close friends, whose support and patience enabled us to maintain the semblance of a social life in the midst of isolated evenings and weekends working. We wish to thank our editor, Clare Siska, who assisted us through weekly cycles of editing, revising, and formatting. The support and enthusiasm of Evelyn Nelson, Manager for ESL/Bilingual Marketing at Addison-Wesley, were particularly important when the book was in the early conceptual stages. We are also indebted to Elinor Chamas, Executive Editor for ESL/EFL at Addison-Wesley, for her continuing support and most particularly for living with unforeseen delays in writing, and to Judith Bittinger, Vice President and Director of Product Development, for her support and interest in the project.

We are always interested in new experiences in assessment and in your own examples describing the link between assessment and instruction. We encourage you to contact us with your ideas so that we can continue to expand the contributions good assessment practices can make to other teachers and to ELL students.

J. Michael O'Malley
Office of Assessment and Evaluation
Prince William County Public Schools
14800 Joplin Road
P. O. Box 389
Manassas, Virginia 22110

Lorraine Valdez Pierce
Graduate School of Education
George Mason University
MSN 4B3
4400 University Drive
Fairfax, Virginia 22030-4444

MOVING TOWARD AUTHENTIC ASSESSMENT

· ·

Over the past decade we have seen a rapid expansion of interest in alternatives to traditional forms of assessment in education (Aschbacher 1991; Herman, Aschbacher, and Winters 1992). The form of assessment used for both standardized testing and classroom assessment for as long as most educators can remember is the multiple-choice test. While this type of test has been a mainstay of educational programs, educators from all backgrounds have raised concerns about its usefulness as a primary measure of student achievement and

are seeking alternatives through multiple forms of assessment. These educators are also seeking assessments that more closely resemble instructional activities in classrooms.

Alternative assessment consists of any method of finding out what a student knows or can do that is intended to show growth and inform instruction, and is an alternative to traditional forms of testing, namely, multiple-choice tests (Stiggins 1991). Alternative assessment is by definition criterion-referenced and is typically authentic because it is based on activities that represent classroom and real-life settings. We use the term *authentic assessment* throughout this book to describe the multiple forms of assessment that are consistent with classroom goals, curricula, and instruction.

The increased interest in authentic assessment is based on two major issues: current assessment procedures do not assess the full range of essential student outcomes, and teachers have difficulty using the information gained for instructional planning. Educators have questioned "fill in the bubble" or multiple-choice tests because these forms of assessment are not adequate to assess the full range of higher-order thinking skills considered important in today's curriculum. Further, these types of tests do not represent recent improvements in our understanding of what and how students learn (Resnick and Klopfer 1989). Multiple-choice tests, while objective and highly reliable for most students, have emphasized the assessment of discrete skills and do not contain authentic representations of classroom activities. The tests therefore lack the content validity considered important to ensure student interest and motivation during assessment. In their classrooms, students read interesting literature, write papers, integrate resource information with personal viewpoints, work on projects cooperatively, share information while summarizing their conclusions, and use information from one content area (like mathematics) to solve problems and display information in other content areas. Little of the knowledge and strategic processes needed to accomplish these tasks is captured in multiple-choice or single-answer tests.

Teachers question the overdependence on a single type of assessment because test scores sometimes disagree with conclusions they have reached from observing how students actually perform in classrooms. Teachers need information to gauge whether students are making progress, if they respond to instructional approaches and materials, and if they accomplish the kinds of complex learning expected in today's curriculum. The information teachers need for instructional planning concerns the very type of complex and varied student learning that is difficult to assess with multiple-choice tests. Teachers need information about

integrative language and content knowledge rather than isolated pieces of knowledge and skills. What teachers gain from daily contact with students is an understanding of the processes by which students learn as well as the products of their learning. They also rely on multiple ways of collecting information that provide them with the type of feedback they need to monitor student progress and to plan for instruction.

In addition to the issues raised by teachers, administrators and education policy analysts have been concerned that the knowledge and skills students will need to function effectively in a future technological and complex society are inadequately represented in multiple-choice tests. Because teachers tend to focus instruction on the skills emphasized in testing, multiple-choice tests have had the long-term effect of limiting the curriculum to isolated and lower-level skills (Resnick and Klopfer 1989). The ability to accurately select one of a number of options to brief questions does not reflect what students will be called on to do in solving complex problems, communicating significant ideas, persuading others on important positions, organizing information and managing human resources, and working cooperatively with others in the workplace (Wiggins 1989, 1993). Policy analysts and administrators are looking for evidence of accountability that schools are successful in producing a new generation of students with skills that will be required in the decades to come. Because teachers and administrators both sense the need for new forms of assessment, the development of new measures has become all the more important and is likely to thrive as an important component of instructional programs.

While there has been a high degree of interest in authentic assessment in general education, as evidenced by the number of articles and books appearing on the topic, there are relatively few articles and monographs on alternative assessment with language minority students (students who speak a language other than English as their first language and/or come from an environment where a language other than English is spoken). The more general articles and books on alternative assessment, while often useful, do not focus on the specific needs of language minority students and often fail to provide specific examples that teachers can use in classrooms. Thus, schools must search deeply to find the information they need to assess these students and to monitor their educational progress. In addition to these instructional needs in assessment, school districts continually have difficulty in making effective decisions about the level of English language proficiency necessary for the participation of English language learning[1] (ELL) students in district or statewide testing programs (O'Malley and Valdez Pierce 1994).

Assessment of English Language Learning Students

. . . .

For at least three decades, teachers and program administrators have struggled to identify appropriate procedures to assess the knowledge and abilities of ELL students. The path has been difficult in part because of the need to identify varying levels of knowledge and proficiency in English and in part because the purposes of assessment with language minority students are so varied and complex. Assessment information is needed by administrators, teachers, staff developers, students, and parents to assist in determining appropriate program placements and instructional activities as well as in monitoring student progress.

Accurate and effective assessment of language minority students is essential to ensure that ELL students gain access to instructional programs that meet their needs. The failure of assessment and instruction to interact effectively is most evident when inappropriate assessment approaches lead to inaccurate identification, improper program place

ments, inadequate monitoring of student progress, and the long-term failure of instruction (Cummins 1984). Conversely, appropriate assessment has the potential to ensure that these students are on course to becoming literate and able participants in English language classroom settings.

With ELL students, assessment is far more complex and challenging than with native speakers of English. Assessment is used for at least six purposes with ELL students:

1. *Screening and identification:* to identify students eligible for special language and/or content area support programs

2. *Placement:* to determine the language proficiency and content area competencies of students in order to recommend an appropriate educational program

3. *Reclassification or exit:* to determine if a student has gained the language skills and content area competencies needed to benefit from instruction in grade-level classrooms[2], (i.e., from all-English programs not specifically designed to address the needs of ELL students)

4. *Monitoring student progress:* to review student language and content area learning in classrooms

5. *Program evaluation:* to determine the effects of federal, state, or local instructional programs

6. *Accountability:* to guarantee that students attain expected educational goals or standards, including testing for high school graduation

Many schools assess skills in the student's native language as well as in English, thereby expanding the range of assessment with ELL students. Because of these varying purposes and audiences, consensus on the appropriate procedures for assessment of language minority students has been difficult to attain.

In spite of this general lack of agreement, most educators do agree that standardized, norm-refer

1. The term *limited English proficient* or *LEP* is typically used to describe non-native speakers of English who experience difficulty in profiting from instruction in English. We prefer the term *English language learners (ELLs)* or *English language learning (ELL)* students because of the more positive emphasis on what the students are learning rather than on their supposed limitations. ELL students are part of a larger population of language minority students who speak a language other than English as their first language and/or who come from a background where a language other than English is used. We use the term *language minority* because of its broader implications in the United States population even though language minority groups may be dominant in some local school districts.

2. The term *grade-level classrooms* is borrowed from Enright and McCloskey (1989) and refers to classrooms with grade-appropriate content materials. In grade-level classrooms, reclassified ELL students learn along with native English-speaking students. We prefer the term *grade-level* over *mainstream*, which has connotations from special education and may be inappropriate where the local student population is largely from language minority backgrounds.

enced tests are inappropriate for ELL students. Traditional forms of assessment such as standardized tests are inappropriate for ELL students for a variety of reasons. Standardized tests use multiple-choice items, a format that may be unfamiliar to students with limited experience in U.S. public schools. Moreover, multiple-choice items assume a level of English language proficiency that ELL students may not have acquired. The subtle distinctions made on various items for vocabulary, word analysis, reading, and listening subtests may produce information on what the student *does not* know but little information about what the student *does* know. This gives the teacher an incomplete picture of student needs and strengths. The language components of standardized tests mainly assess reading and vocabulary knowledge and ignore progress in written and oral language, important components of language-based instructional programs. Standardized tests in content areas, such as math and science, may not assess what ELL students know because of the complexity of the language in which the questions are asked. These tests have not been effective in assessing the higher-order thinking skills students use in solving problems, analyzing texts, or evaluating ideas (Resnick and Klopfer 1989). Virtually all schools administer standardized tests once a year, leaving teachers without regular information throughout the school year on what students have learned. Even formal language testing for oral proficiency is typically conducted only once annually. Without additional assessments tailored to the needs of ELL students, teachers are unable to plan instruction effectively or make accurate decisions about student needs and progress.

The previous discussion does not suggest that there is no role for standardized testing in school district or state assessment programs or in the assessment of former ELL students. Standardized tests have an important role in at least four components of an overall testing program: (1) to compare individual or group performance with an external normative group, (2) to identify relative strengths and weaknesses in skill areas, (3) to monitor annual growth in skills, and (4) for program evaluation (Hoover 1995). With former ELL students, standardized tests can be used for accountability to ensure that these students are progressing effectively in grade-level classrooms once they no longer need special language and/or content area supports (O'Malley and Valdez Pierce 1994). As we have noted, however, these uses of standardized tests do not cover the full range of assessment needs for ELL students.

Past critics of standardized testing with language minority students have had limited success in proposing acceptable alternatives, except to suggest administering tests in the student's native language. Unfortunately, the same type of tests have been recommended in the native language as are typically administered in English, thereby not extending the argument into new areas of assessment and not allowing for multiple ways of assessing knowledge and skills. Recently, educators have offered more varied suggestions for improving the assessment of ELL students (e.g., Fradd, McGee, and Wilen 1994; Garcia and Ortiz 1988; Navarette et al. 1990; O'Malley and Valdez Pierce 1991; Valdez Pierce and O'Malley 1992; Short 1993).

Definition of Authentic Assessment

• • • • • • • • • • • • • • • •

We use the term *authentic assessment* to describe the multiple forms of assessment that reflect student learning, achievement, motivation, and attitudes on instructionally-relevant classroom activities. Examples of authentic assessment include performance assessment, portfolios, and student self-assessment.

Performance assessment consists of any form of assessment in which the student constructs a response orally or in writing (Feuer and Fulton 1993; Herman, Aschbacher, and Winters 1992). The student response may be elicited by the teacher in formal or informal assessment contexts or may be observed during classroom instructional or non-instructional settings. Performance assessment requires students to "accomplish complex and significant tasks, while bringing to bear prior knowledge, recent learning, and relevant skills to solve realistic or authentic problems" (Herman, Aschbacher, and Winters, p. 2). Students may be called on to use materials or perform hands-on activities in reaching solutions to problems. Examples are oral reports, writing samples, individual and group projects, exhibitions, and demonstrations.

Some of the characteristics of performance assessment are the following (adapted from Aschbacher 1991; Herman, Aschbacher, and Winters 1992):

1. *Constructed Response:* students construct a response, provide an expanded response, engage in a performance, or create a product

2. *Higher-order Thinking:* the student typically uses higher levels of thinking in constructing responses to open-ended questions

3. *Authenticity:* tasks are meaningful, challenging, and engaging activities that mirror good instruction or other real-world contexts where the student is expected to perform

4. *Integrative:* the tasks call for integration of language skills and, in some cases, for integration of knowledge and skills across content areas

5. *Process and Product:* procedures and strategies for deriving the correct response or for exploring multiple solutions to complex tasks are often assessed as well (as or sometimes instead of) the product or the "correct" answer

6. *Depth Versus Breadth:* performance assessments provide information in depth about a student's skills or mastery as contrasted with the breadth of coverage more typical of multiple-choice tests

Performance assessment often requires teacher judgment of student responses. To aid in making the judgments accurate and reliable, a scoring scale referred to as a *rubric* is used, in which numerical values are associated with performance levels, such as 1 = Basic, 2 = Proficient, and 3 = Advanced. The criteria for each performance level must be precisely defined in terms of what the student actually does to demonstrate skill or proficiency at that level. One of the characteristics of performance assessment is that the criteria are made public and known in advance (Aschbacher 1991). Accordingly, students can participate in set-ting and using the criteria in self-assessment of their own performance.

Portfolio assessment is a systematic collection of student work that is analyzed to show progress over time with regard to instructional objectives (Valencia 1991). Examples of portfolio entries include writing samples, reading logs, drawings, audio or videotapes, and/or teacher and student comments on progress made by the student. One of the defining features of portfolio assessment is the involvement of students in selecting samples of their own work to show growth or learning over time.

Student *self-assessment* is a key element in authentic assessment and in self-regulated learning, "the motivated and strategic efforts of students to accomplish specific purposes" (Paris and Ayers 1994, p. 26). Self-assessment promotes direct involvement in learning and the integration of cognitive abilities with motivation and attitude toward learning. In becoming self-regulated learners, students make choices, select learning activities, and plan how to use their time and resources. They have the freedom to choose challenging activities, take risks, advance their own learning, and accomplish desired goals. Because students have control over their learning, they can decide how to use the resources available to them within or outside the classroom. Students who are self-regulated learners collaborate with other students in exchanging ideas, eliciting assistance when needed, and providing support to their peers. As they go about learning, these types of students construct meaning, revise their understandings, and share meaning with others. These students take pride in their efforts and in the new meanings they construct because they see the connection between their efforts and learning success. Finally, self-regulated learners monitor their own performance and evaluate their progress and accomplishments (Paris and Ayers 1994). Self-assessment and self-management are at the core of this type of learning and should be a regular part of instruction.

Because we believe assessment is inextricably tied to instruction, our suggestions for using authentic assessment imply changes in instruction. For example, you cannot use portfolios without changing your philosophy of teaching and learning from one which is transmission-oriented to one which is learner-centered. Student input and ownership are defining elements in portfolios and in authentic assessment in general. In learner-centered classrooms, students have input not only into what they learn, but also into how they will be assessed. Student self-assessment and reflection are critical to the view of assessment and learning we propose.

Authentic assessment is important for ELL students as well as for students in grade-level classrooms. Teachers of language minority students have benefited from the interest of the general education community in authentic assessment and are adding to this repertoire of new assessment procedures. With ELL students, teachers using authentic assessment can assess students at all levels of proficiency for language and content knowledge in both English and in their native language.

The use of authentic assessment places greater demands on teachers than the use of single-answer tests. Time and management skills are needed to design and use these assessments, and judgment is required in reaching conclusions about student learning and student progress. Because authentic assessment is relatively new, few teachers have had sustained professional development opportunities on the design, creation, and use of these assessment procedures. The changing models of student learning and instruction also require teachers to understand the reasons for the new directions in assessment and how to link assessment with instruction.

Purposes of This Book and Target Audience

· · · · · · · · · · · · · · · ·

This book is designed for teachers, teacher trainers, administrators, and assessment specialists who work with ELL students. We present an overview and rationale for authentic assessment and a framework for the assessment of ELL students at all grade levels. The book focuses on portfolios and practical examples of assessment procedures used to collect information on ELL students in

English as a second language (ESL) and bilingual programs, and in grade-level classrooms. We describe assessment procedures for second language learners in language arts and in the content areas. The examples we use are largely K-12, although the assessment procedures are often applicable to early childhood and adult settings. We have tried to introduce a variety of assessment procedures and a number of ways of looking at student performance that will provide teachers with a balanced view of learning. We also describe assessment procedures that can be used for identification and placement of English language learners, monitoring of student progress, and reclassification of students who are ready to exit special language programs and enter grade-level classrooms.

The assessment procedures described in this book will benefit all teachers working with students who need to strengthen their language skills. In addition to ELL students, these include students in any second language context and Title I students. Teachers may use these assessment procedures whether they work in their own classroom, on interdisciplinary teams, or with content area teachers in collaborative settings.

While teachers spend as much as 20-30 percent of their professional time involved in assessment-related activities (Stiggins 1988), pre- and in-service programs to date have not familiarized teachers with issues in authentic assessment, nor have they prepared them to design and use this type of assessment for instructional planning. Teachers in some states are not required to take an assessment course, and most college and university courses in assessment tend to be very traditional. Such courses cover the different types of tests used in education, various standardized tests, different types of test items, the meaning of test scores, test construction in classrooms, some rudimentary statistics necessary for classroom testing, and grading practices. These courses do not cover the design, construction, and use of performance assessments, student portfolios, anecdotal records, reading logs, running records, and other types of assessment discussed in the performance assessment literature and covered in this book. Furthermore, these courses for the most part do not address the assessment of language minority and ELL students in any significant manner.

Authentic assessment places heavy demands on teachers' professional skills. In comparison to multiple-choice testing, where judgments are made based on a curve or on the percent of correct items, these new assessment procedures call for more independent judgment and interpretation of student performance (Herman, Aschbacher, and Winters 1992). Furthermore, authentic assessments take time and careful planning to be used effectively. Teachers need staff development and support to design and use performance assessments that effectively address multidisciplinary understanding and critical thinking skills (Khattri, Kane, and Reeve 1995). Without opportunities to collaborate with other teachers, to try out new assessments, and to discuss the assessments they are using, teachers will almost certainly have problems in advancing beyond rudimentary uses of these new approaches.

Overview of the Book

. . . .

We have introduced this book by presenting some background information about general assessment issues, about authentic forms of assessment, and about specific issues in the assessment of language minority students. We view assessment and instruction as interlocking parts of educational programs and believe that assessment must be an integral part of instruction.

We continue in Chapter 2 by presenting an overview of authentic assessment, including performance and portfolio assessments. We describe specific types of authentic assessment and issues in designing these assessments, and bring essential assessment concepts of reliability and validity together with authentic assessment procedures. We also discuss how to design authentic assessments and lay out a series of steps that teachers can apply in working with other teachers to design and use performance assessments and portfolios. This chapter is particularly important for teachers working in grade-level or school teams on authentic

assessments and contains suggestions for staff development.

In Chapter 3 we present a more detailed overview of portfolio assessment and explain how to integrate the information collected from classroom assessment in a portfolio. We describe different types of portfolios, the purposes of portfolio assessment, issues that are relevant to the use of portfolios, specific steps in portfolio design, and suggestions for using portfolios in instruction. Throughout this chapter we describe the changing role of teachers and students in using portfolios. We also discuss procedures for communicating information about portfolios to parents so that portfolios are useful in helping parents understand their children's progress.

Chapters 4-7 discuss assessment approaches that have special relevance to teachers of ELL students and show how these procedures can be used in conjunction with portfolio assessment in classrooms. These chapters focus on assessment of oral language (Chapter 4), reading (Chapter 5), writing (Chapter 6), and assessment in the content areas (Chapter 7). Teachers looking for assessment at the different grade levels will find examples addressing their needs throughout these chapters. The use of separate chapters on the language skills is a convenience only, and does *not* imply that we believe these skills should either be taught or assessed in isolation.

We begin Chapters 4-7 with an overview of the instructional context in each area and highlight advances in thinking about instruction that urge the use of authentic assessment. We review the purposes of assessment in each subject for administrative or instructional applications. We then define specific assessment approaches, give examples that teachers can use, and provide sample scoring rubrics for various assessment procedures. In each of these chapters we point out the importance of self-assessment and indicate methods teachers can use to support student self-assessment. We include numerous tables and figures containing scoring rubrics and assessment techniques throughout the book. At the conclusion of each chapter we discuss how teachers can use the assessments in instruction. While teachers use performance assessment during instruction in a variety of ways—to share performance expectations with students and to introduce project-based tasks (Khattri, Kane, and Reeve 1995)—we also emphasize uses to monitor student progress and to assist in planning for future instruction.

The final chapter provides examples from the classroom in which teachers have used authentic assessment. In these examples, teachers have embedded assessment in instruction so that the result appears to the students (or to an observer) as nothing more than an interesting instructional activity. From these activities, however, teachers and students derive feedback on student performance from self-assessment, from peer evaluation, and/or from the teacher's assessment of the student. These examples illustrate that setting time aside to conduct authentic assessment in classrooms requires the creative integration of assessment with an instructional activity the teacher had already planned. The teachers in these examples relied on their professional leadership qualities to introduce and use innovative approaches to assessment when their background may not have prepared them for using authentic assessment, when other teachers in their school held to more traditional assessment approaches, and when careful preparation and sustained commitment were required to communicate student performance on the new assessments to parents.

DESIGNING AUTHENTIC ASSESSMENT

· ·

This chapter lays the groundwork for designing, developing, and using authentic assessments and introduces a variety of these assessment approaches. We begin with a description of teaching and learning models that underlie authentic assessment and note their implications for assessment procedures. We continue with a general review of various types of authentic assessment and the unique advantages of each. We then describe steps teachers can use to design authentic assessments for classrooms. We include a description of scoring

rubrics and how to score performance assessments, an important consideration with open-ended questions. As in the design of any assessment, two issues that need to be addressed in performance assessment are validity and reliability. Reliability is particularly important when scoring depends on professional judgment. We review procedures to ensure that the performance measures you design are valid and reliable. We conclude this chapter by identifying important issues that are of concern in all assessment practices, such as clarifying the purpose of the assessment, fairness in assessment, and grading practices.

Approaches to Teaching and Learning

• • • • • • • • • • • • • • • • •

In the first chapter we noted that one of the reasons for the increasing attention to complex thinking skills in educational curricula has been improvements in our understanding of what and how students learn. Until recently, education has been based on a "transmission" model of instruction, in which it was assumed that knowledge consisted of discrete facts to be learned by students. In this model, teachers and curriculum designers were presumed to possess the knowledge and skills students needed to learn. The role of teachers was to transmit this information to learners, and the role of students was to acquire this information rapidly and thoroughly. Students needed to learn a common set of basic skills in reading and computation as a foundation for learning more complex skills and applications of information. In this view learning is linear, and once the basic skills are learned, students should be able to combine subskills in order to perform more complex forms of school learning. Textual information is presented to students on the assumption that students will listen to or read this information and be able to answer questions about it accurately. Assessment using multiple-choice tests was considered appropriate because there was always one correct answer and students should be able to select this answer from among a number of alternatives.

In more recent views of teaching and learning, referred to as *constructivism*, all individuals are thought to learn by constructing information about the world and by using active and dynamic mental processes (e.g., Jones et al. 1987; Marzano, Pickering, and McTighe 1993; Resnick and Klopfer 1989). Students learn to read through these active mental processes, and they learn information in the content areas by constructing personal meaning from new information and prior knowledge.

Students learn most effectively through integrative experiences in programs that reflect the interdependence of listening, speaking, reading, writing, thinking, direct experience, and purposeful student interaction. As students listen or read, they question what they need to know, select information of importance, relate it to what they already know, retain what they consider to be important, and apply the information under appropriate circumstances. Students also reflect on what they have learned and relate it to their original learning goals (i.e., they use metacognitive processes in planning, monitoring, and evaluating their own learning). Basically, learning does not proceed by the accumulation of a common set of basic skills but can follow multiple strategies and pathways. Students vary in how they learn, among other ways, by establishing different goals for learning, by selecting different information to use in constructing new knowledge, and by using different strategies to aid in learning (Gagné, Yekovich, and Yekovich 1993; O'Malley and Chamot 1990; Pressley and Associates 1990; Weinstein and Mayer 1986).

IMPLICATIONS FOR ASSESSMENT

This analysis of learning has direct implications for authentic assessment. If students construct information as they learn, and apply the information in classroom settings, assessment should provide the students with opportunities to construct responses and to apply their learning to problems that mirror their classroom activities in authentic ways. If students acquire both knowledge and procedures, they should be called upon to demonstrate familiarity with new knowledge and to exhibit the problem-solving and other skills they have acquired. If complex thinking and academic language skills are important components of today's curriculum, assessment should reflect these emphases. And if students learn complex procedures most effectively when they have opportunities to apply the skills in meaningful ways, then assessments should be authentic reflections of these kinds of meaningful learning opportunities.

Types of Authentic Assessment

There are numerous types of authentic assessment used in classrooms today (Feuer and Fulton 1993). The range of possibilities is sufficiently broad that teachers can select from a number of options to meet specific purposes or adapt approaches to meet instructional and student needs. Teachers already use many of these types of assessments but do so in a relatively informal way that does not provide systematic information about student learning or about the goals of instruction. As you read through the types of assessment, we encourage you to think of the ways in which you already use some of these assessment procedures and to speculate on ways in which you can make these types of assessment better serve your needs in instruction.

We list a range of authentic assessments in Figure 2.1, describe each, and note some of their advantages. In later chapters we describe in detail how these procedures can be used for specific purposes, such as assessing language proficiency or content-area learning. In Figure 2.1 we include a variety of performance assessments—oral interviews, text retelling, writing samples, etc.—plus teacher observation of student knowledge and skills in the classroom. The last item listed, portfolios, is often used to integrate the results of individual performance assessments and to monitor learning over time. We have not listed self-assessment as a separate category because it should be involved in all of the types of assessment identified (apart from teacher observation).

ORAL INTERVIEWS

The oral proficiency of ELL students should be assessed regularly, especially with very young students or when students have yet to acquire sufficient command over the language for written assessments to be appropriate. Students can respond orally to questions about a range of topics that might include their prior knowledge, activities, and interests or preferences. The teacher may be interested either in the substantive information collected or in judging the student's proficiency in responding to the questions, both of which can be used for instructional planning. In this type of assessment, teachers can ask probe questions to determine student comprehension or command over specific aspects of the language. Teachers of ELL students in one school system told us they did not provide instruction for oral proficiency "because it was not being tested by the county." You may listen regularly to students' oral language but may not have a systematic procedure for analyzing oral proficiency or for recording growth in oral language over time. The procedures we describe in Chapter 4 enable teachers to establish oral proficiency assessment as part of their ongoing instruction.

STORY OR TEXT RETELLING

In this type of assessment, students read or listen to text and then retell the main ideas or selected details. As with the other assessment activities listed here, this type of assessment is authentic because it is based on or closely resembles actual classroom activities. What makes it an assessment approach is the systematic collection and recording of information about the performance of individual students. Students respond orally and can be rated on how they describe the events in the story (story structure), their response to the story or text, and/or their language proficiency. Teachers or other students can ask probe questions about the text. Students at all levels of English proficiency can participate in story or text retelling. For example, students who are more proficient in English can read a story to a less proficient peer, who can then retell the story in English or the native language, if preferred. In this way, students who have little proficiency in English are able to participate in the assessment, even in ESL classrooms where the teacher is not proficient in each language spoken by the students. (See Chapter 5 for more on reading assessment.)

WRITING SAMPLES

As part of instruction, students are often asked to generate writing samples to meet a number of different *purposes*. These may include expressive or

Figure 2.1 Types of Authentic Assessments

Assessment	Description	Advantages
Oral Interviews	Teacher asks student questions about personal background, activities, readings, and interests	• Informal and relaxed context • Conducted over successive days with each student • Record observations on an interview guide
Story or Text Retelling	Students retell main ideas or selected details of text experienced through listening or reading	• Student produces oral report • Can be scored on content or language components • Scored with rubric or rating scale • Can determine reading comprehension, reading strategies, and language development
Writing Samples	Students generate narrative, expository, persuasive, or reference paper	• Student produces written document • Can be scored on content or language components • Scored with rubric or rating scale • Can determine writing processes
Projects/Exhibitions	Students complete project in content area, working individually or in pairs	• Students make formal presentation, written report, or both • Can observe oral and written products and thinking skills • Scored with rubric or rating scale
Experiments / Demonstrations	Students complete experiment or demonstrate use of materials	• Students make oral presentation, written report, or both • Can observe oral and written products and thinking skills • Scored with rubric or rating scale
Constructed-Response Items	Students respond in writing to open-ended questions	• Student produces written report • Usually scored on substantive information and thinking skills • Scored with rubric or rating scale
Teacher Observations	Teacher observes student attention, response to instructional materials, or interactions with other students	• Setting is classroom environment • Takes little time • Record observations with anecdotal notes or rating scales
Portfolios	Focused collection of student work to show progress over time	• Integrates information from a number of sources • Gives overall picture of student performance and learning • Strong student involvement and commitment • Calls for student self-assessment

narrative writing (a personal experience, story, or poem), expository or informative writing (writing to explain or clarify a concept or process, often in a content area), persuasive reports (to convince another of a particular position), or some combination of the different purposes. Students can also be asked to write in different *genres*, such as a letter, a journal entry, an essay, a newspaper report, or a research paper (a paper requiring use of reference materials, critical judgment, and citations). Students might produce the writing on demand in a fixed period of time or might be given the time to generate it after completing some readings on a subject, discussing the reading with peers, and editing and revising a draft of the product.

Teachers often have their own criteria for judging student writing and assigning grades. Grades will tend to vary from teacher to teacher unless they are based on specific performance criteria. The assessment procedures we suggest include the use of scoring rubrics for both holistic and analytic scoring in specific domains of writing, such as vocabulary, composition, style, sentence construction, and mechanics. With ELL students, as with other students, self-evaluation of writing promotes a reflective approach to learning and contributes to an understanding of effective writing processes. (See Chapter 6 for additional information on writing assessment.)

PROJECTS AND EXHIBITIONS

Students may complete a project on a specific topic and/or exhibit their work. An exhibition can include displays or models of buildings or objects appropriate to an instructional setting, role-plays, simulations, artistic creations, videotaped segments, charts, graphs, tables, etc. A project may be conducted individually or in small groups and is often presented through an oral or written report. Projects and exhibitions presented orally can be reviewed by a panel of judges rating the content presented, its organization, and/or the language used. Teachers often ask students to develop a presentation on a particular historic period and to generate drawings and written products appropriate to the period. This approach may be particular-

ly effective when ELL students are taught to communicate step-by-step procedures or project descriptions that are supported by diagrams or realia. (See Chapter 7 for additional ideas on assessment in the content areas.)

EXPERIMENTS OR DEMONSTRATIONS

Students might conduct an experiment in science using actual materials, or illustrate how something works (like a microscope). The experiment or demonstration is presented through an oral or written report which describes the steps and materials necessary to reproduce the experiment and any hypotheses that were tested, methods or observations used, or conclusions drawn. Students can be rated on their understanding of the concept, explanation of scientific methods, and/or the language used in the explanation (see Chapter 7).

CONSTRUCTED-RESPONSE ITEMS

This is a type of performance assessment in which students read or review textual materials and then respond to a series of open-ended questions eliciting comprehension and higher-order thinking. The assessment often focuses on how students *apply* information rather than on *how much* they recall of what has been taught. The student might produce a graphic depiction of the substance and organization of the readings (e.g., a semantic map), a brief comment on one or two points made in the readings, or an extended essay discussing or evaluating the text materials. Thus, students are able to respond in a variety of different ways appropriate to their level of English proficiency. Constructed-response items can be used in all of the content areas. In math and in the sciences, these types of questions are often used to ask students how they solved a problem or reached a conclusion. This type of assessment is authentic in that it draws on the kinds of thinking and reasoning skills students use in classrooms, presents problems or questions that are typical of classroom instruction, and encourages students to apply classroom learning in real-life settings (see Chapters 5-7).

TEACHER OBSERVATIONS

Teachers often observe students' attention to tasks, responses to different types of assignments, or interactions with other students while working cooperatively toward a goal. Both spontaneous events and planned classroom activities can be the subject of these observations. Especially with planned classroom activities, teachers can observe students' use of academic language and higher-order thinking skills in task-oriented discussions with other students. Most likely, you already observe daily student interactions to ensure that the students are on-task and working productively. To turn your observations into assessments, you need to record observations systematically over time to note changes in student performance. These changes should be summarized in personal notes for communicating with the student, with parents, or with other teachers. With ELL students, this type of observation is particularly important because we need to document what these students can do and build on existing areas of strength in addition to noting their response to various curriculum or instructional approaches. (See Chapters 4-7 for more on teacher observation.)

PORTFOLIOS

A *portfolio* is a purposeful collection of student work that is intended to show progress over time. The portfolio may include samples of student work, usually selected by the student or by the student and teacher to represent learning based on instructional objectives. Although portfolios have become popular over the past decade, we know that most teachers are not using them to their best advantage: collecting information purposefully and systematically over time to reflect learning with regard to instructional objectives. Each portfolio entry may be scored using a scoring rubric or checklist. The overall portfolio can be scored as well, based on the extent to which instructional goals have been met (see Chapter 3).

In the following chapters we describe these forms of assessment, provide examples of each, and illustrate how to use them. As seen in Figure 2.1, each of these techniques has its own advantages. The one major limitation that some of the techniques have is the amount of time required for the teacher to collect the information or to score the students' performance. We discuss various ways in which teachers can deal with this limitation in the appropriate section as each form of assessment is described. We justify the extra time involved because we believe that authentic assessment is an integral part of instruction rather than a separate piece that imposes on instruction or draws time away from instruction.

Awareness of Authentic Assessments

· · · · · · · · · · · · · · ·

Teachers in different schools have various levels of awareness and interest in alternative assessments. Some teachers will already have tried some form of authentic assessment or may have attended workshops on authentic assessments or performance assessment. They may even be using portfolios containing representative samples of student work to show growth over time. Some of these teachers may have already designed scoring rubrics and provided feedback to students on their performance. On the other hand, there may be others who have only heard about performance assessments and want to know more. Because of these different levels of experience, teachers may find it difficult to reach agreement on the type of professional development needed in a school or district.

The Authentic Assessment Inventory for Goal Setting shown in Figure 2.2 will assist in engaging other teachers in a dialogue about authentic assessment and in setting personal goals for staff development. The Inventory contains questions that can guide discussions with other teachers about goals to set in a school or district and about the development of authentic assessments.

The questions in Figure 2.2 are divided into six (unlabeled) sections. The sections concern level of interest in authentic assessments (questions 1-2), practices related to authentic assessment (questions 3-6), concerns about authentic assessment

Figure 2.2   Authentic Assessment Inventory for Goal Setting

Teacher _____ Date _____

Purpose: This inventory will help you establish goals for further development and use of authentic assessments in your classroom.

Directions: After reading each statement, circle the appropriate number in both columns to indicate (1) how you are using authentic assessment approaches, and (2) your ideal level of use.

1	2	3
Not at all	Somewhat	A great deal

To What Extent Do I:	Where I am Now:			Where I Would Like to Be:		
1. want to use authentic assessments?	1	2	3	1	2	3
2. want to use authentic assessments more effectively?	1	2	3	1	2	3
3. clearly define levels of student performance?	1	2	3	1	2	3
4. plan scoring rubrics before using assessments?	1	2	3	1	2	3
5. compare student performance to a standard?	1	2	3	1	2	3
6. inform students about scoring criteria before judging?	1	2	3	1	2	3
7. find authentic assessments difficult to use?	1	2	3	1	2	3
8. feel concern about the time required to use them?	1	2	3	1	2	3
9. talk to other teachers about authentic assessment?	1	2	3	1	2	3
10. share my assessment strategies with other teachers?	1	2	3	1	2	3
11. share teaching strategies for authentic assessments?	1	2	3	1	2	3
12. ask students to rate their own performance?	1	2	3	1	2	3
13. ask students to rate each other's performance?	1	2	3	1	2	3
14. give students feedback about their performance?	1	2	3	1	2	3
15. give parents feedback about their child's performance?	1	2	3	1	2	3

Use: Review the two right-hand columns to identify differences between where you are now and where you would like to be. Items for which there is a difference of one or two points can become target areas to establish goals for authentic assessment. Circle the statement for those areas.

Adapted from Stiggins (1992).

Figure 2.3 **Checklist for Designing Authentic Assessments**

Design Step	Description	Completion (√)
1. Build a team	1. Create an assessment team of teachers, parents, and administrators.	——————
2. Determine the purpose	2. Determine the purposes of the assessments for use in planning instruction or for other purposes.	——————
3. Specify objectives	3. Specify the instructional objectives to be evaluated with the assessments.	——————
4. Conduct staff development	4. The staff development is for the design team and other teachers on the purposes, use, and development of the assessment.	——————
5. Collect sample assessments	5. Review the sample assessments for suitability in your school or district to meet local purposes and objectives.	——————
6. Adapt existing assessments	6. Where possible, adapt existing instruments to meet local purposes by changing the item content, format, or scoring rubric.	——————
7. Try out the assessments	7. Give the assessments to students, score the papers, and discuss the assessments with students and other teachers.	——————
8. Review the assessments	8. Discuss the assessments with other members of the team and make final adjustments to the assessments or the rubrics.	——————

Adapted from Baker (1993) and Herman, Ashbacher, and Winters (1992).

(questions 7-8), collaboration with other teachers (questions 9-11), student involvement in authentic assessment (questions 12-13), and uses of authentic assessment (questions 14-16). The two columns on the right ask you to indicate "Where I am Now" and "Where I Would Like to Be" with regard to each question. The discrepancies between these two columns indicate potential targets for professional development in authentic assessment. After each teacher interested in authentic assessment completes the Inventory, the results can be used to form a dialogue about staff development needs, as discussed in the next section, and to plan for future professional development. This table can also be used to monitor annual progress toward awareness, interest, and implementation of authentic assessment by looking at responses in the "Where I am Now" column. Some items in Figure 2.2 might also be useful in evaluating workshops focusing on selected aspects of authentic assessment, by simply rewording the heading "To What Extent Do I" to say "This Workshop Helped Me..." (e.g., clearly define levels of student performance).

Designing Authentic Assessments

. . . .

We recommend that you work with at least one or more other teachers at your grade level and gain the support of administrators and parents in using any new assessments. Performance assessments and portfolios represent such a sufficient departure from traditional tests that explorations with your colleagues during development and initial use are necessary to share in the successes and to review strategies for overcoming what appear to be obstacles. You will need to bring parents into the picture because grades will be determined in part from results on the assessments and because the way in which information is sent home may differ from traditional approaches, as when portfolios are sent home at grading periods to illustrate student work. You will need the support of your school administrator to move forward with authentic assessment because teachers often need to

attend district-level workshops on assessment, to have planning time for collaboration, to observe uses of authentic assessments in other classrooms, to share experiences, and to discuss scoring or standards setting. Standards setting requires consensus-building discussions with other teachers. In addition, discussions on scoring are a crucial part of using authentic assessments in order to ensure inter-rater agreement.

The complexity of changing the assessment approach in a school or an ESL/bilingual program warrants a multi-step planning procedure that brings teachers and schools together with parents and administrators. Participation in the process for developing authentic assessments is an important way to gain the cooperation and commitment of those who need to be involved in assessment. We have summarized eight steps for planning and developing authentic assessments in Figure 2.3. These steps are adapted from procedures suggested by Baker (1993) and Herman, Aschbacher, and Winters (1992). A column is provided on the right of Figure 2.3 to check off each step as it is completed. We suggest that you use this table to review progress in planning for authentic assessment and in designing professional development.

1. Build a team. Create an assessment team of teachers, parents, and administrators to begin discussion on an authentic assessment program, why authentic assessment is important, the purposes of the authentic assessments, and the role of the new assessments in instruction and in the school.

2. Determine the purposes of the authentic assessments. Baker (1993) indicates that the end result of effective assessment is to improve teaching and learning. With ELL students, the purposes of authentic assessments can include identification, placement, and reclassification as well as monitoring student performance during instruction. It is through all of these purposes that improvements in teaching and learning are realized. We caution teachers not to expect authentic assessments to meet all school or district needs in assessment. The assessment team can determine how the authentic assessments complement information derived from standardized tests or commercially available language proficiency tests.

3. *Specify objectives*. The assessment team must reach agreement on the objectives that will be assessed using authentic assessments. The objectives should be obtained from the district's curriculum, from state curriculum frameworks, and from standards developed by professional associations (e.g., NCTM 1989). In Chapter 5 on reading and Chapter 7 on content-area assessment, we provide examples of these types of objectives. You can select objectives which will be most effectively assessed with authentic assessments and set aside for later consideration those that would be more effectively assessed with multiple-choice or conventional tests.

4. *Conduct professional development on authentic assessment*. The purpose of this professional development is to share information with the design team and with other teachers about the rationale for authentic assessments, their design, and their use in planning instruction. We have seen teachers conduct this type of professional development themselves and for other teachers after having collected articles on authentic assessment and attended professional conferences or workshops in which authentic assessment was discussed. In some cases, teachers have invited other teachers in the district who are using authentic assessment to make presentations for their school. We have also seen teachers influence the topics on district-wide professional development activities by encouraging presentations or work- shops on authentic assessment at their grade level and for their content area. Where schools have access to local or near-by college or university schools of education, teachers can get help in planning authentic assessment through collaborative efforts with the university. Professional development can be extended by planning information-sharing sessions on teacher work days or at full-staff meetings as teachers gain more experience in the use of authentic assessments. Inviting administrators to attend these staff development activities ensures they are informed about the new types of assessment being used.

5. *Collect examples of authentic assessments*. One of the best ways to begin the development and use of authentic assessments is to look for examples of the assessments that seem consistent with your objectives and the types of assessment you want for students. There are numerous sources for examples of authentic assessment. The examples in this book are intended as a resource for assessment teams planning new assessments for ELL students in their school. A second source is the many new books and articles on alternative assessment that are emerging on a regular basis. A third source is the numerous conferences and workshops specifically devoted to authentic assessment and portfolios. A fourth source is the Center for Research on Evaluation, Standards, and Student Testing (CRESST) at the University of California at Los Angeles. CRESST has a database on performance assessments that is accessible to teachers. A fifth source is the Test Center at the Northwest Regional Educational Laboratory in Portland, Oregon, which contains a lending library for test items and bibliographies on assessment information. Finally, a number of test publishers have introduced performance assessments along with their more conventional forms of assessment (e.g., CTB/McGraw Hill, Psychological Corporation, Riverside Publishing Company). In some cases, the publishers have item banks of performance assessments that teachers can use in designing their own assessments. One major caution about these sources: few of them include performance assessments specifically designed for ELL students. Nevertheless, these sources can provide you with ideas for adopting or adapting assessment procedures for use in your classroom. In addition to collecting examples of performance assessments, you can collect examples of scoring rubrics at the same time.

6. *Adapt existing assessments or develop new ones*. We have found that the process of developing new authentic assessments without adequate examples from other sources or without outside assistance is a burden on teachers. Steps such as carefully reviewing local objectives that can be suitably assessed with authentic assessments, designing sample assessment procedures, reaching agreement on scoring rubrics, trying out the assessments, setting standards, and reviewing the success of the assessments are daunting tasks that are enough to discourage even the most ardent supporters of authentic

assessment. It is for these reasons that we encourage you to look for good examples of authentic assessment and determine if you can adapt them for local use with your ELL population. An assessment team may have ideas about how to adapt these examples to assess local objectives.

7. *Try out the assessments.* Once your assessments have been developed, try them out with students. Working with other members of the assessment team, you can set aside classroom time to ask students to respond to the authentic assessments. Give most of the students enough time to complete most of the tasks. Students should feel a sense of success in responding to authentic assessments. You are interested in how students perform and how they explain or justify their responses. You gain little from knowing the number of items students can complete in a limited time period since test items that have not been completed provide no information about student performance. You gain the most information from seeing how students respond and from justifications they give for their answers. Score the assessments using the scoring rubric you have agreed on with other teachers and select anchor papers that you can share with others also trying out the assessments. Look at specific items to determine if there are some items students did not respond to at all or tended to get incorrect. This could call either for modifications to instruction or to the item.

Ideas for gathering student perceptions of the assessment are shown in Figure 2.4. Student perceptions provide valuable information to assist in planning and using authentic assessment to improve instruction.

In addition to trying out the assessments with your own ELL students, gain the cooperation of grade-level teachers in trying them out with native English speakers of the same grade level. This will accomplish two things. First, you can establish a baseline of performance for typical native English speakers in your school. It is important to realize what standards of performance are appropriate for grade-level classrooms so you can evaluate the performance of your own students realistically. Second, you will find out if the authentic assessments you have designed are also authentic for

grade-level classrooms. That is, you will determine if the activities you have designed reflect actual classroom instruction for those students.

8. *Review the assessments.* Discuss the assessments with other members of the assessment team. Share not only how well your students did but the students' perceptions of the assessments. Make adjustments or changes in the assessments if you find that students are consistently unable to respond to certain items, provided that low performance is not resulting from a curriculum-assessment mismatch or inadequate instruction. Some possible ways to change the items for ELL students include providing a diagram or chart that will clarify the question, simplifying the wording, changing the directions, and changing the scoring rubric. Decide on one or more of these changes and then try out the assessment with a different group of students similar in ability or proficiency. Review the results and determine if performance has been improved. If it has, keep the changes, and if it has not, keep making adjustments in the items until you are satisfied.

Technical Quality of Authentic Assessments

Demands for the technical quality of assessments focus on their reliability and validity. *Reliability* is the consistency of the assessment in producing the same score on different testing occasions or with different raters. The most important types of validity for performance assessments are *content validity*, or the match between the content of the assessment and the content of instruction, and *consequential validity*, or the uses of assessment for instructional planning and improvement.

RELIABILITY

In contrast to multiple-choice tests, which are scored objectively, authentic assessments require teacher judgment to produce a score. This introduces the possibility of subjectivity and lack of consensus with other teachers. *Inter-rater reliability* is

Figure 2.4   **How to Identify Student Reactions to Authentic Assessment**

Purpose: to obtain students' perceptions of authentic assessment.

Approach: Work on an assessment team with other teachers at or near the same grade level. Administer a multiple-choice test on information covered in class and score the results, providing scores on the number and percent correct. Use an end-of-unit test, if available.

Next, identify an authentic assessment to use with students, such as a writing prompt and scoring rubric. The prompt should reflect a topic covered in class. Make an easily understood checklist from the rubric that students can use as a reminder when they edit their own papers. Have each teacher on the team use the prompt and rubric in a writing assessment with the following steps:

• Introduce and discuss the scoring rubric with students. Ensure that students understand the rubric will be used to score their written work.
• Administer the writing assessment, mentioning again that the rubric will be used to score their papers.
• Give students the opportunity to edit and revise their papers using the rubric.
• Collect the papers, score them, and give feedback to the students. As an option, ask students to use the rubric to score the paper of another student. Then discuss the papers and answer any questions about the rubric.

Ask the class their opinions on such questions as the following:

• How was this different from other tests you have taken?
• Did this task assess things that you learned in school?
• Would you like more tests to look like this?
• How would you suggest that other students prepare for this kind of test?

After the papers have been scored, you can also ask students some of the following questions:

• How is the information you get back from this type of assessment different from what you get back on a multiple-choice test?
• Can you use the results of this type of assessment to learn better?
• Can the results of this type of assessment be used in grading?
• How can the results be communicated best to your parents?

Take notes on the students' comments so you can share them with other members of your assessment team. Students should see a substantial difference between feedback they receive from an authentic assessment and from the percentage correct on a multiple-choice test. They may have some creative ideas on how to use the assessment information for their own learning and in grading.

Comments: The students' perceptions communicate valuable information to other teachers in your school who may be curious about the effect of this type of assessment on students and how it can be used to plan instruction.

important mainly to ensure consistency and fairness (Herman, Aschbacher, and Winters 1992). Without reliability, some teachers may give students the impression of "rating hard" while others are "rating easy." Further, teachers can give the impression of rating students inconsistently, as in the familiar comment about papers thrown in the air to determine which ones receive the highest grades (those which stick to the ceiling).

You will want to have confidence that a score or grade was based on the actual student performance rather than some idiosyncratic or indefensi-ble application of the scoring criteria. Scores can be based on a scoring rubric or a scoring scale that assigns a numerical value to the performance depending on the extent to which it meets pre-designated criteria. Two types of scoring rubrics are holistic rubrics and analytic rubrics.

An example of a *holistic rubric* for writing assessment will suffice to illustrate why establishing reliability is difficult. Assume that you have selected a writing prompt that will elicit writing from students on topics that are familiar and interesting to them. You are using a narrative genre in which students are asked to write about an experience that had personal meaning to them. For example:

Write about an experience in which someone said something very important to you. Who was the person? What was said? Why was it important?

A scoring rubric for a holistically-scored writing assessment is shown in Figure 2.5. This scoring rubric was designed by ESL teachers in Fairfax County Public Schools, Virginia for use with ELL students. A six-point scale is provided to enable teachers to make fine distinctions among beginning writers. Other than providing an interesting holistic system for rating written products, this rubric illustrates an important point: different teachers might assign different scores to individual papers based on their understanding or their application of the criteria. The scoring rubric contains six levels ranging from Early Writer to Exceptionally Fluent. At each level, the following domains are addressed:

- focuses on a central idea, uses clear introduction, fully develops ideas, and presents a conclusion

- uses appropriate verb tenses and varied grammatical and syntactic structures, uses complex sentences effectively, and uses smooth transitions

- uses varied, precise vocabulary appropriate to the purpose

- uses accurate capitalization, punctuation, and spelling

Each level of the scoring rubric requires slightly more demanding performance from the student on each of the criteria. The difference between the levels is essentially the degree of control the student has over each of the domains of scoring. The ESL teachers who designed this rubric felt that the components and the descriptions at each level represented the types of writing they most often see among their ELL students. However, obtaining inter-rater agreement is complicated because a student's performance could easily fall into one level of the rubric on one of the criteria but at another level on other criteria. The question is how to ensure that you reach reasonable levels of agreement with other teachers in judging the papers submitted by students.

In using an *analytic scoring rubric*, a separate rating is given to each of the separate components in the scale. That is, separate ratings are assigned to Idea Development/Organization, Sentence Fluency/Structure, Word Choice, and Mechanics. If inter-rater agreement is difficult to establish with holistic scoring, you can see that it might be even more difficult to establish with analytic scoring. Rather than agreeing on the overall score, raters using an analytic rubric might be called on to reach agreement for each component. Detailed examples of analytic rubrics are provided in Chapters 4-6.

RATER TRAINING

In developing and using authentic assessments, there is no substitute for effective professional development. There are at least six staff development activities that can help teachers reach agreement in scoring any authentic assessment (adapted from Herman, Aschbacher, and Winters 1992). While the example we use is of writing assessment, these steps are also applicable to the assessment of oral language, reading, or assessment in the content areas. The steps assume that teachers have already established a writing prompt or prompts and a scoring rubric and have administered the assessment to their students. A clearly defined scoring rubric is an essential first step in developing consistency in scoring among teachers. Without a clearly defined rubric, the remaining steps are not likely to be successful. As with the rubric in Figure 2.5, you need to define student performance at each level of the scoring scale. The steps also assume that the assessment team has reached consensus on the selection of *anchor papers* that define each level of the scoring rubric. Finally, a staff developer or a teacher plays the role of facilitator or trainer with colleagues.

1. *Orientation to the assessment task.* The staff developer or teacher playing the role of staff developer introduces the purposes of the assessment, describes who will use the assessment results, discusses the objective being assessed, describes the prompts and student directions, and gives an overview of the scoring rubric. Participants in the

Figure 2.5 Sample Holistic Scoring Rubric for Writing Samples

Rating	Criteria
6 Proficient	• Writes single or multiple paragraphs with clear introduction, fully developed ideas, and a conclusion • Uses appropriate verb tense and a variety of grammatical and syntactical structures; uses complex sentences effectively; uses smooth transitions • Uses varied, precise vocabulary • Has occasional errors in mechanics (spelling, punctuation, and capitalization) which do not detract from meaning
5 Fluent	• Writes single or multiple paragraphs with main idea and supporting detail; presents ideas logically, though some parts may not be fully developed • Uses appropriate verb tense and a variety of grammatical and syntactical structures; errors in sentence structure do not detract from meaning; uses transitions • Uses varied vocabulary appropriate for the purpose • Has few errors in mechanics which do not detract from meaning
4 Expanding	• Organizes ideas in logical or sequential order with some supporting detail; begins to write a paragraph • Experiments with a variety of verb tenses, but does not use them consistently; subject/verb agreement errors; uses some compound and complex sentences; limited use of transitions • Vocabulary is appropriate to purpose but sometimes awkward • Uses punctuation, capitalization, and mostly conventional spelling; errors sometimes interfere with meaning
3 Developing	• Writes sentences around an idea; some sequencing present, but may lack cohesion • Writes in present tense and simple sentences; has difficulty with subject/verb agreement; run-on sentences are common; begins to use compound sentences • Uses high frequency words; may have difficulty with word order; omits endings or words • Uses some capitalization, punctuation, and transitional spelling; errors often interfere with meaning
2 Beginning	• Begins to convey meaning through writing • Writes predominately phrases and patterned or simple sentences • Uses limited or repetitious vocabulary • Uses temporary (phonetic) spelling
1 Emerging	• No evidence of idea development or organization • Uses single words, pictures, and patterned phrases. • Copies from a model • Little awareness of spelling, capitalization, or punctuation

Adapted from a rubric drafted by the ESL Teachers Portfolio Assessment Group, Fairfax County Public Schools, Virginia.

staff development then actually take the assessments themselves and score their own papers. One important purpose of taking the assessment is to ensure that teachers understand the mental processes that are being called on as students take the assessment.

2. *Clarification of the scoring rubric.* Participants discuss the scoring rubric and its components in small groups in order to gain a better understanding of the information derived from the rubric. Teachers think back on the mental processes they used while writing. This discussion enables them to understand the kind of thinking processes that are called for in responding to the prompt and how the rubric taps into these processes. Think about the following questions:

- Are the thinking skills you used assessed in the scoring rubric?

- Are the thinking skills assessed by the scoring rubric important?

- Do these thinking skills represent the objective the assessment is designed to evaluate?

Now review the anchor papers and answer these questions:

- Do the anchor papers at each level of the scoring rubric represent effective and less effective performance?

- Can you write a description justifying why a particular paper is representative of the level on the rubric to which it was assigned?

- If needed, how would you change the anchor papers?

- Do you have other anchor papers that you prefer at any of the levels of the scoring rubric?

Replace the original anchor papers with the versions preferred by your team if you have more appropriate substitutes.

3. *Practice scoring.* Each teacher should score one or two papers at a time, with discussion following each paper. That is, two teachers might each rate one paper, exchange papers, rate the new paper, and then discuss the two papers they rated. In the discussions, teachers should focus on their reasons for assigning a score to each paper and refer to the

rubric to establish a common ground. Teachers should take notes while they are rating, if needed, to describe why they assigned a score to a particular paper. Taking notes is important so teachers can review the reasons why they assigned scores as they rate additional papers. You can expect these judgments to be difficult. Different teachers may have different reasons for assigning their scores. At this point, teachers should strive for establishing consensus in their ratings.

4. *Record the scores.* In order to proceed to the next step, checking the reliability, you will need to design a system for recording the scores for each student. The rater training should cover the process for recording the scores as well as the process for assigning the scores. Raters should operate independently, assign their scores to about 20-25 papers, and then combine their scores onto a single record sheet. For example, one system for recording the scores would be to list the student names or identification numbers down the left column and indicate one score for each rater in the remaining columns, as shown in Figure 2.6. To ensure objectivity on the part of teachers, student names could be removed or replaced with number codes.

5. *Check reliability.* Teachers can use reliability checks to compare their own scoring with the scores assigned to anchor papers by teachers who are expert in use of the scoring rubric. A simple table such as the one shown in Figure 2.6 can be used to record the ratings. Scores given by the teacher undergoing training are placed under the column for Rater 1 and scores given by teachers who are expert in the system can be entered under the column for Rater 2. If ratings on anchor papers are not available, scores for any two teachers undergoing training can be entered on the table. Subtract the scores for Rater 2 from those for Rater 1 and enter the difference in the Difference column of Figure 2.6. The training has been successful if individual teachers tend to be in agreement with ratings assigned to the anchor papers by expert raters or are in agreement with each other.

How much agreement is desirable? Most raters are content if they agree within ±1 score point in 90 percent of the papers rated (e.g., 18 out of 20) on a rubric with a 1-4 or 1-6 scale. Achieving this

Figure 2.6   **Rater Scoring Record**

Student Name/Number	Rater 1	Rater 2	Difference
1. 0001	4	3	1
2. 0002	4	4	0
3. 0003	2	4	2
4.			
5.			
6.			
7.			
8.			
9.			
10.			
11.			
12.			
13.			
14.			
15.			
16.			
17.			
18.			
19.			
20.			
21.			
22.			
23.			
24.			
25.			

level of consistency for most teachers takes about a half day of training for a holistic scoring rubric like the one shown in Figure 2.5. For analytic scoring rubrics, with scores assigned to each of a number of domains, training can take a full day. When scores are assigned on a number of domains, the criterion for agreement should be reached on each domain. The 90 percent criterion for inter-rater agreement may be relaxed to 80 percent if decisions being made from the results of the assessment are not particularly critical in determining student placement (Herman, Aschbacher, and Winters 1992). However, reliability checks should always be part of staff development even when no critical decisions are being made from the assessment results.

One possible source of rater error is the tendency to rate high or rate low. That is, some teachers will agree with a criterion ±1 about 80 percent of the time but consistently rate toward the high or the low end of that range. This tendency can be checked by simply adding the Difference column in Figure 2.6. Assume the criterion ratings are in column 2. If the difference between Teacher 1 and the criterion are about +1 for each student, Teacher 1 tends to rate high. Conversely, if the differences are consistently about -1, Teacher 1 rates low. This tendency should be corrected through retraining because rater drift can become even more pronounced after the teacher has been back in the classroom a while.

What should be done if one or more teachers seems unable to reach acceptable levels of agreement? The best approach is to review the scoring criteria, discuss the written justification teachers have made for their ratings, review the anchor papers, provide new sample papers for these teachers to score, and engage these teachers in discussions with the new sample papers. There is always a possibility that some teachers will never attain the level of agreement preferred.

6. *Follow-up.* There should be follow-up activities with peer coaching (Joyce and Showers 1987) or continuing staff development in which teachers review their scoring with each other in pairs, in small groups, or at departmental meetings. It is always a good idea for the teacher team using

authentic assessments to return to the anchor papers, review the original criteria in the rubric, and discuss their ratings. The teachers can bring for discussion additional examples of papers from their students that have been difficult to score. This continued staff development keeps a focus on the authentic assessments, prevents rater drift from the original criteria, and provides opportunities for discussion about uses of the assessment in classroom practice.

VALIDITY

Two types of validity are of most concern with authentic assessments. The first is *content validity*, or the correspondence between curriculum objectives and the objectives being assessed. The second is *consequential validity*, the way in which the assessment is used to benefit teaching and learning processes and to benefit students (Darling-Hammond 1994; Shepard 1993).

Consideration of content or *curriculum validity* is particularly important to ensure correspondence between local curriculum objectives and the content of the assessment. In programs for ELL students, objectives may be stated for English language outcomes, for content-area knowledge and skills, and for affective outcomes. These objectives may be contained in a specific curriculum document for ELL students or may be drawn from objectives for all students. Objectives may be contained in a state curriculum framework or in local curriculum action plans. Presumably, these objectives will have undergone considerable review by teachers so that they represent valued learning outcomes. To gain community input, parents may be asked to review local objectives.

Content validity is also important to ensure the assessments represent thinking skills in your local curriculum. Many local curricula are beginning to emphasize higher-order thinking skills to match complex reasoning processes advanced by professional organizations (e.g., NCTM 1989) and by curriculum reform advocates (e.g., Marzano et al. 1988; Resnick and Klopfer 1989). For example, Marzano et al. suggest a number of core thinking skills are important that go beyond the traditional analysis, synthesis, and evaluation (Bloom et al. 1956). *Core thinking skills* are a means to a particular goal. They are essential to the functioning of other thinking activities and may be used in the service of metacognition, cognitive processes, or critical and creative thinking. Representative core thinking skills include: *focusing*—defining problems and setting goals; *organizing*—comparing, classifying, ordering, and representing information; *analyzing*—identifying attributes and components, relationships and patterns, main ideas, and errors; *generating*—inferring, predicting, and elaborating; and *establishing criteria and verifying conclusions*. Marzano et al. encourage teachers to ensure that these core thinking skills are reflected throughout instruction and assessment. These skills can be used at any point in critical thinking and may be used repeatedly. The thinking skills can be taught effectively for most students by integrating them with classroom tasks and curriculum concepts.

Because authentic assessments provide in-depth assessment of student knowledge and skills, curriculum validity is all the more important. If students are asked to demonstrate knowledge and skills in physical sciences on a performance assessment when the curriculum objectives at that grade level emphasize earth sciences, their low scores must be attributed to the curriculum mismatch rather than to instruction. Thus, the assessment provides little of use for teachers in planning, as the in-depth information is being provided in the wrong area of the curriculum. This points out why teachers cannot simply adopt someone else's assessments without adapting them to local curriculum expectations. This applies especially with ELL students.

This discussion of the usefulness of assessments for instruction leads directly to consequential validity. Assessments have consequential validity to the extent that they lead teachers to focus on classroom activities which support student learning and are responsive to individual student needs. One of the major considerations in the design of assessment is authenticity with respect to classroom activities. If assessments are in fact authentic, the teacher will naturally include the results of the assessments in instructional planning. Because performance assessments should be used on an ongoing basis, teachers should have the information they need to review student performance to verify that students are profiting from instruction. Having this information available enables teachers to investigate the effects of their teaching on student learning and to reformulate their instruction so that it becomes more effective.

It is this insight into what students are really doing, thinking, and learning that is one of the greatest contributions of authentic assessment to teacher development. (Darling-Hammond 1994, p. 24)

PERFORMANCE STANDARDS

One of the additional benefits of performance assessment is in supporting teachers' attempts to specify standards of student performance. There are at least two basic types of standards: content standards and performance standards (Marzano and Kendall 1993). *Content standards* "articulate the important declarative knowledge and procedural knowledge specific to a given content domain" (Marzano and Kendall, p. 24). While declarative knowledge consists of *what* you know, or knowledge of concepts and facts, procedural knowledge is *what you know how to do*, the "how" of performance and learning (Anderson 1983, 1990; Jones et al. 1987). Content standards specify the curriculum objectives, the knowledge students must have in each content area, and the skills they must be able to apply successfully. We present a variety of content standards in Chapter 7 that can be used to assist in standards setting.

Performance standards are more specific; they complement content standards by identifying specific activities on which declarative and procedural knowledge can be demonstrated and often the conditions under which students are asked to demonstrate these achievements (Marzano and Kendall 1993). Moreover, performance standards identify the level of performance on a specific assessment task and scoring rubric that students must attain in order to function at a basic, proficient, or advanced level (Freed 1993). Typically, there are verbal descriptions accompanying these general standards, as with the scoring rubric shown in Figure 2.5. This scoring rubric had six levels: Proficient, Fluent, Expanding, Developing, Beginning, and Emerging. Teachers working in a team might agree that all students should be at least at the Developing level of proficiency in writing by the end of the quarter, and that 85 percent of the students should attain the Fluent level or better by the end of the year. Other teachers might specify a different standard or might individualize the standard depending on where the student starts. However, the standards these teachers select should be compatible with overall district standards of performance.

Performance standards are also established in content areas such as mathematics and science. Curriculum objectives identify the types of knowledge and skills that are important in the content areas but do not indicate *how* successful students must be in accomplishing the objectives. That is the role of performance standards. Often teachers identify *benchmark standards* of performance or standards that are expected at selected developmental levels, and discuss the *benchmark grade levels* at which students should reach this level of attainment.

The percentage of students who are considered to be proficient will vary. For example, the percent of students meeting high standards of performance might vary from 20 to 40 percent. Whatever percent results from the criterion score established, the primary guide to locating the performance standard should always be the curriculum objectives, the scoring rubric, and the content standard. Teachers involved in setting the performance standard should not ease the standard simply because it is difficult to attain. High standards of performance often present a challenge that requires changes in curriculum and instruction.

Issues in Designing Authentic Assessment

. . . .

Whether authentic assessments are designed by individual teachers or by a school district, a number of issues will emerge that need to be addressed

concerning assessment in general and the use of assessment with ELL students. These include the purpose of the assessment, fairness, and grading.

PURPOSE

The purposes of authentic assessment with ELL students can include identification, placement, reclassification, and monitoring student progress, as discussed in Chapter 1. The first three purposes involve extremely important ("high-stakes") decisions that affect whether or not ELL students receive special language-based instruction, the type of instruction, and the duration over which the instruction continues. For these reasons, the assessment should be conducted accurately and reliably, and multiple assessments should be used to ensure that the decisions made are consistent with all that is known about the student. The decisions should be based on a combination of formal language proficiency testing, subject area assessments, and records of classroom performance, where available. Furthermore, ESL and bilingual teachers should join together with grade-level teachers and with district assessment staff in making these decisions. Observations should be carefully documented if they are to play a role in this type of assessment.

Assessments conducted by individual teachers to monitor student progress or to plan instruction can be less formal because high stakes are not involved. Such assessments may not have to meet the highest standards of inter-rater reliability to be useful and could include observations and anecdotal records. Authentic assessments and portfolios are often used to monitor student progress as well as for grading.

FAIRNESS

All students taking performance assessments should have reasonable opportunities to demonstrate their expertise without confronting barriers. As suggested by the National Council on Education Standards and Testing (1992), ELL students should be "provided opportunities to learn and to demonstrate their mastery of material under circumstances that take into account their special needs" (p. 10). Critics of multiple-choice tests have indicated that the tests are culturally biased owing to the unfamiliar item format and to content that is not representative of the educational experiences of ELL students. As Mohan (1986) notes, the item content in conventional standardized tests often contains references to cultural conventions that are unique to the experiences of students reared in the country where the test was developed and normed but which are not taught directly in school. Apart from simple language differences, students from other cultures or other countries might be at a disadvantage in demonstrating their ability to read or understand the implications of some of this kind of information.

Not all problems with fairness in using multiple-choice tests with ELL students are solved by shifting to authentic assessments. In fact, some new difficulties might be introduced. One problem is that the performance called for in authentic assessments is often highly language-dependent, either oral or written. ELL students might be at a disadvantage in responding to these types of questions, depending on their level of proficiency in English. A second problem is that the responses called for in performance assessments involve complex thinking skills. Many of these students have not had the opportunity to learn how to express complex thinking skills in English because they are continually exposed to curricula that focus on basic skills in the English language. Third, authentic assessments are often used to measure student knowledge in depth in a particular area. ELL students who have had limited opportunities for exposure to the full curriculum might easily find the knowledge and skills that they do possess missed altogether. And finally, the use of authentic assessments might exacerbate the problem mentioned above with culturally unfamiliar content. Authentic measures usually ask a small number of questions about applications of knowledge to a single theme rather than ask a large number of questions about a broad range of topics. If the content related to the single theme is unfamiliar, the stu-

dent may be unable to respond to any of the questions contained in the assessment.

One of the ways to address the concern about the excessive dependence of performance assessments on language is to provide the student with opportunities to respond in other ways. Students can respond by drawing pictures or diagrams, making semantic maps of the structure and concepts in textual materials, and giving shorter answers than the conventional extended responses called for in some performance assessments. For example, in describing scientific contributions in the 20th Century, students might be asked to select the three most important innovations from a given list and choose words from another list that explain why those particular three were selected. Similarly, in responding to a question about the causes of a specific historical event, students can indicate their understanding by labeling a cause-effect diagram. We describe a number of these assessment procedures in Chapter 7 and indicate how they can be used.

Most concerns about content coverage with authentic assessment can be addressed by bringing the assessments into closer alignment with the local curriculum. That is, the focus of authentic assessments on higher-order thinking skills should be addressed by ensuring that the local curriculum for ELL students includes complex thinking from the earliest levels of instruction onward. This can be accomplished most readily by *scaffolding* (providing temporary contextual supports for meaning, including modeling, visuals, and hands-on experiences) and reducing the language demands of instructional tasks while maintaining the requirement for complex thinking (Chamot and O'Malley 1994a; Jones et al. 1987). Alignment of the assessment measures to the curriculum will also ensure that students will not be asked to respond to in-depth questions that have barely been covered in the curriculum. Further, the students will not be asked to respond to culturally unfamiliar messages, thereby reducing the likelihood of a mismatch between the student's experiences and the content of the assessment measure.

GRADING

Report card grades are an important part of the communication among teachers, students, and parents (Stiggins 1988). Grades have two basic purposes in the classroom: to reflect student accomplishments and to motivate students. While grades may indicate the level or rank order of student performance, there are questions about their success in serving as an incentive for students to exert greater effort. Teachers often comment that not all students see grades as motivating (Stiggins, Frisbie, and Griswald 1989). Grades are extrinsic motivators and are often contrasted with intrinsic motivation derived from self-determined criteria, as in learning out of interest and self-created goals. Moreover, as Kohn (1994) notes, people who are promised extrinsic rewards for an activity "tend to lose interest in whatever they had to do to obtain the reward" (p. 39). Wiggins (1993) puts it even more bluntly. He indicates that grades can be a disincentive to some students because, particularly when teachers grade on a curve, somebody always loses, and a portion of the class is made to feel inept.

The problems with assigning grades are even more evident with group grades. Group grades are typically an attempt to grade the final product of student teams who worked on a project, essay, or presentation. Group grades can undermine motivation because they do not reward individual work or hold individual students accountable (Kagan 1995). The poor performance of a single person can lower the group grade, thereby undermining the motivation of high achieving students and rewarding low performers who are fortunate to have a high achiever on the team. In this sense, the group grade is due to forces outside the control of the high achieving student. Students need to know that they and other students are individually accountable for their work.

Surveys of grading practices indicate that teachers consider factors other than achievement or growth in determining grades, such as perceived level of effort, attitude, ability, behavior, and attendance (Alverman and Phelps 1994). Two problems are evident in considering factors other than growth or achievement in assigning grades. First,

the intermingling of achievement with other factors can have an unintended negative effect because students receive a mixed message on their accomplishments: You tried hard but didn't succeed anyway. The second problem is in the extreme variation in grading from teacher to teacher. Teachers vary not only in the factors they use in grading, they also vary in the criteria they use to assign grades on classroom tests. Among the methods teachers use in grading classroom tests are the following (EAC-West 1992):

- percentages (90-100% = A, 80-90% = B, and so on)
- mastery (80% = mastery, 60-79% = partial mastery, <60% = nonmastery)
- grading on a curve (top 7% = A, next 24% = B, middle 38% = C, next 24% = D, and lowest 7% = F)
- gap grading (assigning grades to suit large gaps in a score distribution, e.g., 94-100% = A, 90-93% no scores, 83-89% = B, 79-82% no scores, 68-78% = C, etc.)

In determining final grades from classroom tests, some teachers average numerical scores on these tests, while other teachers average the grades received on the tests. The latter approach reduces the impact on final grades from a single high or low test score. For example, an extremely low numerical score such as 3 out of 100 will have a far greater impact on the mean of all the tests than a single F will have on the mean of the corresponding grades. Teachers can also assign different weights to tests, papers, presentations, and classroom participation in determining final grades. In sum, not only does each teacher decide what will be evaluated and how much each activity will count, but teachers also determine how the final grade will be calculated. Because of this variation in grading practices and in criteria used to assign grades on classroom tests, we could expect a great deal of variation from teacher to teacher in the final grades students receive even given a common set of papers or products to rate.

One final difficulty in grading practices stems more from the tests on which grades are based than from the grades themselves. In the past, classroom tests have tended to assess lower-level skills even when teachers claim to value and teach complex thinking (Stiggins, Frisbie, and Griswald 1989). Inevitably, the resulting grades assigned will be based on lower-level skills instead of on the real objectives and content of classroom instruction.

Despite the problems we have identified with grading practices, our experience leads us to believe that grades can be useful if they are based on authentic assessments and are assigned following certain guidelines. Grades are requested regularly by parents as a guide to their child's performance and are useful as an overall indicator of student achievement. When combined with illustrative samples of student work and with informative scoring rubrics, grades can provide parents and other teachers with a comprehensive picture of student growth and achievement. Part of the usefulness of grades depends, however, on establishing relatively uniform criteria for grades in a school or among classrooms.

The introduction of authentic assessment (including portfolios) to accompany more innovative forms of instruction expands considerably the alternatives that can be used to establish classroom grades. Teachers using authentic assessments evaluate students on representations of classroom performance that include reports, projects, group work, and so on. With authentic assessment, integrative knowledge and complex thinking can be assessed beyond simple knowledge of isolated pieces of information, and the processes by which students derive answers can be assessed as well. In authentic assessment, student performance is often rated using scoring rubrics that define the knowledge students possess, how they think, and how they apply their knowledge.

Because the rubrics are specific (or at least should be) their use tends to reduce teacher-to-teacher variations in grading, especially if the teachers base their ratings on a common set of anchor papers. With the use of portfolios, teachers can provide parents with specific examples of student work to illustrate the ratings they give to students on the scoring rubrics. Furthermore, with authentic assessment, teachers often establish standards of performance that reflect what students should know or be able to do at different levels of performance or that reflect different levels of mastery. Finally, teachers using authentic assessment share the criteria for scoring student work openly and invite discussions of the criteria with students and parents.

With these new opportunities comes a challenge: to define the procedures by which scoring rubrics and rating scales are converted to classroom grades. In rating individual pieces of student work, one option is to directly convert rubrics on a 1-4 scale to corresponding letter grades. This could work acceptably provided that the points on the rubric represent what you consider to be "A-level" performance, "B-level" performance, and so on. While this may be effective in some cases, it is not always a good practice because definitions of what students know and can do at the different levels on the rubric do not always correspond to what is considered to be A or B performance. Further, it may be unwise to confuse the informed feedback provided by a scoring rubric with the external reward of a grade (Kohn 1994). Thus, a second option is to establish independent standards of performance corresponding to letter grades. That is, identify in advance exactly what students receiving an A, B, etc. are expected to know and do in meeting the course objectives. Then obtain a student grade by comparing the student's actual performance with the standard established. The standard corresponding to grades can reflect overall student performance across activities or projects, thereby avoiding the difficulty of having to create standards for grades on each student product. The score on a rubric for each activity provides effective informed feedback to students on their work, and the standard provides them with direction on what they need to accomplish.

Our recommendations in grading and communicating student performance with authentic assessment are as follows:

- Assign scores to individual student achievement or growth based on a scoring rubric or agreed on standard to reflect mastery of classroom objectives.
- Assign weights to different aspects of student performance as reflected in class assignments (e.g., projects, reports, class participation).

- Multiply each rating by the weight and sum the ratings or scores on individual papers or performances to obtain an overall numeric score.

- Reach agreement with other teachers and with students on the interpretation of the summed score with respect to grades.

- Do not assign grades for effort and especially do not combine effort and achievement in a single grade.

- If you assign grades for group work, assign separate grades for the group product and for individual contributions.

In using anecdotal records to support grades:

- Use the language of the rubric to help you write anecdotal comments, describing specifically what each student should know and be able to do, and using examples.

- Link your comments to instructional goals, and (where appropriate) distinguish between language proficiency and content-area knowledge and skills.

- In expressing concerns, focus on (1) what the student knows and can do, (2) your plan or strategies for helping the student improve, and (3) what the parent can do to help.

- Discuss growth over time in addition to current performance.

- Use anecdotal comments to provide feedback on group work and group participation.

- Use enclosures: a one-page class or course overview, samples of the student's work, the student's self-evaluation, a letter from you or from the student to parents, etc.

We believe that teachers should explore alternative forms of assessment and grading that are adapted to their instructional methods and to the scoring rubrics they use in evaluating student performance. In one such approach (Brodhagen 1994), a grade-level middle school teacher attempted to accomplish three goals: to establish a grading system that was consistent with an integrative (thematic) curriculum, to involve students in the design of classroom assessment and grading,

and to avoid the stigma attached to grades of D and F by giving students opportunities to improve their work. She and a cooperating teacher agreed to assign only grades of A, B, C, or I (Incomplete), and graded only if the student turned in 80 percent of required work because anything less would be insufficient to grade. Students were given through the next quarter to complete their work and still receive a grade. Students were involved in the assessment of their own learning and also in the design of this system. One of the student recommendations was to attach to the grade report a list of assignments to date and identify which ones the student had completed. Students selected five or six pieces from a portfolio to represent their "best work," wrote a self-evaluation of the quarter's work, and wrote goals for the next quarter. The teacher used all of this information in a quarterly parent-teacher-student conference with considerable success and a high degree of student participation in the system.

Conclusion

The types of authentic assessments discussed in this chapter and in subsequent chapters are forward-looking with regard to models of teaching and learning. These assessments enable students to construct information rather than simply choose response alternatives, and challenge students to use their language to communicate their understandings and applications of knowledge. These types of assessments pose significant challenges in use with ELL students because they tend to rely on oral and written responses, yet provide flexibility by enabling students to demonstrate their knowledge and skills in a variety of ways. However, as with all assessments, the major challenges are to ensure that the assessments help improve instruction and benefit students.

APPLICATION ACTIVITIES

1. In a group, use Figure 2.1 to discuss the types of authentic assessment you are familiar with or have experience using.

2. On your own, complete Figure 2.2. Then talk with a partner about where you are now with regard to goal setting and authentic assessment and where you would like to be. Share this information with other teachers and use the information to decide what type of staff development you prefer.

3. Form a team of teachers and administrators working to design and use authentic assessments. Use Figure 2.3 to begin a discussion and develop an overall plan for authentic assessment in your school or program.

4. Try out one authentic assessment in a classroom and then share your experience. For example, try out a writing assessment using the scoring rubric in Figure 2.5. Select writing prompts appropriate to your curriculum or to topics being discussed in class. Modify the rubric to match local language arts objectives.

5. Check the inter-rater reliability of a scoring rubric. Work with one other teacher to identify two or three anchor papers that exemplify different points along the continuum on a scoring rubric. Then use Figure 2.6 to compare your score with those of others. In case of disagreement, engage in a discussion to clarify and revise the rubric, if needed, or to resolve differences.

PORTFOLIO ASSESSMENT

· ·

The number of professional publications emerging on the topic of portfolios continues to increase rapidly. Yet, even with the proliferation of materials, not one addresses in any significant way the use of portfolios with English language learners (ELLs). In this chapter we provide an overview of portfolio assessment, including its whole language base, implications for assessment, and advantages for ELL students. We also describe basic features of portfolios and elaborate on two essential ele

ments: student self-assessment and goal setting. As part of this discussion, we identify different kinds of portfolios and varying levels of portfolio use. In addition, we address the teacher's role in collaborative assessment. Finally, we provide suggestions for getting started with portfolios, managing portfolios, and using portfolio assessment in instruction. Examples presented throughout this chapter are meant as models to be modified by teachers or school teams for their particular needs.

Instructional Context

. . . .

Portfolios have been most often associated with the arts, where aspiring artists carry their "best" pieces and sketches in progress in order to display their talents. In 1987, researchers began collecting information on portfolios in language arts classrooms and found little information and virtually no research on the topic (Tierney, Carter, and Desai 1991). What they did find was that teachers more often advocated portfolio use than knew how to implement portfolios systematically in their classrooms. This finding has been substantiated by others (Calfee and Perfumo 1993; Gottlieb 1993; O'Malley et al. 1992; Valdez Pierce and O'Malley 1993).

One important instructional context that has supported and extended the use of portfolios has been provided by the whole language approach.[1] A *whole language* approach emphasizes holistic instruction and assessment rather than a skills-based approach to learning. Whole language instruction often involves thematic curriculum or the teaching of skills in the context of authentic reading and writing (e.g., trade books instead of basal readers). In a whole language classroom, activities are learner-centered, meaningful, and authentic (Goodman 1986; Freeman and Freeman 1992). A whole language approach provides a context for learning. It makes use of students' prior knowledge, experience, and interests and supports active construction of knowledge. It also provides meaning and purpose for learning and engages students in social interaction to develop both oral and written language. Rather than ignore basic skills, a whole language approach supports the integration of specific features of language in a meaningful context across the school curriculum (Cazden 1992). Whole language approaches have taken hold in more elementary than secondary classrooms and are evident not only in language arts classrooms but also in integrated curriculum programs (Hedgecock and Pucci 1993).

In a whole language approach, the roles of the teacher and student change from those in traditional classrooms. Instead of transmitting information based on a pre-determined curriculum and textbooks, the teacher provides an environment where both teacher and students have input into the nature of each day's plans and activities. This is a challenging (if not frightening) role for many teachers. Some tend to see it as giving up "power," while others see in it the potential for empowering both teachers and students (Cummins 1989). The student's role changes from one of passive absorber of information to one of active, self-directed learner and evaluator. The student becomes a critical, creative thinker who analyzes and applies facts rather than just repeats them. Clearly, these changing roles imply radical changes for assessment as well as instruction.

IMPLICATIONS FOR ASSESSMENT

As in whole language classrooms, the roles of teachers and students using portfolios for assessment change. Portfolio assessment is very much learner-centered, which means that the student has input on not only what goes into the portfolio but also on how the contents will be evaluated. In addition, the student has a role in assessing his or her own progress in the classroom. This learner-centered feature of portfolios is what some have called the "spirit" of the portfolio classroom (Tierney, Carter, and Desai 1991).

We encourage you to integrate these new roles for teachers and students into your classroom so that portfolios can become part of a learner-centered, collaborative assessment program, rather than one which is teacher-centered. In portfolio assessment, students and teachers become partners who confer on portfolio contents and their interpretation. It is not a matter of who has the last word but of reaching consensus. Because of this, it takes considerable time and experience on the part of both teacher and students to learn their new roles. It takes trust and respect between both parties as well.

---

1. An *approach* refers to a philosophy toward teaching encompassing a number of instructional techniques rather than a single instructional method (Richards and Rodgers 1986).

ADVANTAGES OF PORTFOLIOS

One of the most valuable aspects of portfolio assessment is that it links assessment with instruction. That is, student performance is evaluated in relation to instructional goals, objectives, and classroom activities. Portfolio contents should represent what ELL students are doing in the classroom and reflect their progress toward instructional goals. In this way, portfolios can be said to have *content validity* (see Chapter 2); that is, the contents reflect authentic activities through which students have been learning in the classroom. In addition, compiling portfolios does not take an inordinate amount of time away from classroom-based activities when the contents reflect the curriculum. In a way, portfolios go beyond assessment. They do this by trans-forming instruction and learning. Successful teachers have found that portfolios increase the quantity as well as the quality of writing and contribute to students' cognitive development (Dellinger 1993). For an example of a first quarter portfolio, see the Appendix.

Unlike single test scores and multiple-choice tests, portfolios provide a multidimensional perspective on student growth over time. Portfolios reveal much more about what students can do with what they know than do standardized tests. The use of portfolios encourages students to reflect on their work, to analyze their progress, and to set improvement goals. Portfolios can be tailored not only to individual classes but also to individual students, and portfolio results can be used to plan instruction. Portfolios can contain samples of work in the native language as well as in English, depending on the medium of instruction and the goals of each class.

What a Portfolio Is and Isn't

. . . .

Portfolios mean different things to different people. Although there is no single definition of portfolios that will suit everyone, here we will define the essential elements of a portfolio and describe different types of portfolios being used in classrooms today. We will also indicate the uses of portfolios in classrooms and schools, and at broader administrative levels.

ESSENTIAL ELEMENTS OF PORTFOLIOS

From among the diverse types of portfolios being used today, we identify several key elements. These include: samples of student work, student self-assessment, and clearly stated criteria.

Samples of Student Work   We know that most portfolios consist of a sample of student work that shows growth over time. The sample can consist of writing samples, audio or videotapes, mathematics problems, social studies reports, or science experiments. The contents may depend on student or teacher preferences, the purposes of the portfolio, or the instructional goals the portfolio is designed to reflect. Tierney, Carter, and Desai (1991) indicate that the whole point of having portfolios is to individualize them as much as possible—not only to suit classroom goals, but to suit each student's goals as well. Because of this, no two portfolios may ever be alike.

Although portfolios may differ considerably from one classroom to another, they can nevertheless be used as systematic collections of student work. Systematic collections need to be carefully planned, just like instruction. That is, if we plan our instructional goals, objectives, materials, and activities, we should also plan a way to gather evidence of student achievement toward learning goals. We need to determine not only the process by which we and our students will evaluate progress but also the system for bringing all the information together and for sharing it with students and their parents, other teachers, and program administrators. Portfolios can provide such a system. We can begin by asking students to collect baseline samples of their work (e.g., the first piece of writing for the year, the first story retelling, and/or the first oral interview) and updating these as the year progresses.

Student Self-Assessment   Without self-assessment and reflection on the part of the student, a portfolio is not a portfolio (Paulson, Paulson, and Meyer 1991; Tierney, Carter, and Desai 1991;

Valencia 1990). That is, a portfolio is not just another assessment measure that is done to a student by a teacher or someone else. A portfolio is a unique opportunity for students to learn to monitor their own progress and take responsibility for meeting goals set jointly with the teacher. Portfolios that call for reflection on the part of students lead to several outcomes: students take responsibility for knowing where they are with regard to learning goals; they broaden their view of what is being learned; and they begin to see learning as a process, thereby getting a developmental perspective on their learning (Wolf 1989).

How do students do self-assessment with portfolios? Three kinds of self-assessment have been described: documentation, comparison, and integration (Paulson and Paulson 1992). In *documentation*, the student provides a justification for the items selected for the portfolio. Students asked to select their "best work," for example, might indicate that they chose a piece because they liked what they had said, because the work had good spelling, or because they liked the topic. In self-assessment through *comparison*, students compare a recent piece of work with an earlier one by looking for ways that they have improved as writers. For example, students might comment on their improved editing or ability to keep to a central theme in more recent writing. In the third kind of self-assessment, *integration*, students address their learning in a more general way. They use the portfolio to provide examples of their growing strengths in oral or written language or their independence as a learner. All of these forms of self-assessment are important for ELL students as they go about mastering new skills.

Despite the advantages of student self-assessment, many teachers do not yet feel comfortable with it. In fact, teachers have told us that they do not believe in giving up this much control to students, whom they do not believe to be capable of self-assessment. This assumption calls for instruction on two sides: instruction for the teacher and instruction for the student. Both parties need to learn about their new roles in assessment and acquire experience through them. Tierney, Carter, and Desai (1991) suggest that the new role for teachers includes providing time for work that encourages decision making, drafting, reflecting, discussing, reading, and responding, as well as using information gathered from interactions with students about their portfolios to guide instruction. Students need to learn how to choose writing topics and materials, engage in self- and peer assessment, and set goals for learning. These aspects of portfolios will be discussed more fully later in this chapter.

Clearly Stated Criteria   Students need to know how their work will be evaluated and by what standards their work will be judged. Specifying criteria and standards and providing representative samples of what these look like helps students set goals and work toward them. Rather than making students guess at how the teacher is grading or applying criteria, the teacher involves students in setting the standards and clarifying them. Teachers need to make time for students to discuss criteria and engage in goal setting. In addition, goals that many students in a class have in common can be used to direct instructional activities, such as mini-lessons designed to address students' need for help in formulating summaries or using transitions in written discourse (Clemmons et al. 1993; Tierney, Carter, and Desai 1991).

In portfolio assessment, criteria can be identified for selecting the work samples that go in portfolios as well as for judging the quality of each sample (Herman, Aschbacher, and Winters 1992). Since one of the principles of performance assessment is public and discussed criteria, criteria for portfolio assessment need to be clear to students and parents.

Our experience in working with ESL teachers using portfolios indicates that even when teachers have identified a focus for portfolios and guided students in engaging in self-assessment, they may still be grading samples of student work without having clearly stated criteria for each sample or type of work. Later in this chapter we describe how teachers can teach students to set criteria and standards for their work.

TYPES OF PORTFOLIOS

When we think of portfolios, most of us think of collections of student work, including samples of their best work. However, in our interactions with teachers of ELL students, we've realized that portfolios tend to mean different things to different people and are by no means standardized to suit every student's needs. A number of attempts have been made to describe different types of portfolios (NEA 1993; Gottlieb 1995), but it is our impression that there are three basic types of portfolios: showcase portfolios, collections portfolios, and assessment portfolios.

Showcase Portfolios   *Showcase portfolios* are typically used to display a student's best work to parents and school administrators. As showcase pieces, entries in the portfolio are carefully selected to illustrate student achievement in the classroom. Some schools sponsor a "portfolio night" where portfolios can be discussed with teachers, students, and parents. The limitation to showcase portfolios is that, in showing only students' best work, they tend to leave out the path by which students arrived. The process itself is missing. A showcase portfolio is one which tends to hold only finished products and therefore may not successfully illustrate student learning over time.

Collections Portfolios   A *collections portfolio* literally contains all of a student's work that shows how a student deals with daily class assignments. These are also called *working folders* and may include rough drafts, sketches, works-in-progress, and final products. This type of portfolio may contain evidence of both process and product and has the advantage of containing everything produced by the student throughout the year. However, it becomes rather unwieldy for assessment purposes because it has not been carefully planned and organized for a specific focus.

Assessment Portfolios   Unlike showcase and collections portfolios, *assessment portfolios* are focused reflections of specific learning goals that contain systematic collections of student work, student self-assessment, and teacher assessment. The contents are often selected to show growth over time. Each entry in the portfolio has been selected with both student and teacher input and is evaluated based on criteria specified by both student and teacher. These criteria may take the form of rubrics, checklists, rating scales, and so on. Whereas the portfolio itself does not receive a grade or a rating, the different entries may be weighted to reflect an overall level of student achievement.

Our experience indicates that portfolios are more often used as showcase and collections portfolios than as assessment portfolios. This may be because the idea of quantifying student work goes against the notion that portfolios are reflections of student work and belong to students themselves. It may also be because most teachers have not received any guidance on how to plan portfolios as assessment management systems. For whatever reason, portfolios planned and used systematically for assessment purposes are currently not being widely used at the classroom level. They are, however, beginning to be used for such purposes at the district-wide and state levels, with mixed results (Abruscato 1993; Herman and Winters 1994). In cases where portfolios are mandated on a large-scale basis, this practice may actually undermine their value for individual student reflection and self-assessment (Case 1994).

LEVELS OF PORTFOLIO USE

The use of portfolios in classrooms has sufficient advantages that it has recently become an alternative to traditional assessment at the school level and in statewide assessment programs. However, uses at other than the classroom level change the original purpose and usefulness of portfolios for instructional planning.

Classrooms   At the classroom level, portfolios reflect classroom instruction and activities and have the potential for linking assessment and instruction in ways that externally-imposed assessment does not. Portfolios can capture both process and product by focusing not only on the answer to a problem but also on how students approached the problem-solving situation. For example, let's say you are working with low literacy students in a high school ESL program. How would you go about using a portfolio for assessment? First, you would define your instructional goals. Then you would review how you are documenting student progress toward those goals and whether your approaches need to be revisited in light of what we know about how students learn. Finally, you would help students generate criteria by which their work would be evaluated, as well as criteria for selecting what should go into the portfolio. Low literacy students will need extra support in using portfolios until they have been in your class for at least a quarter or semester.

Schools At the school level, portfolios can follow students to the next ESL/bilingual or classroom teacher. In this context, portfolios contain valuable evidence of how far a student has come toward meeting classroom or program goals. An assessment portfolio is useful for this purpose because the contents can illustrate student growth and achievement. On a district-wide level, portfolios can accompany students from school to school in cases of transfer or promotion, again providing follow-on teachers with concrete evidence of what the student has accomplished and how far he or she still needs to go. In many cases, district ESL programs are passing along folders with test results and some alternative assessments as the student moves from teacher to teacher, but these cannot be called portfolios. Instead, they serve as placement folders for which the data are collected only twice or several times a year. Assessment portfolios inherently require continual updating and maintenance and include student input, self-assessment, and goal setting.

Statewide Assessment Not much empirical evidence exists regarding the use of portfolios for large-scale assessments (Herman and Winters 1994). Also, little information exists regarding the validity and reliability of portfolio assessment used for high-stakes purposes (e.g., to qualify students for high school graduation). The Vermont statewide portfolio assessment program reported low inter-rater reliability with some of its portfolio components. Nevertheless, self-reports from teachers indicated that portfolio assessment had positive effects on instruction, in particular, on

the curriculum content and instructional strategies (Koretz 1993).

Self-Assessment: The Key to Portfolios

• • • • • • • • • • • • • • • • • • •

The key to using portfolios successfully in classrooms is engaging students in self-assessment. Effective assessment involves students and enables them to see possibilities for reflection, redirection, and confirmation of their own learning efforts. Students often need support in understanding the importance of self-assessment, in becoming independent evaluators of their own progress, and in setting goals for future learning.

IMPORTANCE OF SELF-ASSESSMENT

Why is self-assessment important? If we see ELL students as active learners who construct their own knowledge, then surely asking students to map their route and check their progress along the way are part of the learning process. Apprising students of the performance standards and criteria to which they will be held accountable helps students focus on precisely what it is that their work must show. Teachers indicate that when students become actively involved in self-assessment they become more responsible for the direction their learning takes (Rief 1990; Tierney, Carter, and Desai 1991; Wolf 1989).

LEARNING ABOUT SELF-ASSESSMENT

ELL students at beginning levels of proficiency in English need time not only to acquire the language but also to be able to communicate their ideas and plans. Because of this, these students will need extra support in using portfolios until they've been in your classroom for at least one or two full grading periods.

Teachers should learn how to support students in evaluating their own progress. Even students as young as kindergartners can learn to identify essential aspects of good work (Clemmons et al. 1993; Sperling 1993). The following discussion draws on the work of Clemmons et al. and Tierney, Carter, and Desai (1991), whose discussions of self-assessment in grade-level classrooms we have adapted for our own purposes with ELL students.

If you are new to student self-assessment, you should start small. That is, begin with one assessment at a time and gradually build a repertoire of self-assessment approaches and techniques that most closely match your instructional goals. We have included some sample self-assessment formats in this chapter for you to adapt or modify as you choose. By beginning with an assessment model that closely reflects your instructional goals, you will be halfway toward using student self-assessment. Every model will need to be tailored to your students' needs. However, it is important to remember that self-assessment is a *process* through which students must be led. Self-assessment is not about forms or checklists. Teaching students to evaluate their progress begins with realizing that students will be learning new skills. As such, they will need plenty of opportunities to learn and apply these skills with feedback from you on how they're doing.

Setting Criteria   In order for students to evaluate their own work or performance, they need to be able to see examples of good work and understand by what standards it has been judged. This means that you need to *work with students to specify the criteria* by which different kinds of work will be evaluated. For example, you could discuss the elements of good oral proficiency, reading comprehension, writing, problem solving, or working in groups. In helping students to evaluate their own work, you can also *provide samples of exemplary work* (called *benchmarks*) and less than exemplary work. These examples let students see what good work looks like and develop a clear idea of how their work will be evaluated. To do this, you can keep samples of student performance from each quarter or grading period in a notebook, or use samples of student performance from a previous year and share these with students.

Ask students to *identify the characteristics of exemplary work* which they think makes it good or outstanding. You can put a sample on the overhead projector or give every student a copy of several samples of student work (oral or written performances). As students name the characteristics, you could write these on the board or on chart paper. These become *criteria charts*. Criteria charts should contain as many essential criteria as students can generate, even if these are added a few at a time. If students initially identify only a few characteristics, you might ask probe questions to guide them in looking at aspects of performance not yet mentioned. State criteria in positive terms, such as "I can…" or "I put…" Examples of student-generated criteria can be found in Figure 3.1. These criteria appear as they might on a criteria chart developed in a typical classroom. You can place the chart on the wall of your classroom and refer to it from time to time as you discuss student writing. Have students *work in cooperative learning groups* to examine samples of good work and extract criteria. Younger students and those with lower proficiency can use fewer criteria and language appropriate to their level.

The use of the criteria chart is similar to a writers' workshop, where the teacher leads students through mini-lessons to focus on aspects of their work that need improvement (Calkins 1994; Graves 1983; Samway 1992). You can present mini-lessons to students on specific criteria for evaluating oral language, reading comprehension, writing, and content area progress. One mini-lesson might focus on the use of punctuation in writing (a concern ESL teachers often raise for beginning and intermediate students). One way to get students to focus on this aspect of their writing is to provide them with two samples of writing, one with appropriate punctuation and one which lacks punctuation. By having students compare and discuss the two writing samples, you can be sure that they will come away with a better idea of why effective punctuation is essential to good writing. As criteria evolve, you can add these to the student-generated list. Students can refer to the criteria for different aspects of their oral language, reading, writing, and/or content area achievement. As students internalize the criteria, they will no longer need to refer to a wall chart.

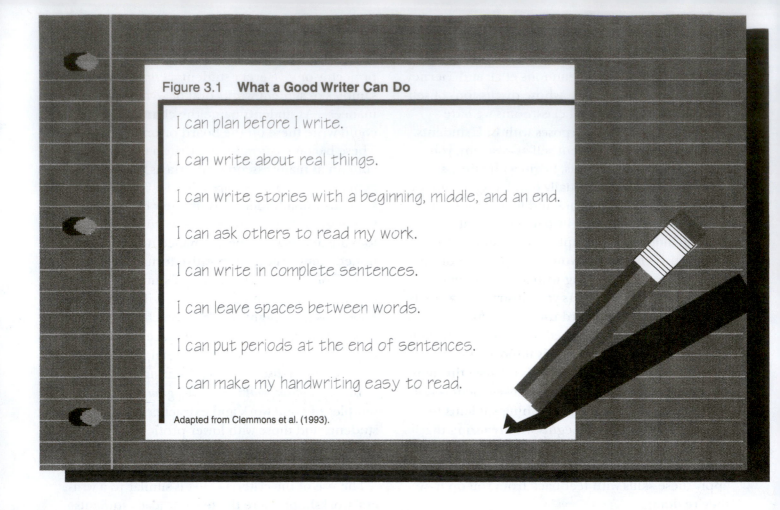

Figure 3.1 What a Good Writer Can Do

I can plan before I write.

I can write about real things.

I can write stories with a beginning, middle, and an end.

I can ask others to read my work.

I can write in complete sentences.

I can leave spaces between words.

I can put periods at the end of sentences.

I can make my handwriting easy to read.

Adapted from Clemmons et al. (1993).

Applying Criteria Once students have participated in identifying criteria to assess their work, they need opportunities to *apply the criteria as a group* to actual work samples. You can begin by having students work in pairs or in small groups. Ask students to identify the strengths and weaknesses of a sample selected from their own work. The criteria they use will be drawn from the criteria chart or a handout. The group can then share their assessment with the rest of the class, perhaps using a transparency of how they applied the criteria. The class can then discuss this assessment as a whole and suggest revisions of the product. When students have done this a number of times, they are ready to *begin assessing their own work individually.* You will need to provide opportunities for students to make the transition from the group process to self-assessment with varied types of writing or other products.

Another way to advance students toward individual self-assessment is by having them work with a *portfolio partner* (Clemmons et al. 1993). Ask students to select a work sample that they want to put in their portfolio. Together with another student, their portfolio partner, they can evaluate one of their own entries using the criteria developed by the class. On 3″ x 5″ index cards, students can jot down the strengths and weaknesses of their partner's work sample and attach the card to the portfolio entry, as suggested in Figure 3.2. This can be done with all types of student work samples, including oral language samples, reading comprehension activities, writing samples, and content area work samples. You can ask students to reflect on their own work by considering what their partner's assessment says about what they have learned. From peer assessment *students can then move to independent self-assessment.* Although they will need to rely on the criteria chart or handout initially, the more practice they get in applying the criteria to their own work, the more independence they will develop in assessing it.

Setting Goals   By engaging in self-assessment activities, students begin to identify strengths and weaknesses in their work. Weaknesses become improvement goals. For ELL students, you will probably need to give numerous examples of your own personal improvement goals, such as reading one best-seller each month or jogging two miles every other day. Ask students for examples of their own personal goals, then write these on the board and discuss how they might be applied to their portfolio entries. For example, Clemmons et al. (1993) suggest that teachers guide students in setting realistic goals by putting forth humorous examples, such as, "My goal is to read a hundred books this week."

Have students begin by setting improvement goals for the work samples used previously in establishing criteria. As a class, identify areas of need in the work samples or performances and then jot down improvement goals for each work sample. In this way, students begin to get a feel for how to identify their own improvement goals. By working together in pairs or groups and getting feedback from the class, students get practice in identifying weaknesses in their work and in setting realistic goals. Once students set goals for others' work, they can set goals for themselves with a portfolio partner and then individually. Students can record their goals on index cards attached to their work sample, as shown in Figure 3.3.

Working Toward Goals   Students will need help in remembering to work toward their learning goals. One of the ways to make sure students remember is to have them jot down their goals on an index card or a sheet of paper and attach this to their notebook or to their desk where they can refer to it from time to time. Another way is to meet with students in small groups to discuss their progress toward goals. Encourage students to

Figure 3.2   **Portfolio Partners**

Your Name _____   Date _____

Your Partner's Name _____

1. Review your partner's work sample.

2. What do you think the sample shows your partner can do?

3. What do you think your partner did well?

4. What do you think your partner could make better?

Adapted from Clemmons et al. (1993).

Figure 3.3 **Setting Improvement Goals**

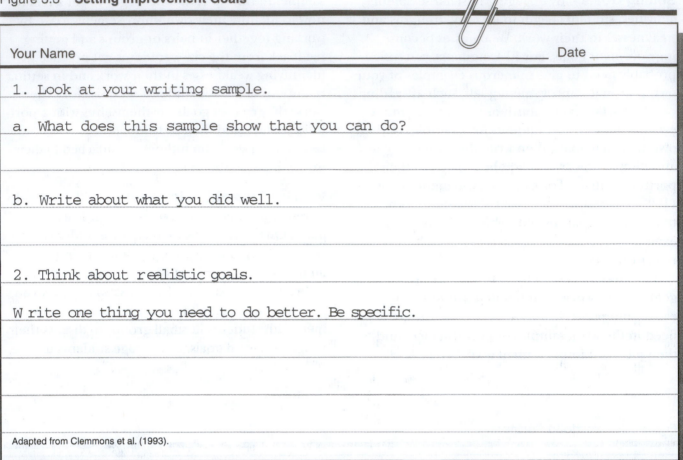

Your Name _____ Date _____

1. Look at your writing sample.

a. What does this sample show that you can do?

b. Write about what you did well.

2. Think about realistic goals.

Write one thing you need to do better. Be specific.

Adapted from Clemmons et al. (1993).

make suggestions to each other in small groups. Clemmons et al. (1993) suggest that after these group meetings teachers ask students to restate their goals and their plans for achieving them. Still another way is to ask students to report their progress to you in writing each week on a card or sheet of paper. Have students aim for goals they can work on each quarter or grading period, and meet with them to discuss these goals at least halfway through the period and then again at the end.

Using Goals to Improve Instruction In addition to making time for students to set and discuss goals, teachers also need to make time to allow students to work toward those goals in daily class activities. This is an optimal opportunity for linking assessment with instruction. By identifying goals that students have in common, either as a

class or as a small group, you can plan mini-lessons aimed at those areas that need improvement. Not only does this make your classroom more learner-centered, it also gives you feedback on the effectiveness of your instruction (Herman and Winters 1994; NEA 1993; Tierney, Carter, and Desai 1991).

Teacher Assessment

. . . .

Given the student's role in assessment, what then is the teacher's role? The teacher's role in authentic assessment of students is multifaceted. The teacher models approaches to learning and assessment, facilitates student self-assessment, and manages the evidence of learning. The teacher provides guidance and support to students as they generate and apply evaluation criteria, reflect on their learning, set goals, and organize samples of their work in their portfolios. The teacher plays a crucial role in providing feedback to students, in setting realistic goals, and in evaluating student pro-gress. The teacher periodically evaluates samples of student work after students have evaluated their own work and set goals for themselves. By spot-checking students' self-assessments and representative samples of their work, teachers save time and avoid the redundancy of going back over everything students have already evaluated. Teachers can confirm that students have made progress toward meeting their goals and suggest additional goals.

To help students focus on goals, teacher comments should be brief and address specific work samples. Comments should include both strengths and weaknesses in student work. Some brief comments on index cards or notes attached to the work samples can go a long way toward giving students useful diagnostic information. Teacher assessments can also take the form of anecdotal records, checklists of student performance, rating scales, and conferences. We have supplied numerous examples of these types of assessments throughout the chapters in this book (see the Index of Figures and Reproducibles).

Collaborative Assessment

· · · · · · · · · · · · · · · ·

Once teacher and student have each had the opportunity to evaluate the student's work, they are ready to participate in a *portfolio conference* to discuss student progress. It is here that teacher and student face the student's growth together. Portfolio conferences can be mutually informative for students and teachers alike. That is, not only do students learn more about their strengths and weaknesses and the status of their personal goals, the teachers learn about how each student sees his or her own work and the effectiveness of classroom activities. Students get individual feedback on how to set and achieve goals, and teachers gets individual feedback on how to make instructional activities more meaningful and useful to students. It is

in this way that students and teachers engage in collaborative assessment as part of the portfolio process. A list of questions for teachers to use in portfolio conferences on reading and writing assessment is presented in Figure 3.4.

Prepare for the portfolio conference by reviewing each student's portfolio and planning to make some positive observations regarding its organization and contents. Begin the conference by asking students to reflect on their growth and the status of their goals in regard to learning objectives, whether these are in reading and writing, oral language development, or content area achievement. The portfolio conference is not meant to put students on the defensive (see sample questions below); rather, it is meant to get students actively involved in reflection and self-assessment and to provide teacher feedback.

ELL students can be prepared for the portfolio conference by providing them with questions on a Portfolio Review Guide, as shown in Figure 3.5. Guiding questions can include the following:

- What does your portfolio tell you about your (oral language, reading, writing, math, science achievement, etc.)?

- What can you do well in (oral language, reading, writing, math, science achievement, etc.)?

- What goals do you need to continue working on in (oral language, reading, writing, math, science achievement, etc.)?

ELL students may initially need more probing questions to get them to reflect upon their work and to express their evaluation of it. Older ELL students may have been schooled in a system in their native country where teacher-centered modes of instruction did not invite student participation in assessment. These students may need more time to adjust to portfolios and portfolio conferences.

Many teachers we have spoken to recommend holding portfolio conferences at the end of the grading period. However, we recommend wherever possible holding a portfolio conference in the middle of the grading period, as well. In this way, students begin to understand how their work will

Figure 3.4 **Portfolio Conference Questions**

Student _____ Date _____

Reading

1. Tell me about your favorite stories/books. _____

_____

2. What do good readers do to understand what they read? _____

_____

3. What does your portfolio show about you as a reader? _____

_____

4. Did you meet your reading goals from last quarter? _____

_____

5. What are your goals for becoming a better reader next quarter? _____

_____

Writing

1. Tell me what you like to write about. _____

_____

2. How do you make your writing better? _____

_____

3. What does your portfolio show about you as a writer? _____

_____

4. Did you meet your writing goals from last quarter? _____

_____

5. What are your goals for becoming a better writer next quarter? _____

_____

Adapted from Clemmons et al. (1993); Glazer and Brown (1993); and Yancey (1992).

Figure 3.5 Portfolio Review Guide

Name _____ Grade _____

Your teacher will soon have a conference with you about your portfolio.
Review your portfolio and prepare for the conference by answering the following questions:

1. How has your English improved since the last report period? _____
_____
_____

2. What can you do now that you could not do before? _____
_____
_____

3. How has your reading improved? _____
_____
_____

4. What do you like to read? What makes it interesting? _____
_____
_____

5. What are you doing to become a better reader? _____
_____
_____

6. How has your writing improved? _____
_____
_____

7. What are you doing to become a better writer? _____
_____
_____
_____

Adapted from a form developed by ESL teachers P. Conrad and K. Huston (1994).

be evaluated at the end of the quarter. On the average, portfolio conferences take about fifteen minutes and can be conducted a few each day as other students are engaged in small group or independent work (Clemmons et al. 1993). You can obtain the help of colleagues, teacher aides, and parents during the portfolio conference period. Helpers can work with the rest of the class while you confer with students. On the other hand, some teachers have told us that they show parents how to conduct portfolio conferences and that this enables them to meet with more students in a shorter period of time.

Getting Started with Portfolios

• • • • • • • • • • • • • • • • •

A number of steps will help to ensure that student portfolios provide you with the assessment information needed to make decisions regarding student progress. Steps include setting a purpose, matching contents to purpose, setting criteria, setting standards of performance, and getting students and parents involved (Valdez Pierce and Gottlieb 1994).

SETTING THE PURPOSE

This first step is the most important step, and yet many teachers skip it altogether. Getting ready to use portfolios for assessment means specifying the assessment purpose. The purpose may be oriented toward classroom use or toward school and district use. Potential purposes in classrooms are to encourage student self-evaluation, to monitor student progress, to assess student performance relative to curriculum objectives, to showcase student products, to communicate student performance to parents, to maintain a continuous record of student performance from one grade to the next, or all of these.

Uses of portfolios at the school or district level often concern accountability. The focus is on determining if the student meets expected standards of performance relative to the district's benchmark objectives (e.g., in language arts and mathematics). The classroom and school-level pur-

poses are sometimes combined. For example, selected work from a collection portfolio, which contains all student products, can be entered into a showcase portfolio, which shows best work in a particular area. In turn, selected products from showcase portfolios in language arts and mathematics can then be combined in an assessment portfolio for district accountability.

Part of stating the assessment purpose of a portfolio is to decide in which curriculum areas the portfolio will be maintained. For example, most portfolios are literacy or reading/writing portfolios. There are also math, science, and social studies portfolios as well as integrated portfolios. If you would like to focus on how students use higher-order thinking skills, you might be interested in using portfolios to give you information on how students apply thinking skills across the curriculum (see Chapter 7). For ELL students, portfolios can also be used to assess oral language development. These portfolios may include oral language tapes, rating scales and scoring rubrics, self-assessment forms, and so on (see Chapter 4).

Pull-out ESL teachers working with students already using portfolios in grade-level classrooms or in bilingual programs can collaborate with grade-level colleagues to determine the assessment purpose and help the student identify entries from ESL activities. Through this type of collaboration everyone benefits: the grade-level teacher, the student, and you. If you are a novice portfolio user, start small and focus on only one class or area of instruction at a time in order to keep from being overwhelmed. If you begin with one area and feel comfortable with the process over a period of time, you may then want to incorporate another instructional area addressed in your curriculum.

MATCHING CONTENTS TO PURPOSE

Once you have identified your assessment purpose, you can begin to think about the kinds of portfolio entries that will best match your instructional outcomes and reflect the type of work students are doing in your class. Begin by taking stock of your current assessment approaches and deciding which might provide the most useful kind of information in a student portfolio. Now is also the time to try out new approaches to assessment if you would like to include something in the portfolio which you are currently not doing in your classroom. For example, you may have heard of teachers doing reading/writing portfolios and using reading logs, anecdotal records, and student self-assessment checklists for reading strategies application. You may be using none of these approaches at present. Select one or two approaches you would like to try out each grading period and see how they work. You may need to revise your approach many times before you are happy with the results, but this is a natural part of trying out innovative assessment techniques.

In the process of proposing entries to match your instructional outcomes and assessment purpose, consider having two types of entries for all students: required and optional entries. *Required* or *core* entries provide the primary basis for assessment of student work. These should include student self-assessment, samples of student work, and some type of teacher assessment. The number of required entries you include depends on your experience and comfort level in working with portfolios. Teachers have told us that they generally begin with two or three entries each grading period and build up to about five required entries after several grading periods. *Optional* or *supporting* entries provide additional information that complements information contained in the required entries. Have students gather evidence of not only what they have produced but also the processes involved in the problem solving, the story writing, or the preparation of the research report.

A sample Portfolio Summary Sheet is illustrated in Figure 3.6. This form was adapted from one used in the secondary ESL program in Arlington County Public Schools, Virginia. Note that the contents have both optional and required components and focus on reading and writing. You could easily add an audio or videotape to the portfolio to expand the contents to include all language skills. The four columns for the school quarters suggest that not all materials might be collected in each quarter. This is an option you have in determining whether you need information only at the beginning and end of the year or on a more continuous

basis. Spaces are provided for you to enter marks for each entry in the portfolio in each quarter. What you enter in these spaces may be a simple check mark to indicate that the entry is contained in the portfolio, a score on some kind of rating scale reflecting performance relative to district objectives, or the date of the entry. Space is provided on the form to enter results from more formal end-of-year assessments conducted for reclassification. When combined with the contents of the portfolio, the Portfolio Summary Sheet contains information that will be useful for making reclassification decisions from multiple data sources. Space is available at the bottom of the sheet for placement recommendations and comments.

SETTING CRITERIA

In portfolio assessment, you will need to develop clear, objective criteria for judging student work. This is to let anyone reviewing the portfolio know exactly how the student is doing. You can do this by including evaluative criteria for each sample of student work in the portfolio. For example, if a portfolio holds writing samples, it should also contain specific criteria for evaluation of writing. These may take the form of rating scales, rubrics, or checklists (see Chapter 6). Reading comprehension can be assessed by including teacher checklists, reading texts with comprehension questions attached, cloze tests, etc. (see Chapter 5). The criteria for evaluation of student work must be in place and clearly understood by students before their work is evaluated and placed in their portfolios.

In most classrooms, teachers assign grades to student work. Grades communicate rank order of performance (A is better than B, etc.) and are useful in communicating with parents, who often insist on knowing the grade their child received. However, the criteria underlying grades are often ambiguous. Students tend to be unclear on what criteria were used for grading and therefore have difficulty in identifying areas of need. Scoring rubrics are specifically designed to address this problem and to clarify for both students and parents the criteria for assigning scores. You can convert ratings and checklists to grades at the end of the period by deciding what level of performance

Figure 3.6 **Portfolio Summary Sheet**

Student _____ Grade _____

Teacher _____ School _____

Required Contents	School Quarter			
	1st	2nd	3rd	4th
1. Sample reading text with questions				
2. Reading strategies checklist				
3. Writing sample				
4. Student choice of writing				
5. Self-assessment				

Optional Contents

1. List of books read				
2. Reading interest inventory				
3. Pre/post reading scores				
4. Literacy checklist				
5. Samples from content areas				

Placement Test Scores

Reading _____   Grammar _____   Listening _____

Recommended Placement

Comments

Adapted from a form developed by secondary ESOL HILT teachers, Arlington County Public Schools, Virginia.

is associated with different grades, as discussed in Chapter 2. When making this conversion, you should make the basis for your grading and its relationship to the scoring rubrics explicit to both students and parents.

SETTING STANDARDS OF PERFORMANCE

Along with criteria for evaluation, you will need to assist students in understanding what assessment results mean and how to interpret them. You can do this by explaining how criteria reflect standards. Whether you are using a holistic or analytic rubric, a teacher checklist, or a percentage of correct responses, you will need to decide cut-off points for at least three levels: *exceeds the standard, meets the standard,* and *approaches the standard.* If using a holistic rubric, we recommend at least a four-point rating scale in order to allow for more differentiation in the middle range of performance. As you evaluate student work, you can revise these cut-off points as needed.

Besides sharing with students clear standards of performance, you can also provide examples of standards through samples of student work or benchmark papers. You share these with students currently in the class as well as with students in future classes. By providing benchmarks, you are helping students visualize the standards of performance and how they can improve their own work to meet the standard.

GETTING STUDENTS INVOLVED

Once you have identified your assessment purpose, proposed portfolio contents, and thought about setting criteria and standards, you can begin to plan how to get students involved with *their* portfolios. Think about what role the students will play in selecting portfolio entries, providing input for assessment criteria and standards for each entry, and assessing their own work and the work of others. As you plan, you will also need to consider how you will make all of this part of your instruction. That is, you will need to determine how and when you will teach students to do each of the things that will get them involved in reflecting upon their own progress in your class.

Three reasons why students are more likely to become involved in their own learning when portfolios are used effectively are that portfolios (Sweet 1993):

1. Convey to students the features or criteria of quality performance so they can apply these criteria to their own work and internalize them.

2. Engage students in meaningful activities that are likely to result in products worth sharing with others and retaining for review.

3. Allow students to chronicle their own work and open new channels for communication with teachers that are focused on their own classroom products.

GETTING PARENTS INVOLVED

Parents should also become partners in the portfolio process. They should be informed at each step of the way—from setting criteria to selecting portfolio entries. Parents can be involved in at least three ways: (1) as home collaborators who provide input on student progress, (2) as portfolio conference participants who come in to listen to their child talk about their portfolio, and (3) as an audience for and contributors to both the students' portfolios and methods for reporting student progress. Parents should be informed early and often about the purposes, procedures, and benefits of using portfolios. We encourage you to begin communication with parents about portfolios through the school newsletter or with a more personal letter. A sample letter to parents is contained in Figure 3.7.

You can invite parents to portfolio or parent nights or other meetings to inform them of how portfolios work in your classroom. You can also use this time to encourage students to showcase their accomplishments. Tierney, Carter, and Desai (1991) suggest the following guidelines for getting parents involved:

1. Give parents advance notice about upcoming conferences.

2. Invite parents by phone or in person or in conjunction with other parental meetings.

3. In the conference, provide each student's portfolio for parents and students.

Figure 3.7 Sample Parent Letter

_____
(Date)

Dear Parents:

Your child, (_____) will be putting
(Student's Name)

together a portfolio this year. This portfolio will contain samples of his

or her work that show what he/she is learning. I will use the portfolio

to identify each student's strengths and weaknesses and to plan

appropriate instructional activities.

At various times throughout the year, I will be asking you to review

the portfolio and to comment on your child's work. After you have

reviewed your child's portfolio, please make comments on the Portfolio

Summary Sheet and initial it at the bottom. Please call me if you have

any questions or would like to come in for a parent-student portfolio

conference. I am looking forward to working closely with you.

Sincerely,

_____
(Teacher's Name)

_____
(Teacher's Telephone Number)

Adapted from De Fina (1992).

4. Use an interpreter for non-English-speaking parents and meet in a comfortable setting.

5. Focus conversation in the conference on each student's progress (interests, strengths, needs).

6. Ask open-ended questions about the student.

7. Write a summary of the conference and give or send parents a copy.

When sending portfolios home with students, send a note to parents in both English and the native language regarding the importance of returning the portfolios. Invite parent comments on samples of the student's work. A number of teachers have indicated to us that parental support for the portfolio is essential to maintaining student interest in the portfolio. An uninvolved parent who expresses no interest in looking at or who dismisses the student's carefully prepared portfolio can seriously undermine student motivation in the classroom.

Managing Portfolios

. . . .

One of the major concerns we have heard teachers express regarding portfolio assessment relates to the management of portfolios. In this section, we address this concern and indicate how teachers can organize portfolio contents, make time for assessment, and communicate portfolio results.

ORGANIZING CONTENTS

The portfolio contents need to be organized effectively in order to communicate student progress to students, parents, and teachers. First, every entry must be dated so that you and your students can identify clear signs of growth. Second, a cover sheet should be used as a table of contents for the portfolio. A sample cover sheet was provided in Figure 3.6. Third, you can organize contents by indicating whether the entries are required or optional. The sample cover sheet in Figure 3.6 allows for this distinction.

One way that some teachers identify the contents is by listing them on the left side of the inside cover of a portfolio folder. They have the school district print shop print these contents on a number of folders they anticipate using for the year. This has the advantage of easing the burden on individual teachers, but it assumes a considerable amount of planning among teachers who are collaborating in portfolio use. In addition to having the contents of the portfolio listed on the left side of the inside cover, these teachers use the right side of the inside cover to list the scoring rubrics for the student work to be included in the portfolio. In this way, both students and teachers are reminded of the criteria by which the products will be evaluated every time they place an entry in or update the portfolio.

MAKING TIME FOR ASSESSMENT

Portfolios become easier to use once they become part of a regular routine in your classroom. However, initial efforts at using portfolios will seem time-consuming. Herman and Winters (1994) reported that portfolios make substantial demands on teacher time in terms of learning new assessment approaches, teaching students to compile portfolios, developing portfolios, applying criteria to student work, and reflecting on and revising instructional and assessment practices. We believe there are a number of positive steps you can take to alleviate the time demands of using alternative assessment and portfolios.

Instead of seeing portfolios and alternative assessment approaches as things that take time away from instruction, these approaches should be seen as part of instruction and as bringing much-needed information to it. Rather than looking at portfolios as something extra and beyond the number of tasks allowed by your daily schedule, you can plan creatively by examining your current instructional approaches and activities and identifying those you can use to provide authentic assessment for student portfolios. You need to make time for assessment, just as you make time for instructional activities. Some ways to make time for assessment are:

1. *Learning centers.* A learning center is a niche in the classroom where hands-on materials and

objects are available for a specific instructional purpose. An example is a science learning center or a reading center. Activities at the center can be teacher or student-directed. Students can spend a specific amount of time at each learning center and have choices of centers to use. One of the centers can be a portfolio center, where students can work independently, in pairs, or with the teacher in reviewing their portfolio.

2. *Small groups.* Assessment can also be conducted while students work in groups to complete team projects, engage in peer conferencing, do lab work, or engage in other learning activities. Groups can be assessed for how well they work together as well as for the quality of their work.

3. *Staggered cycles.* Individual students can be assessed in staggered cycles where only two to three students are assessed per class period or day until all students have been assessed. This would work best for oral language interviews, reading strategies, and portfolio conferences.

4. *Self-assessment.* When students are taught to reflect on their learning and apply criteria in self-assessment, the teacher can ask them to do this with little guidance. Teachers can spot-check student self-assessments periodically and assess major student products as needed for grading.

5. *Daily classroom activities.* Use teacher observation checklists or rating scales to evaluate student performance while students are actually engaged in the learning activities, such as taking part in a role-play, doing a science experiment, or working in groups. We provide a number of examples of these checklists and rating scales in other chapters of this book (see the Index of Figures and Reproducibles).

COMMUNICATING PORTFOLIO RESULTS

Once portfolios become part of your routine, you will need to plan how you will best capture and communicate portfolio contents to students, parents, and other teachers. Among your options are: a cover sheet, a narrative summary, a portfolio evaluation summary, a parent letter, and a letter to the follow-on teacher. A *cover sheet* is a table of contents that describes portfolio entries and the date they were entered (see Figure 3.6). A *narrative summary* consists of a one-paragraph description of student progress as illustrated by the portfolio and written by the teacher; the narrative summary may appear on the cover sheet. A *portfolio evaluation summary* indicates whether or not a student has met performance standards in various areas.

For assessing a bilingual student, the portfolio evaluation summary can document student performance in both first and second languages. The sample Portfolio Evaluation Summary shown in Figure 3.8 allows for indicating the performance of the student in each language (native language and English) for oral language, written language, reading, and an overall summary of performance. Student performance on this form is rated in terms of pre-set standards of performance you may have set for your classroom or that have been established by your school district.

A parent letter is essential to inform parents of the purpose and results of the portfolio. Parents should be asked to review the portfolio and respond to it. A sample parent letter was provided in Figure 3.7.

Students sometimes use the portfolio to communicate with the next year's teacher. We have seen students write to their next year's teacher to identify important things they want the teacher to know about them, what they have learned, what they want to work on next year, and what their learning needs are. This type of letter encourages the kind of reflection students benefit from and is an important entry for ensuring that the careful work you and the student have put into the portfolio will be used in the future.

Using Portfolio Assessment in Instruction

. . . .

Evaluating portfolio contents means planning how you will use portfolio entries for decision making. What does the portfolio reveal about the student's strengths and educational needs? Does the student perform assignments independently or does the student need guided support from you or from

Figure 3.8 **Portfolio Evaluation Summary**

Student _____ Grade _____ Date _____

Teacher _____ School _____

First Language (L1) _____ Second Language (L2) _____

Directions: Circle L1 or L2 to indicate if student meets the standard.

Curriculum/ Assessment Area	Does Not Meet Standards		Meets Standards		Exceeds Standards	
Oral Language	L1	L2	L1	L2	L1	L2
Written Language	L1	L2	L1	L2	L1	L2
Reading	L1	L2	L1	L2	L1	L2
Overall Summary	L1	L2	L1	L2	L1	L2

Comments

Adapted from M. Gottlieb in Valdez Pierce and Gottlieb (1994).

peers? On which topics or assignments has the student done well? Not done well? Does the student respond favorably to both individual and small group work? Are there special instructional approaches to which the student responds well (e.g., hands-on experiences, visuals, demonstrations, or other scaffolded supports)? Are there particular content areas the student prefers, such as language arts or mathematics? Do the student's self-assessments provide clues to these questions? Answers to all of these questions can be obtained by reviewing the contents of the portfolio and relating them to the type of instructional activities provided. A framework for noting observed strengths and needs is provided in the Portfolio Review Notes in Figure 3.9.

In making decisions about student performance, you will be thinking about ways to combine the various pieces of information and student work in the portfolio. Will you assign weights to each of the entries to calculate a rating or grade? How will you weight the entries with regard to instructional goals and students' strengths and needs? You will also be thinking about the kinds of decisions you will make based on evidence in the portfolio. Will you modify instruction for this student? Provide more hands-on experiences, small group work, or try different materials? Will you use portfolios to determine if ELL students are ready to leave the ESL program and enter grade-level classrooms? If so, what will be the minimum criteria required for leaving the program?

The most important information a portfolio can provide for decision making is to indicate to what extent students are benefiting from instruction. By conducting portfolio conferences with students at least twice during each quarter, you can discuss student progress and plan future learning goals. At the end of the year, you and the students can decide which entries will remain in the portfolio if it is to be a permanent folder used the next year. Portfolios can also be used to show parents and administrators evidence of growth. While parents may be interested in reviewing actual work samples, principals may be more interested in looking at a list of portfolio entries and seeing how these relate to instruc- tional goals (Valencia 1990).

Portfolios can be particularly useful for students who are not making progress in either language-based or grade-level classrooms. By focusing on actual student work, teachers can share information with child study teams, assessment teams, and parents as part of the decision-making process. Because assessment portfolios are focused, they can serve as vehicles for observing gradual change and for helping teachers make professional judgments about individual students.

Conclusion

This chapter described the instructional context for portfolios, including the changing roles of students and teachers in assessment. In particular, with portfolio assessment students become self-directed learners who monitor their own progress. The teacher takes part in a collaborative assessment process where students receive individual feedback while the teacher uses assessment results to plan instruction. The greatest advantage of using portfolios comes from the information they can provide on how ELL students are benefiting from instructional activities.

We described different types of portfolios and the key elements they have in common. We also discussed how portfolios are being used in settings beyond the classroom. The key element in portfolio assessment is student reflection through self-assessment. Teachers need to guide students to engage in self-assessment in meaningful ways that will help them set learning goals for themselves. This means that students need to know the criteria and standards by which their work will be judged, and even take part in shaping them.

We provided guidelines for getting started with portfolios, including setting a purpose, matching portfolio entries to that purpose, setting criteria and standards, and getting students and their parents involved. We also addressed managing portfolios and making time for assessment. Finally, we made suggestions for communicating portfolio results with students, parents, and other teachers.

Figure 3.9 **Portfolio Review Notes**

Student	M. S.	Teacher	L. D.

Quarter	1st	ESL Level	2	Date	10/11

Observed Strengths	Needs	Instructional Options
M. has good reading comprehension and likes to read a variety of books.	Doesn't seem able to write a coherent paragraph.	Need to link reading interests with writing activities; schedule mini-lessons for writers' workshop.

Adapted from Glazer and Brown (1993).

In using portfolios with English language learners, the following key points should be kept in mind:

1. Portfolios are student-centered and used to help increase learning rather than to rank or punish students.

2. Portfolios can be used to guide students in taking a more active role in monitoring their own progress.

3. Portfolios must be selective in order to be useful for assessment purposes.

4. Portfolio assessment is collaborative: teachers and students confer on the meaning of student work.

5. Portfolio entries should come from actual classroom activities.

6. Assessment portfolios must include three key elements: samples of student work, student self-assessment, and clearly stated criteria.

7. Portfolio entries must be clearly organized in order to communicate student progress to parents and other teachers.

8. Portfolios allow for a number of ways to involve parents in monitoring the academic progress of their children.

9. Portfolio assessment requires making time for planning and managing assessment activities.

APPLICATION ACTIVITIES

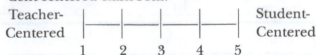

1. Using the scale below, indicate where you think you are with regard to having a teacher- or student-centered classroom.

Teacher-Centered						Student-Centered
	1	2	3	4	5	

Jot down three things you can do to make your classroom more student-centered. Get feedback from a partner.

2. Take a few minutes to share your experience in using portfolios with a partner. Have you been using showcase, collections, or assessment portfolios? Explain your choice.

3. Work with a group to develop a criteria chart for students. If one of the members of your group is currently teaching, that member can ask his or her students to identify characteristics of exemplary work which they think make it good or outstanding. You can use any task in this activity—a writing sample or a tape of an oral presentation, for example.

4. Talk with a partner about the value of student self-assessment. Explain why you think self-assessment is important. Then make a plan for engaging students in the self-assessment process.

5. With a partner, decide how you will involve students in the development of a portfolio. Which entries will students be able to select? On which criteria will students provide input?

6. Form a group with other teachers who teach at approximately the same grade level. Decide on a purpose for student portfolios and decide whether you want required or core entries. What optional or supporting entries are important for your purpose? Develop a Portfolio Summary Sheet like the one in Figure 3.6.

7. Discuss with a partner how to involve parents as early as possible in the development of the portfolio. Write a letter to parents, like the one in Figure 3.7, describing the purposes of portfolios and how they will be used. Role-play discussions of the portfolios in parent conferences. Explain scoring rubrics used in rating student papers.

ORAL LANGUAGE
ASSESSMENT

• •

In this chapter we examine the nature of oral language, with a focus on oral language in school, and discuss implications for assessment. We propose steps for assessing oral language, including identifying purpose, planning for assessment, developing rubrics and scoring procedures, and setting standards. We also make suggestions for involving students in self- and peer assessment. In a key part of the chapter, we describe in detail specific classroom activities and approaches for recording teacher observations that can be used for assessment of oral language. For bringing all of

the information together, we recommend developing an oral language portfolio. We conclude with ideas for using oral language assessment in instruction.

One of the major responsibilities of any teacher working with English language learners (ELLs) is to enable students to communicate effectively through oral language. With an increasing focus on collaborative classrooms, teachers are more often incorporating pair and group activities into their daily lesson plans. Many of these classroom activities have the potential for being used in assessment. However, there are at least three challenges facing teachers who assess oral language in the classroom: making time, selecting assessment activities, and determining evaluation criteria. Perhaps with the exception of those in K-3 classrooms, most teachers do not assess oral language on a systematic, on-going basis over the course of a school year or marking period. Either they cannot find the time or they do not have procedures or assessment activities that can readily be incorporated into their lesson plans. If you find yourself in this situation, we suggest that you look at your instructional activities and begin to identify those you are using now that could be used for the purpose of assessing oral language.

By making assessment reflect instruction, you are increasing the validity and reliability of your assessment approach (see Chapter 2). You can begin by identifying learning goals and activities that provide a representative sample of all oral language tasks you expect students to be able to accomplish in your classroom. The activities or tasks should elicit performance that provides a valid picture of your students' abilities and can be scored reliably (Hughes 1989). This means that you have provided students with opportunities to develop the language and skills needed to perform well on the assessment tasks. You also need to plan for assessment, and this means making time to observe students and document their performance. Finally, you need to determine, with student input, how their performance will be evaluated. In this chapter, we provide examples of how classroom-based oral language activities can serve as opportunities for assessment, how to make time for assessment, and how to develop criteria for evaluation.

Nature of Oral Language

. . . .

To begin our discussion of assessment approaches for oral language, we first need to have a clear understanding what we are assessing. What are the differences between spoken and written language? How does a listener come to understand what is said in a second or foreign language? And how

does the same listener put together a message in order to communicate his or her intended meaning? What do listeners have to work with in order to make meaning out of what they hear? What roles do the native language and prior experience play in oral language development of a second language? How is oral language used in school? For what purposes do students listen and speak?

We start by considering the nature of oral language, the differences between oral and written language, and implications for assessment. Characteristics of spoken language are quite different from those of written language. For example, native speakers do not typically use complete sentences when speaking, and they use less specific vocabulary (with many pronouns) than in written language. They also use syntax in a loosely organized manner and make frequent use of discourse markers (e.g., *well, uh-huh,* etc.) (Brown and Yule 1983). Information is packed less densely in oral language than in written language, with much more use of phrases and simple sentences. In addition, oral language varies depending on the age, gender, and dialect of the speaker. An implication for teaching and assessment includes the need to assess language as it is typically used in speaking rather than demand an oral representation that resembles formal, written language.

Part of being a proficient speaker is listening to oral language and understanding what is said. Listening is not a passive or receptive skill, as is commonly assumed. Research suggests listening is an interactive, dynamic, interpretive process in which the listener engages in the active construction of meaning (Bachman 1990; Littlewood 1981; Murphy 1991; O'Malley, Chamot, and Küpper 1989). Anyone who has attempted to communicate in a foreign language knows how fatiguing it can be to listen for long stretches at a time because of the effort involved in trying to comprehend the incoming messages.

What do listeners attend to, what do they comprehend, and what do they retain? Richards (1983) used research on native language listening processes to suggest that the basic unit of meaning in oral communication is the proposition or idea. The listener's task is to determine the propositions in an utterance or speech event. The listener does this by using knowledge of syntax and of the real world. Syntactic knowledge allows the listener to "chunk" incoming discourse into segments, and knowledge of the world helps listeners determine the most plausible meaning of spoken language. Most importantly, it is the meaning of propositions that is retained, not the actual words or grammatical structures uttered. The example that Richards provides is:

> Tom said that the car had been fixed and could be collected at five.

Richards suggests that the listener will recall that the car is ready to be picked up, but not whether it "is fixed" versus "had been fixed" or "could be collected" versus "will be ready to be collected." This points to the importance of having students summarize the main points or gist of oral communication rather than relate the exact words.

O'Malley, Chamot, and Küpper (1989), in their examination of listening strategies in second language acquisition, found processes similar to those used in a first language. Specifically, effective listeners used prior knowledge or elaboration, inferencing, and self-monitoring, while ineffective listeners focused on the meanings of individual words. Instead of being an all-or-nothing notion, listening comprehension is actually the "process of arriving at a reasonable interpretation" (Brown and Yule 1983, p. 57) of the speaker's intended meaning; this is how native speakers of the language process spoken language input.

Because oral communication involves the negotiation of meaning between two or more persons, it is always related to the context in which it occurs. Speaking means negotiating intended meanings and adjusting one's speech to produce the desired effect on the listener. It means "anticipating the listener's response and possible misunderstandings, clarifying one's own and the other's intentions, and arriving at the closest possible match between intended, perceived, and anticipated meanings" (Kramsch 1986, p. 367). Speaking in a classroom entails interacting with the teacher and peers, depending on how classroom activities are organized. It follows that teachers who use more oral interaction activities in the classroom will have more opportunities to assess oral language. Listening and speaking are interdependent oral language processes and need to be taught and assessed in an integrated manner (Murphy 1991). For example, pronunciation and grammar should be taught and assessed in context. Ideally, the teaching of oral language skills should be based on priority learning needs evident in how students actually use language (Carruthers 1987).

The American Council of Teachers of Foreign Languages (ACTFL) suggests that different kinds of speaking activities (and consequently assessment tasks) are appropriate at different levels of proficiency. This principle applies to ESL and bilingual classrooms, as well. For example, for beginning and intermediate language learners, oral language assessment will include tasks using predictable, familiar language and visual cues, such as listening for the gist, matching descriptions to pictures, making a physical response, and inferring the meaning or implications of an oral text. Also, while formal oral reports and public speaking performances may be appropriate for intermediate or advanced students, they will probably not be suitable for beginners. On the other hand, advanced beginners can make oral presentations with plenty of support or scaffolding (e.g., if they read what they themselves have written, describe a chart they have prepared, describe steps in conducting a science experiment, or tell how to solve a problem). For more advanced learners, tasks might include summarizing, note-taking, and use of fewer visual cues. High intermediate and advanced students who are in grade-level, content area classrooms should be engaged in listening and speaking activities which prepare them to participate in listening for the same purposes as native speakers, such as listening for the gist of the message, taking notes, analyzing, and evaluating (Murphy 1991; Omaggio Hadley 1993).

One problem in assessing oral language in the classroom has been a lack of authenticity. Authenticity in oral language assessment relates to both the type of language used and the task to which that language is applied. In an analysis of authentic listening activities, Porter and Roberts

(1987) identified at least thirteen differences between authentic spoken language and listening texts prepared especially for second language learners. The prepared texts included inauthentic use of complete sentences, intonation, enunciation, and formality, as well as distinct turn-taking and limited vocabulary. Listening activities should provide students with opportunities to hear and attempt to decipher language representing, as much as possible, that which occurs in the real world. Similarly, speaking activities should provide occasions for students to use language for authentic purposes. *Authentic activities* refer to those which call for purposeful exchanges of information, not those that provide information already known to the listener or speaker (Brown and Yule 1983).

ORAL LANGUAGE IN SCHOOL

Oral language assessment of English language learners in school aims to capture a student's ability to communicate for both basic communicative and academic purposes. Communicative or conversational skills involve face-to-face interaction where meaning can be negotiated and is supported by contextual cues, such as the situation itself, gestures, facial expressions, and intonation (Cummins 1989). Daily conversational interactions are typically *context-embedded* (occur in a meaningful social context with many paralinguistic cues) and *cognitively-undemanding* (call for relatively familiar language and tasks). This is seldom the case for academic language, which tends to become increasingly *context-reduced* (little information is provided besides that obtained from teacher lectures or from the textbook itself) and *cognitively-demanding* (new information and new language items are presented) as students advance through the grades. ELLs need to acquire proficiency in academic language in order to succeed in school. Academic language proficiency, then, is the ability to make complex meanings explicit in either oral or written modes by means of language itself rather than by means of paralinguistic cues such as gestures or intonation. Academic language is typically found in the content areas, where students are asked to use language in decontextual-

ized settings in order to learn and on standardized achievement tests to show what they have learned.

The communicative/academic language distinction was first made by Cummins when he reported on studies indicating that second language learners take less time to acquire a language for basic communicative purposes than for academic purposes (Cummins 1980). Since then, Cummins has made clear that this distinction is not a dichotomy but a continuum of language proficiency (Cummins 1989). Over the past decade, research has confirmed that students may be able to use oral language to communicate fluently in English after only two to three years of all-English schooling but may take longer, between five and ten years, to reach grade-level norms on standardized achievement tests in English.

The time required to reach grade-level norms depends on a number of factors, including years of schooling in the native language and age upon entry to an all-English system (Collier 1987; Collier 1989; Collier and Thomas 1988; Cummins 1981, 1984). Collier (1989) found that even for middle or upper-middle class English language learners with a strong educational background in the native language, it took a minimum of four to nine years to achieve grade-level norms on standardized tests in English. Cummins (1989) suggests that less advantaged students can be expected to take even longer. This research should not be interpreted to mean that instruction in the content areas for ELLs should be delayed until students are proficient enough in English to benefit from all-English classrooms. Nor should these findings be used to lower expectations for ELLs. On the other hand, the research does support the movement toward content-based ESL and bilingual classrooms that provide students access to math, science, social studies and other content areas either with native or English language support. Through these types of instructional settings, ELLs have a much better chance of obtaining the academic language proficiency needed for succeeding in school. (See Chapter 7 for ideas on assessment in the content areas.)

Figure 4.1 Communicative Language Functions

Communicative Language Function	Student Uses Language to:	Examples
1. Greetings/ Leave-takings	Meet and greet others; say good-bye	Uses common expressions, such as *How do you do?* and *Nice to meet you.*
2. Requesting Information/ Assistance	Ask for information or help	Can formulate questions using courtesy formulas as in: *Excuse me, could you please tell me where Room 208 is?*
3. Giving Information/ Assistance	Provide information or assistance in response to a request	Comprehends requests and responds appropriately, as in: *Sure, it's down this hall, first door on your right.*
4. Describing	Tell about a place, thing, or idea	Uses descriptive language to convey an image, as in: *Well, it's about 12 feet by 15 feet, has lots of light, and is big enough for 30 students.*
5. Expressing Feelings	Relate what he/she feels or thinks	Describes emotions, as in: *Yes, I feel a little nervous about being interviewed.*

LANGUAGE FUNCTIONS

Whether in or out of classroom settings, English language learners use language functions to express meaning. *Language functions* refer to how individuals use language to accomplish specific tasks (Halliday 1975; Wilkins 1976). The most commonly used language functions are those used to describe or give information or to express feelings (Bachman 1990). Language functions have been identified for both social/communicative and academic purposes by Chamot and O'Malley (1994) and Wilkins. *Communicative language functions* are those used to express meaning in a routine social context that is not cognitively demanding (Cummins 1984). Communicative language functions include greetings and leave-takings, requesting and giving information, requesting and giving assistance, and others such as those listed in Figure 4.1.

Academic language functions are those that are critical for success in grade-level classrooms (Cummins 1982, 1984). Academic language functions may be global in that they can be used across various content areas, or they may be content-specific, particular to a single content area (Chamot

and O'Malley 1994a; Hamayan and Perlman 1990; O'Malley 1992). Academic language functions may include describing, explaining, informing, comparing, debating, persuading, evaluating, and others listed in Figure 4.2. In the ESL/bilingual or grade-level classroom, both communicative and academic language functions are used, but reliance on academic language functions tends to increase as a function of grade level (Chamot and O'Malley 1994a).

IMPLICATIONS FOR ASSESSMENT

Given the preceding discussion of the nature of oral language, what are some implications for assessment? Assessment of oral language should focus on a student's ability to interpret and convey meaning for authentic purposes in interactive contexts. It should include both fluency and accuracy. Cooperative learning activities that present students with opportunities to use oral language to interact with others—whether for social or academic purposes—are optimal for assessing oral language.

Teachers need to use assessment tasks that are as authentic as possible in a classroom setting. This

Figure 4.2 **Academic Language Functions**

Academic Language Function	Student uses language to:	Examples
1. Seeking Information/ Informing	Observe and explore the environment, acquire information, inquire; identify, report, or describe information	Use *who, what, when, where,* and *how* to gather information; recount information presented by teacher or text; retell a story or personal experience
2. Comparing	Describe similarities and differences in objects or ideas	Make/explain a graphic organizer to show similarities and contrasts
3. Ordering	Sequence objects, ideas, or events	Describe/make a timeline, continuum, cycle, or narrative sequence
4. Classifying	Group objects or ideas according to their characteristics	Describe organizing principle(s), explain why A is an example and B is not
5. Analyzing	Separate whole into parts; identify relationships and patterns	Describe parts, features, or main idea of information
6. Inferring	Make inferences; predict implications, hypothesize	Describe reasoning process (inductive or deductive) or generate hypotheses to suggest causes or outcomes
7. Justifying and Persuading	Give reasons for an action, decision, point of view; convince others	Tell why A is important and give evidence in support of a position
8. Solving Problems	Define and represent a problem; determine a solution	Describe problem-solving procedures; apply to real-life problems and describe
9. Synthesizing	Combine or integrate ideas to form a whole	Summarize information; incorporate new information
10. Evaluating	Assess and verify worth of an object, idea, or decision	Identify criteria, explain priorities, indicate reasons for judgment, confirm truth

Adapted from Chamot and O'Malley (1994).

means: (1) using authentic language in listening/speaking activities; (2) setting real-world tasks, such as getting the gist of a message, listening selectively, describing, giving directions, and giving opinions; and (3) giving students opportunities to use language in situations based on everyday life. It is important to expose students to authentic language and help them work out strategies for dealing with less than total comprehension (Porter and Roberts 1987).

In your lesson planning, articulate learning goals and objectives in terms of those language functions students need to learn first. Be sure to include language functions that reflect both social and academic language. Within this context, the areas of grammar and pronunciation can be addressed, instead of being assessed as discrete items. In all cases, assessment should be instructive, challenging, engaging, and even enjoyable (Underhill 1987; Wiggins 1992).

Authentic Assessment of Oral Language

. . . .

Using instructional activities for assessment takes preparation and organization. The key is to include assessment right along with daily and weekly lesson plans in order to document student progress in a systematic manner. You can do this by looking for assessment opportunities within actual classroom tasks. It has been our experience that teachers who do not plan for assessment tend to overlook it. Steps in preparing for oral language assessment are: identifying purpose, planning for assessment, developing rubrics and/or scoring procedures, setting standards, involving students in self- and peer assessment, selecting assessment activities, and recording information. We discuss each of these steps below.

IDENTIFYING PURPOSE

The oral language of English language learners is typically assessed for one of three purposes:

1. For initial identification and placement of students in need of a language-based program such as ESL or bilingual education.

2. For movement from one level to another within a given program, (e.g., beginning to intermediate levels of ESL).

3. For placement out of an ESL/bilingual program into a grade-level classroom.

Rarely do we hear of assessment to monitor growth in oral language proficiency in the classroom, either for diagnosis or instructional planning. We believe that teachers do not conduct ongoing assessments of oral proficiency because they do not receive training in how to do this. Teachers may also see the three purposes of oral language assessment as being separate from instruction and taking time away from it; because of this, they may not want to assess oral language more often than the minimum required by their school program. It may also be that teachers do not see oral language assessment as being as important as the assessment of reading and writing, since these are the areas typically assessed in grade-level classrooms and in district and statewide assessments. We strongly encourage you to conduct regular, ongoing assessment of oral language along with assessment of reading and writing in order to assemble a complete profile of each student's language proficiency.

In identifying the purpose of oral language assessment, an analysis must be made of the learners' needs. What do students need to be able to listen to and respond to? Part of a needs assessment is conducted by reviewing local curriculum guides and the research literature to identify expected goals and levels of performance. Another part is to conduct surveys or interviews with learners to determine their needs (Richards 1983). A baseline assessment of student strengths and needs in oral language should be conducted to determine instructional objectives. By combining the purposes for which oral language will be used with a learner needs assessment and individual language assessment profiles, teachers can produce appropriate instructional goals, objectives, and assessment activities.

PLANNING FOR ASSESSMENT

After identifying assessment purposes, you can begin planning for classroom-based assessment of oral language by *identifying instructional activities or tasks* you are currently using that can also be used for assessment. In this way, you not only establish a direct link between instruction and assessment, you also save valuable time and energy otherwise spent in designing assessment activities unrelated to classroom activities. One way to describe your instructional activities or tasks is in terms of language objectives. You can also describe and categorize instructional activities in terms of language functions, as shown in Figure 4.2.

Part of planning for assessment is deciding when to assess students individually and when to assess them in groups. For example, let's assume that you use cooperative learning techniques to encourage students to solve problems in groups. How might you use this activity for assessment? This is the kind of question you need to ask of each instructional activity as you plan for ongoing, systematic assess-

Figure 4.3   Oral Language Assessment Planning Matrix

Language Function	Activity	Individual/Pair/Group	Type of Rating Scale/Rubric	Week of:
Informing	Information Gap	Pairs	Rubric for Information Gap	Oct. 15-20
Informing	Picture-cued Descriptions	Individual	Rubric for Oral Language	Nov. 11-16
Persuading	Improvisations	Pairs	Improvisation Checklist	Dec. 5-10
Solving	Simulations	Groups	Self-Assessment for Groups	Dec. 13-17

Adapted from a grid developed by ESL teacher S. Copley (1994).

ment of oral language development. There are several possible answers to the question. First, you might want to assess students' ability and willingness to talk and take turns in small groups. Second, you could assess the group's ability to carry out a given task or solve a problem. Third, you could assess language functions that are important for completing the assignment, such as classifying and informing. Fourth, you could ask students to reflect on the effectiveness of the group process itself or their level of participation in it. The assessment option you choose will depend on your purpose for doing the assessment.

One important step in planning for assessment is to *outline the major instructional goals or learning outcomes* and match these to learning activities and/or performance tasks. We have adapted an Assessment Planning Matrix developed by an ESL teacher (see Figure 4.3) to help you do this, as well as to help you determine whether the assessment will be conducted with individuals, student pairs, or groups; the kind of rubric or rating scale to use; and so on.

Part of planning for oral language assessment involves deciding *whether or not to make an audio or video recording* of student performance. Brown and Yule (1983) suggest that a tape for each student be used if oral language is an essential part of instruction. They also suggest that students be recorded conducting different types of tasks, such as describing a picture or event, telling a story, or expressing an opinion. By assessing different kinds of performances the teacher gets valuable feedback on student needs and is able to focus instructional goals accordingly. Recording oral language provides options such as (1) rating the performance at a later time, (2) getting a second rater to rate the performance, (3) asking students to do a self-assessment of the performance, and (4) enabling students to look back at their progress over time (Underhill 1987). Planning for assessment also means having ready any equipment or supplies needed (such as cameras, videotapes, etc.) in order to proceed as smoothly as possible.

Another important part of planning for assessment is deciding *how often to collect information.* Teachers whose purpose it is to monitor student progress will need to collect information more often than those whose purpose is for reclassification decisions, which may require assessment only twice a year. Teachers who wish to monitor student progress should plan to incorporate assessment into their instruction regularly so that a small amount of information is collected on individual students periodically over time and across a variety of oral language tasks.

A final key component in planning is deciding when and how to *provide learners with feedback.* How soon after oral language assessment should learners be provided with feedback on their performance? Certainly students want to know how they did immediately after a task, but there is another reason for providing feedback as soon as possible after assessment: the feedback will have more meaning and perhaps make more of an impact. The feedback can best be provided verbally in a mini-conference with the student but can also be provided by ratings on a scoring rubric with annotated comments that help the student in preparing for the next oral performance. These comments can be written on an individual student rating form and distributed after the performance is observed.

DEVELOPING RUBRICS/SCORING PROCEDURES

For teachers, parents, and students, classroom-based assessment of oral language aims to answer the questions: How am I [are we] doing? and How can I [we] do better? (Herman, Aschbacher, and Winters 1992). To answer the questions, students need to know the purpose of the assessment activity, the expected performance, and the criteria for each task. Setting criteria is a crucial part of assessment; without criteria or standards of performance, performance tasks remain simply a collection of instructional activities (Herman, Aschbacher, and Winters 1992). Based on student performance, teachers can revise assessment tasks and standards as well as instructional objectives and activities to better meet learners' needs.

You can establish criterion levels of oral language proficiency based on the goals and objectives of classroom instruction *before* using instructional activities for assessment. Next, operationalize these criteria (modify by trial and error) based on actual student performance. As an example, if most students do not provide evidence of a specific criterion in your scoring rubric (e.g., no errors in pronunciation), and if performances are exceptional on other criteria, you may want to consider revising the rubric. Either eliminate those criteria or use them exclusively to distinguish between the upper levels of performance.

Set criterion levels of performance by designing a scoring rubric, rating scale, or checklist. Begin by using a model rubric or scale; revise it to reflect your instructional objectives and then ask colleagues for feedback. Check the dimensions or aspects of oral language that you want to assess. These might typically include communicative effect or general comprehensibility, grammar, and pronunciation. If overall communicative effect is more important than pronunciation, then it should be given more importance in the rubric. Share your rubric with students, and get their input on it. Revise the rubric until both you and the students agree on what it means and how it looks in terms of student performance. (See Chapter 3 for steps used to involve students in setting criteria and engage in self-assessment.)

Brown and Yule (1983) suggest rating procedures that describe essential elements of effective communication; these can become the highest level of performance, with less effective performances listed at lower levels on the rating scale. Gonzalez Pino (1988) reminds us that the dimensions or features of oral language to be assessed depend on the level of proficiency of the class and instructional goals. For example, beginners can be rated for overall communicative effect, with vocabulary and grammar being slightly less important and pronunciation and fluency being least important. Wherever possible, rubrics should highlight what students *can do* rather than what they *cannot do.* Of course, at lower levels of proficiency, what students can do with oral language will be limited.

When using a holistic scale, you may discover that students do not always fit neatly into one category or another. This is because each student is unique and may not conform totally to a single category. You should assign the rating that most closely fits the student's actual performance. Making this decision will take practice and may benefit from a colleague's feedback. If scoring holistically, you need only about three to six levels of performance; you do not want to use more levels than you need. If you find yourself using half-step ratings (e.g., 4.5, 3.5), you may need to redefine the levels in order to avoid calculations with decimals in developing an overall score. Analytic and weighted rating scales, while complicated and time-consuming to use, are most effective for communicating diagnostic information, such as students' strengths and needs. You may want to save these for making placement decisions. Underhill (1987) suggests a balanced approach to using holistic and analytic rating scales, as in assessing for communicative effect or grammatical accuracy. An example of a rating scale for oral language which has been produced in both a holistic and analytic format is provided in Figures 4.4 and 4.5.

When rating oral language in the classroom, use more than one rater periodically to spot-check for inter-rater reliability. Play an audio or videotape of student performance and ask other teachers to rate it using the rubric. Begin with obviously high and low performances before rating less clear-cut cases (Hughes 1989).

SETTING STANDARDS

Once scoring rubrics and procedures have been established, you will need to set standards of oral language performance. Setting standards involves clearly specifying what students should know and be able to do at different levels of oral language proficiency. Standards can be set by establishing a cut-off point on a scoring rubric that meets a specific level of performance. For example, to specify an "advanced" level of proficiency on a rubric with a range from 1 to 6, you might require a score of 5 or 6. A "basic" level of proficiency may require a score of 1 or 2. In either case, the description for the criterion score (given on the rubric) is your key to understanding what each level on the standard means in terms of student performance. The levels on the scoring rubric are always tied to your curriculum objectives in the language or content area being rated. This link established between the scoring rubric, your local curriculum objectives, and the standards you set is essential.

You may decide to use performance on the standard to monitor progress or reclassify students.

ESL teachers in Fairfax County, Virginia are piloting the use of the oral language rating scales provided in Figures 4.4 and 4.5. They are considering that students scoring at a Level 6 would have developed oral language comparable to that of native English-speaking grade-mates. This would mean that Level 6 has been set as the standard of performance for leaving the ESL program. Students scoring at Levels 4 and 5 on the rubric would probably benefit from being placed in the highest level of the ESL program. Students at Level 3 would most likely be placed at the intermediate level of the ESL program, while students at Levels 1 and 2 would be placed at the beginning level of the program. Because placement decisions should always be based on multiple sources of information, these teachers would have to corroborate the information obtained from this rubric with that acquired from other sources.

For the classroom teacher, standards may be used to monitor student performance, to determine who needs extra help, or to assign grades. If, instead of holistic scales, you are using analytic scales, you will need to determine what scores meet the criteria on each dimension of performance. For example, when setting standards for pronunciation, you will need to decide between comprehensible pronunciation and pronunciation that interferes with communication.

INVOLVING STUDENTS

In authentic assessment, involving students in their own assessment is critical. By reflecting on and assessing their own work and that of their peers, students get the opportunity to apply criteria to work samples and to set learning goals.

Self-Assessment   An essential step in preparing for oral language assessment is planning how to engage students in self-assessment. By providing learners with the skills needed to independently monitor their learning, we enable them to take greater responsibility for that learning. Students can be involved in generating criteria for assessment by being given the opportunity to listen to good and poor performances and asked to describe characteristics of effective performance

Figure 4.4   Holistic Oral Language Scoring Rubric

Rating	Description
6	• Communicates competently in social and classroom settings • Speaks fluently • Masters a variety of grammatical structures • Uses extensive vocabulary but may lag behind native-speaking peers • Understands classroom discussion without difficulty
5	• Speaks in social and classroom settings with sustained and connected discourse; any errors do not interfere with meaning • Speaks with near-native fluency; any hesitations do not interfere with communication • Uses a variety of structures with occasional grammatical errors • Uses varied vocabulary • Understands simple sentences in sustained conversation; requires repetition
4	• Initiates and sustains a conversation with descriptors and details; exhibits self-confidence in social situations; begins to communicate in classroom settings • Speaks with occasional hesitation • Uses some complex sentences; applies rules of grammar but lacks control of irregular forms (e.g., *runned, mans, not never, more higher*) • Uses adequate vocabulary; some word usage irregularities • Understands classroom discussions with repetition, rephrasing, and clarification
3	• Begins to initiate conversation; retells a story or experience; asks and responds to simple questions • Speaks hesitantly because of rephrasing and searching for words • Uses predominantly present tense verbs; demonstrates errors of omission (leaves words out, word endings off) • Uses limited vocabulary • Understands simple sentences in sustained conversation; requires repetition
2	• Begins to communicate personal and survival needs • Speaks in single-word utterances and short patterns • Uses functional vocabulary • Understands words and phrases; requires repetitions
1	• Begins to name concrete objects • Repeats words and phrases • Understands little or no English

Adapted from a rating scale developed by ESL teachers Portfolio Assessment Group (Grades 1-12), Fairfax County Public Schools, Virginia.

Figure 4.5 Analytic Oral Language Scoring Rubric

Focus/Rating:	1	2	3	4	5	6
Speaking	Begins to name concrete objects	Begins to communicate personal and survival needs	Begins to initiate conversation; retells a story or experience; asks and responds to simple questions	Initiates and sustains a conversation with descriptors and details; exhibits self-confidence in social situations; begins to communicate in classroom settings	Speaks in social and classroom settings with sustained and connected discourse; any errors do not interfere with meaning	Communicates competently in social and classroom settings
Fluency	Repeats words and phrases	Speaks in single-word utterances and short patterns	Speaks hesitantly because of rephrasing and searching for words	Speaks with occasional hesitation	Speaks with near-native fluency; any hesitations do not interfere with communication	Speaks fluently
Structure		Uses predominantly present tense verbs; demonstrates errors of omission (leaves words out, word endings off)	Uses some complex sentences; applies rules of grammar but lacks control of irregular forms (e.g., *runned, mans, not never, more higher*)	Uses a variety of structures with occasional grammatical errors	Uses a variety of grammatical structures	Masters a variety of grammatical structures
Vocabulary		Uses functional vocabulary	Uses limited vocabulary	Uses adequate vocabulary; some word usage irregularities	Uses varied vocabulary	Uses extensive vocabulary but may lag behind native-speaking peers
Listening	Understands little or no English	Understands words and phrases, requires repetition	Understands simple sentences in sustained conversation; requires repetition	Understands classroom discussions with repetition, rephrasing, and clarification	Understands most spoken language, including classroom discussion	Understands classroom discussion without difficulty

Adapted from a rating scale developed by ESL teachers Portfolio Assessment Group (Grades 1–12), Fairfax County Public Schools, Virginia.

(Brown and Yule 1983). (See Chapter 3 for a description of the self-assessment process.) Self-assessment may take various forms, depending on the age, language proficiency, and reading skills of each learner. For example, students who are reading independently can be expected to complete their own written self-assessments. With young children and pre-readers, teachers can ask open-ended questions to engage students in self-assessment orally and take notes on student comments. Learners may be asked to reflect on a specific performance or on language development over time.

Preparing self-assessment formats for oral language requires careful wording so that the assessment itself does not become an exercise in reading comprehension. If possible, directions for self-assessment should be given at the developmental or reading level of the student or in the native language (where students share the same native language) (Underhill 1987). Each statement should be expressed in the first person (e.g., "I can…") in order to take the learner's perspective from the onset. Self-assessments can take the form of *yes/no* statements, question/answer, rating scales, sentence completion, and learning logs. These are not typically graded or scored by the teacher. Instead, they are used to focus learners on their performance and progress in learning, to give the teacher an idea of the accuracy of the learners' assessment of their performance, and as points of departure for student/teacher conferences to discuss student progress. Students should be guided and given options in setting goals for overall communicative effectiveness, fluency, and accuracy in vocabulary, grammar, pronunciation, stress, intonation, and style. Figure 4.6, adapted from Bachman and Palmer (1989), asks students to rate themselves on six oral language tasks at four levels of difficulty. Students can also do a self-assessment of how well they can use language functions, as shown in Figure 4.7.

An example of self-assessment of communication strategies developed by an ESL teacher for oral communication tasks is presented in Figure 4.8. A self-assessment for speaking developed by another ESL teacher is shown in Figure 4.9. For individual self-assessment of oral language used in groups, students can be provided with questions similar to those shown in Figure 4.10.

Peer Assessment   For pair or team activities, students can be asked to rate each other as well as their functioning as a group. Underhill (1987) suggests that peer assessment is an authentic assessment approach because peers are asked to rate the effectiveness of communication by others. However, students will need to be taught how to evaluate each other as fairly as possible using guiding questions or some kind of rating scale. The natural reluctance some students may have in rating their peers may be partially overcome by providing students with numerous opportunities for engaging in peer assessment.

An example of a peer assessment to determine the effectiveness of using oral language to explain a process has been modified from an instructional activity designed by an ESL teacher (see Figure 4.11). The process described in the oral presentation might be anything ranging from following directions to conducting a science experiment.

SELECTING ASSESSMENT ACTIVITIES

Part of planning for assessment of oral language involves identifying instructional activities that can also be used for assessment. These activities should reflect what we know about the nature of oral language. In particular, they should assess authentic language use in context, both communicative and academic language functions, and the ability to communicate meaning. Assessment of oral language is most effective when it is based on the performance of a task. This means that students are required to do something in response to what they hear, whether it's taking notes, charting a route on a map, or answering questions (Ur 1984). Tasks should be designed to challenge the proficiency level(s) of your students without frustrating them.

Oral language assessment can take various forms depending on your purpose for assessment, students' level of language proficiency, and the purposes for which students use oral language in the classroom. Assessment tasks for oral language dif-

Figure 4.6   **Self-Assessment of Oral Language**

Name _____ Date _____

Check (√) the box that shows what you can do. Add comments.

What Can You Do in English?	Difficulty Level				Comments
	Not Very Well	Okay	Well	Very well	
1. I can ask questions in class.					
2. I can understand others when working in a group.					
3. I can understand television shows.					
4. I can speak with native speakers outside of school.					
5. I can talk on the phone.					
6. I can ask for an explanation.					

Adapted from Bachman and Palmer (1989).

Figure 4.7 **Self-Assessment of Academic Language Functions**

Name _____ Date _____

Check (√) the box that best describes how well you can use English. Add comments.

Task	Not Very Well	Okay	Well	Very Well	Comments
1. I can describe objects and people.					
2. I can describe past events.					
3. I can listen to and understand radio programs.					
4. I can listen to and understand video and television.					
5. I can state an opinion.					
6. I can agree and disagree.					
7. I can summarize a story.					
8. I can give an oral report.					

Figure 4.8 Self-Assessment of Communication Strategies in Oral Language

Name _____ Date _____

Circle the answer that shows how often you do the following things.

When I have problems talking in English, I:

1. use my native language.	Never	Sometimes	Often
2. ask for help.	Never	Sometimes	Often
3. use gestures or facial expressions.	Never	Sometimes	Often
4. avoid communication totally or partially.	Never	Sometimes	Often
5. use a synonym or a description.	Never	Sometimes	Often
6. make up new words.	Never	Sometimes	Often
7. simplify what I want to say.	Never	Sometimes	Often

Adapted from a form developed by ESL teacher S. Copley (1994).

Figure 4.9 **Self-Assessment of Speaking Ability**

Name _____ Date _____

Part 1: Place an X on each line to show how much you agree or disagree.

This week I used English to talk with _____ .

1. I think that I was successful.   Disagree I——I——I——I——I Agree

2. The person I spoke to understood me.   Disagree I——I——I——I——I Agree

3. I felt comfortable speaking with   Disagree I——I——I——I——I Agree
   another person in English.

4. I understood everything that this   Disagree I——I——I——I——I Agree
   person said to me.

5. I could do this again with no problem.   Disagree I——I——I——I——I Agree

Part 2: Complete the sentences below.

6. When someone doesn't understand me, I _____ .

7. When I don't understand someone, I _____ .

8. Now I know _____ .

Adapted from a form developed by ESL teacher M. Crossman (1994).

Figure 4.10 **Self-Assessment of Participation in Groups**

Name _____   Date _____

How often did you do the following things in your group today?
Put a check (√) in the box that best describes your response and add comments.

Task	Rarely	Sometimes	Often	Comments
1. I listened to others in my group.				
2. I summarized what others said.				
3. I asked for information.				
4. I gave information.				
5. I gave an opinion.				
6. I agreed or disagreed.				
7. I asked for clarification.				

Adapted from a form developed by ESL teacher M. Crossman (1994) and Nourse, Wilson, and Andrien (1994).

Figure 4.11 **Peer Feedback Form: Explaining a Process**

Speaker's Name _____ Date _____

Your Name _____

Part 1: Circle the word *Yes, Some,* or *No* to tell how you feel about the speaker's report.

1. I understood what the speaker was talking about.	Yes	Some	No
2. The speaker described how everything worked.	Yes	Some	No
3. The speaker explained in steps I could follow.	Yes	Some	No
4. I think I could do this myself now.	Yes	Some	No
5. The directions were clear.	Yes	Some	No

Part 2: Complete the following sentences.

6. I liked when the speaker_____

_____

_____.

7. The speaker was good at _____

_____

_____.

8. Maybe the speaker could _____

_____

_____.

Adapted by ESL teacher M. Crossman
from Hill and Ruptic (1994).

fer with regard to whether they call for the use of static relationships (such as in describing a picture or giving directions), dynamic relationships (telling a story or taking part in a role-play), or abstract relationships (giving an opinion) (Brown and Yule 1983). These relationships correspond to an increase in difficulty levels; that is, it is easier to describe a picture than to give an opinion in one's second language. You need to consider the purpose of the assessment, the format (individual, pairs, groups), students' level of proficiency, language functions used in daily classroom activities, and the level of student preparation needed for each assessment activity before choosing it. You also need to consider the difficulty of tasks with regard to both linguistic and cognitive load; the tasks should be developmentally appropriate and authentic. The important thing is to give students continued opportunities to engage in authentic oral language activities before using these same activities for assessment.

If you are like most teachers, you are probably already asking yourself where you are going to find the time to assess students individually for oral language. Although with careful planning individual assessment is possible, more often than not you will need to use interactive student pairs or groups for oral language assessment. An interactive setting is actually more authentic than an interviewer/interviewee setting or a format where a student responds to a recording (Underhill 1987). How-ever, individual assessment may be preferred when the needs and strengths of a new student in your classroom are being assessed, when conferencing with individual students, or when conducting quarterly portfolio conferences.

Use as wide a variety of assessment activities as possible to make your assessment more authentic and reliable (Herman, Aschbacher, and Winters 1992; Hughes 1989; Underhill 1987). Also, be sure that your assessment task is not one students can memorize from written notes (unless it is to be a formal presentation, and even that should not be memorized or read aloud) but which reveals their general ability to produce an extended segment of oral language appropriate to a situation (Brown and Yule 1983).

In developing tasks for oral language assessment, teachers can evaluate activities using the following criteria, as adapted from Richards (1983):

1. *Content validity.* Does the assessment measure listening comprehension, speaking, or something else? Have activities been used as part of instruction?

2. *Task validity.* Does the task assess listening comprehension or speaking, or does memory play a significant role?

3. *Purposefulness and transferability.* Does the assessment task reflect a purpose for listening that approximates authentic real-life listening or speaking?

4. *Authenticity.* To what degree does the assessment measure actual spoken language?

In this section, we suggest a number of instructional activities that can also be used for assessment. If these activities provide teachers with the opportunity to try out new techniques in assessment, we suggest that they can also provide ideas for effective language teaching. The instructional and assessment activities described here include: oral interviews, picture-cued descriptions or stories, radio broadcasts, video clips, information gap tasks, story/text retellings, improvisations/role-plays/simulations, oral reports, and debates (Bachman and Palmer 1989; Genishi 1985; Gonzalez Pino 1988; Hughes 1989; Oscarson 1989; Underhill 1987).

Guidelines for using each of these activities at different levels of language proficiency are given below. We have organized assessment activities by format (e.g., individuals/pairs/groups), by level of language proficiency, and by level of student preparation. For a brief overview of all activities described here, see Figure 4.12. We provide examples of scoring rubrics for these activities where the language is sufficiently generalized that a generic rubric is appropriate. In other cases, as in story retelling, the language produced will require a rubric that is specific to the task, or in this case, to the structure of the genre involved. We have also indicated which language functions are most likely to be elicited with each activity, as shown in Figure 4.12. Results of oral language assessment

Figure 4.12   Oral Language Assessment Activity Matrix

Assessment Activity	Format	Level of Language Proficiency	Student Preparation	Language Functions
1. Oral Interview	Individual/pairs	All levels	None	• Describing • Giving information • Giving an opinion
2. Picture-cued Descriptions or Stories	Individual	Beginning, intermediate	None	• Describing • Giving information • Giving an opinion
3. Radio Broadcasts	Individual, groups, whole class	Intermediate, advanced	None	• Listening for the gist • Listening for specific information • Listening for descriptions, directions • Summarizing
4. Video Clips	Individual, groups, whole class	All levels	None	• Describing • Giving information
5. Information Gap	Pairs	All levels	None	• Describing • Giving information • Giving directions
6. Story/Text Retelling	Individual	Beginning, intermediate	None	• Describing • Giving information • Summarizing
7. Improvisations/ Roleplays/ Simulations	Pairs, groups	All levels	Some preparation	• Greetings/leave-takings • Asking for/giving information • Requesting assistance • Agreeing/ disagreeing • Giving/evaluating an opinion • Giving advice • Giving directions • Suggesting • Persuading • Encouraging
8. Oral Reports	Individual	All levels	Extensive preparation	• Describing • Explaining • Giving/asking for information
9. Debates	Groups	Intermediate, advanced	Extensive preparation	• Describing • Explaining • Giving/asking for information • Persuading • Agreeing/ disagreeing

activities can be systematically gathered and interpreted in an oral language portfolio (described later in this chapter).

Oral language should be assessed for each student at least twice during each quarter or semester. This provides baseline data as well as information on improvement of language proficiency on a continuous basis. Unless this information is gathered frequently and systematically, it will be of limited use. Teachers can set up a rotating schedule for assessing students in order to avoid assessing all students at once in a short period of time. In this way, assessment becomes an ongoing part of daily or weekly instruction.

Oral Interviews   Oral interviews can be conducted with individuals or pairs at all levels of language proficiency and require no preparation on the part of the student. In a classroom setting, interviews can take the form of discussions or conversations with the teacher and with other students. Interviews can be used to elicit the following language functions: describing, giving information, or giving an opinion.

To prepare to interview individual students, you will want to prepare a list of guiding questions or tasks. These questions/tasks should be appropriate for the language proficiency and developmental levels of the student, reflect the students' interests and classroom activities, and avoid cultural bias. To check for cultural bias, consult a native speaker of the students' native languages or someone familiar with the students' cultures. Be sure that students understand the tasks they are being asked to perform and the criteria by which they will be evaluated. Some examples of performance tasks to check for in an oral interview are suggested by Underhill (1987):

Can the learner:

- use courtesy formulas? (e.g., Greet the student and evaluate his or her response, or ask the student: *What do you say when you meet someone for the first time?* or *What do you say when you hurt someone by mistake or accident?*)

- ask simple information questions? (e.g., Ask the student: *What questions do you have for me?* or *How can I help you?*)

- describe a series of events in the past? (e.g., Ask the student: *What did you do yesterday, from morning until night?* or *Tell me about what you did last weekend, beginning with Friday night.*)

- produce a smooth stream of speech? (e.g., Tell the student: *I want you to talk for as long as you can without stopping. I will not interrupt you. Now, what can you tell me about... ?*)

Asking simple information questions is an extremely important language task in school. When students are able to ask questions, especially in a classroom setting, they can obtain clarification on information that they might have misunderstood or on which they need help. This is why this language function should take priority in planning which language tasks to assess. Checking all students on the same performance or using similar questions to ask all students will increase the reliability of your assessment by focusing on the performance of similar tasks by different students. Questions will vary, however, with the proficiency level of students and classroom instructional goals and activities. Some sample interview questions are:

For beginners:

- *Can you tell me about your family?*

- *Where have you studied English?*

- *What subjects did you study in your last school?*

- *Ask a friend if you can borrow his book.*

- *Ask a teacher to repeat the directions for doing homework.*

For intermediate level students:

- *Describe what you did last weekend.*

- *Tell me about the kinds of movies you like.*

- *What is your favorite class and why?*

- *Ask for directions to the school gym.*

- *Ask a teacher how to solve a math problem.*

For advanced students:

- *How do you feel you are doing in this class and why?*

- *What has been your favorite subject this quarter and why?*

- *Tell me about how you spend your free time.*

- *Compare this school with your last one.*

- *Ask a teacher how you will be graded on an assignment.*

To conduct the interview with pairs of students, you can share the list of prepared questions with students and have them interview each other. This gives you the opportunity to assess both students during a single session. With prepared questions, you limit the possibility of one student dominating the conversation, either student getting off the topic, or shy students speaking very little. Although there is the danger of the teacher talking too much during a one-on-one interview, this disadvantage can be eliminated when pairs of students are asked to do most of the talking.

To rate the interview, use a holistic (see Figure 4.4) or analytic (see Figure 4.5) rating scale (a rubric) or a checklist of language skills. Wherever possible, it is advisable not to rate students during individual interviews; it can be disconcerting and unnerving for some students. Rate the student as soon as possible after the interview or tape the interview for rating at a later time. We know of teachers who prefer to conduct ratings of oral language as they walk around the classroom observing student interactions. Students will become accustomed to being rated when they understand the purpose of the assessment and the criteria used in the rating. Be sure to make these clear to students if you want to do the ratings while students are interacting.

Picture-cued Descriptions or Stories

Picture cues can be used for assessment of individual students and are probably most appropriate for beginning and intermediate learners. Picture cues require no prior preparation on the part of the student and can be used to elicit the following language functions: describing, giving information, or giving an opinion.

To prepare, obtain a variety of black and white or color pictures or photographs that elicit the kind of language you want to assess. Pictures should be appropriate for the age and interest levels of your students. You can choose either single pictures or a series of pictures. Pictures should be of real people rather than of cartoon characters in order to ensure appropriate interpretation.

Pictures should also be relatively free of cultural bias. For example, can students be expected to be familiar with most items in the picture, or are items particular to our culture only? Pictures should not call for skills that are not being assessed (such as creativity). Pictures should also call for approximately similar types of oral language. For example, Brown and Yule (1983) suggest that a way to make picture descriptions more difficult is to increase the "communicative stress" involved in the description. Selecting pictures that tell stories involving several characters of the same gender calls for more referential and explicit language than those with only one or two characters. Other elements needing clear reference, depending on the story line depicted by the pictures, are changes in location and sequence.

Students can either describe or tell a story about the picture(s). You might ask students to order the pictures in a preferred sequence and describe what is occurring. However, be careful to rate the student's ability to communicate meaning rather than the creativity of the storytelling. For example, if you are assessing a new student about whom you know very little, you may want to use pictures that represent persons from different ethnic groups engaged in typical activities, such as eating, playing, or shopping. If you are assessing students in your class to see if they can use language functions introduced in class, such as describing persons, then you will want to provide a variety of pictures that call for descriptions of persons and reflect the vocabulary and structures presented and used in class.

A convenient way to organize your pictures is to keep a picture file. Collect large photographs representative of persons of different ages and cultures. Brown and Yule (1983) propose using a set of photographs that tell a story, such as eliciting an "eyewitness account" of an automobile accident. In this activity, students are asked to piece together by inference the story related by the pictures. As a listening activity, the listener could be asked to identify the pictures that match the accident being described or make a diagram of the accident.

Whether using single pictures or a series of pictures, allow students whenever possible to choose the picture or series of pictures they want to talk about. Giving students options in choosing pictures to talk about puts them more in control of the situation and at ease with their ability to communicate. Give each student a few minutes to examine the picture before trying to elicit language. The biggest challenge in this kind of assessment is to keep the process from becoming an interview, where the teacher asks a question and the student responds. In oral interviews, teachers tend to do at least 50 percent of the talking. To keep teacher talk to a minimum, tell the student that you want him or her to tell you what the picture is about or to tell you a story about the picture(s). Then ask the student to tell you as much as possible for as long as he or she can. This strategy may work more effectively with older learners than with younger learners. If younger students or shy students appear reticent, you may need to ask a few open-ended questions to elicit language. Asking other than *yes/no* questions will elicit more language with more proficient students. You can expect students at the beginning level to be able to label or name people, objects, colors, and other surface features of the pictures. At more advanced levels of English proficiency, students will compose a story describing relationships, events, background information about the pictures, and implications. To rate student performance, use rating scales or checklists similar to those used for the oral interview. As with the interview, rate student performance after the student has completed the task and returned to his or her desk.

Radio Broadcasts

Radio programs of news, music, weather, and commercials can be used to assess oral language in authentic contexts. Using authentic spoken language to assess listening and speaking can be highly motivating to students because it relates to daily life and calls for use of shared background knowledge (Porter and Roberts 1987). Listening to news reports and weather forecasts can be used to teach and assess listening with a purpose, listening for the gist of the message, and listening with less than total comprehension.

Radio broadcasts used for instruction and assessment are useful with individuals, groups, or whole classes. They are probably most appropriate for middle and high school students having more than a beginning level of proficiency, and require no preparation on the part of students. Language functions that may be assessed through the use of radio broadcasts include: listening for the gist, listening for specific information, listening for descriptions, listening for directions, and summarizing. Learning strategies used in these activities may include making inferences, predicting, asking for clarification, and comparing.

Songs of interest to learners can be used to assess their ability to understand what the song is about and to guess at the meanings of words from context. Of special interest to adolescents are popular songs played on the radio Top 40. Students can be assessed for their ability to identify the topic and the singer's feelings or for completing the words to a song given a partial text. Radio commercials can be used for teaching and assessing students' ability to scan for important information, such as the nature of a product, its name, and its purported benefits. They can also be asked to evaluate the commercial for honesty, reality, and true value. For example, given an automobile or cereal commercial, students can be asked to identify the product from a set of products in the same category. All of these listening activities can easily be conducted in conjunction with speaking activities, such as discussing, engaging in role-plays, or working in small groups. Reading and writing can also be made part of listening assessment, as long as the focus is on accuracy in listening, not on reading and writing.

For news broadcasts, students can predict what they think they will hear, then scan the message to confirm their predictions. They can also listen to a news report recorded later in the day or the next day to update their information and compare what they hear with written news accounts. With weather reports, students can be assessed for listening selectively, summarizing, completing a weather map or short statements or worksheets, discussing results in small groups, or even deciding which clothes to wear in response to the forecast.

To use radio broadcasts for assessment of oral language, select recordings of short texts (one to two minutes) with clear, predictable, and repetitive formats, if possible. To rate comprehension of radio broadcasts, a variety of procedures can be employed, from answering questions, to matching items, pictures, or diagrams to the message, to filling in a grid with pre-specified information.

Video Clips   Use of short videotaped segments or video clips (two to three minutes) to assess oral language can be highly motivating to students, who may typically spend hours watching television or videos outside of school. Video clips can be used at all levels of proficiency, but the things students are asked to do with oral language will differ depending on their level of proficiency. Video clips can be used with individuals, groups, or whole classes. Video can even be used with young children, especially to provide stimulation and motivation to learn about culture and language (Tomalin 1992). Video clips require no preparation on the part of the student and most often will elicit language functions for describing or giving information. On the other hand, at higher levels of proficiency students can be asked to respond to issues presented on the clips or to categorize a series of clips based on instructional goals. For example, a teacher intern we observed used video clips to get her intermediate high school ESL students to talk in pairs about the nature of the clips and to categorize them according to previous class discussions. In this case, the class had been studying violence on television and was being asked to categorize various video clips with regard to type of violence, whether the scenes presented were real or fictitious events, and what type of program was represented (e.g., documentary or reality-based police show). Students were asked to talk with a partner in order to fill out their response sheets/grids with the various questions/categories indicated. Not only were students thoroughly engrossed in the activity, they welcomed the opportunity to talk about the video clips and clarify points presented. For an example of a Student Response Sheet, see Figure 4.13.

Stempleski and Arcario (1992) have written on the use of authentic videos in the ESL classroom. They suggest using only very short clips (two to

three minutes), giving students a purpose for viewing, and providing repeated viewing. Worksheets or tasks requiring written responses can help students focus on what to look for in a video clip. To rate student comprehension of video clips, determine criteria (vocabulary, grammar, language functions, content) based on your instructional goals and activities.

Information Gap   Of all the activities described here, an information gap may provide one of the clearest indicators of the ability of one person to give information to another. An information gap is an activity where one student is provided information that is kept from a partner (Underhill 1987). Jigsaw activities and two-way tasks also provide situations where one person has information that the other does not; each person must provide the information using oral language. This information may involve descriptions of pictures, maps, or manipulatives. Information gap calls for detailed descriptions of physical objects and a linguistic command of colors, shapes, sizes, directions, locations, and sequences. Learners are evaluated on their effectiveness in bridging the information gap. Brown and Yule (1983) suggest that repeating an information gap activity several times as the speaker does not lead to significant improvement, whereas taking a role as the listener does. This is because when a student is on the receiving end of poor descriptions or instructions, he or she realizes the need to organize the message and be explicit. The information gap activity is prepared by the teacher but requires no preparation on the part of students. It is probably useful with students at all levels of language proficiency, from beginners to advanced. Information gap activities typically assess the following language functions: describing, giving information, and giving directions.

In preparing information gap activities, be careful not to design problem-solving activities that call for analysis by the learner. Otherwise, you will be assessing analytical ability as well as oral language proficiency (Underhill 1987). Decide whether your classroom activities involve describing or giving directions or instructions. If describing, choose pictures or manipulatives that elicit vocabulary

Figure 4.13 **Video Clip: Student Response Sheet**

Number of TV Clip	Type of TV Program (Pick from the list below.)
#1	
#2	
#3	
#4	
#5	
#6	
#7	
#8	

News	Quiz shows
Cartoons	Educational shows
Reality shows (*COPS, 911, Code 3*)	Talk shows
Comedies	Dramas
Sports	MTV

familiar to students. For giving directions, design maps of the school or community for students to use. For giving instructions, have listeners draw pictures or diagrams based on their partner's description. Students can also be asked to fill in graphs or grids based on what they hear. Examples include taking a telephone message or filling in details on a table or chart (Omaggio Hadley 1993).

In one kind of information gap task, the listener must identify or construct a model based only on a description provided by the partner. The first student describes a picture or physical model made of manipulatives (such as Legos or Cuisinaire rods) to the second student, who cannot see the first student's picture or model. The first student cannot see the second student's reconstruction and therefore does not know how effective his or her description is. In a basic form, information gap is one-way, with the speaker describing and the listener reconstructing. In a variation, the listener can ask questions of the speaker to clarify understanding. Alternatively, the first learner can describe one of several pictures which are similar except for minor but important details. The second learner does not know which picture the first learner is describing and must rely on the description provided to determine which it is. Learners switch roles and repeat the task with a different model. A useful reference with reproducible pictures for such activities is *Back and Forth: Pair activities for Language Development* (Palmer, Rodgers, and Winn-Bell Olsen 1985).

In another kind of information gap activity, the goal is to find the difference between two pictures which are similar but vary in a number of small details. The first learner describes the picture to the second learner, who responds by noting the differences in the picture. A good resource for this kind of activity is *Look Again Pictures* (Winn-Bell Olsen 1984).

In a third kind of information gap activity, listeners are given a series of unordered pictures or cartoon strips while their partners relate a story about the sequenced pictures. The speaker's task is to tell the story well enough so that the listener arranges the series of pictures into the appropriate sequence (Brown and Yule 1983).

To rate an information gap activity, evaluate the speaker on accuracy and clarity of the description as well as on the resulting reconstruction. The listener should be rated on ability to follow directions or complete the task. Accuracy—rather than speed or description of fine details—should be considered. An example of a scoring rubric for information gap activities designed by an ESL teacher is provided in Figure 4.14.

Story/Text Retelling Story/text retellings involve having students retell stories or text selections that they have listened to or read. If you ask a student to read a story silently, however, you should first ensure that the text is at his or her reading level. Otherwise, this activity becomes an assessment of the student's reading skills in addition to oral skills. It is especially important with retelling to be clear of the purpose of the assessment. Retelling can also be used to determine students' understanding of story structure; we address this purpose in Chapter 5.

In retelling, choosing to read a story or text orally to students means that you will be assessing both listening comprehension and speaking skills. Retellings are appropriate for individual assessment of students at the beginning and intermediate levels and require no preparation on the part of the student. Language functions most likely used in story/text retelling are describing, giving information, and summarizing.

To prepare for the story or text retelling, choose a story or text with which the student is familiar and that is appropriate for the age and grade-level of the student. For example, if you have been reading folktales in class or a scientific text on how volcanoes form, you can use these texts to read aloud to students. Students can also read stories they themselves have written or that the teacher has written for them. Plan on reading aloud approximately six to ten sentences (Underhill 1987). As with the oral interview and picture cues, be sure that the passage you have selected does not contain vocabulary or concepts that are culturally-biased or unknown to the student. You may tape-record the student's retelling for later rating or rate it shortly after the student has finished.

Figure 4.14　Oral Language Scoring Rubric: Information Gap

Rating	Demonstrated Competence
4	• Uses a variety of descriptive vocabulary and expressions • Communicates effectively, almost always responding appropriately and developing the interaction • Uses a variety of structures with only occasional grammatical errors • Speaks with little hesitation that does not interfere with communication
3	• Uses a variety of descriptive vocabulary and expressions • Communicates effectively, often responding appropriately and developing the interaction • Uses a variety of structures with more than occasional errors • Speaks with some hesitation that does not interfere with communication
2	• Uses some descriptive vocabulary and expressions • Communicates acceptably although sometimes responding inappropriately or inadequately or developing little interaction • Uses a variety of structures with frequent errors or uses basic structures with only occasional errors • Speaks with some hesitation that interferes with communication
1	• Uses basic vocabulary and expressions • Communicates marginally; mostly responding inappropriately or inadequately • Uses basic structures with frequent errors • Speaks with much hesitation that greatly interferes with communication

Adapted from a scoring rubric developed by ESL teacher S. Copley (1994).

To conduct the story/text retelling, give clear directions to the student so that he or she understands the nature of the task and how he or she will be evaluated. If the student can read the text independently, allow him or her to read it silently. If the student cannot read the text, then you can read aloud the selected passage. Read the text clearly and at a natural pace, or pre-record it on tape. Then ask the student to tell you in his or her own words what the story or text is about. Avoid the question/answer format of the interview because it leads to increased teacher talk. The advantage of a story/text retell lies in the potential for eliciting an extended amount of talk from the student.

To rate a story/text retelling, use a holistic or analytic rating scale or checklist of oral language skills. Some essential criteria of a story retelling may include accuracy in describing the setting, the characters, or a sequence of events; range of vocabulary; and appropriate syntax (Brown and Yule 1983). Performance tasks can be graded by difficulty along any of the above dimensions. That is, the more complicated the setting, the more similar or numerous the characters, or the more involved the sequence of events, the harder the task will become.

Improvisations/Role-Plays/Simulations

Drama techniques can be particularly effective in developing oral language skills of English language learners. These activities are authentic because they involve language use in interactive contexts. They provide a format for using elements of real-life conversation, such as repetitions, interruptions, hesitations, distractions, changes of topic, facial expressions, gestures, and idiolects (individual variations of dialect) (Forrest 1992). Although they require differing degrees of preparation, improvisations, role-plays, and simulations invite students to speak through the identity of another and/or to lose themselves in plots and situations which are engaging but without real consequences. Dramatic activities have been shown to reduce anxiety, increase motivation, and enhance language acquisition (Richard-Amato 1988).

Improvisations call for students to generate language given an oral or written cue called a *prompt*.

Students interact following the directions on cue cards provided by the teacher (Gonzalez Pino 1988). For example, cue cards might instruct students to ask for directions to the public library from the school. Students typically get no time to prepare what they are going to say.

Role-plays assign distinct roles to each student and ask them to speak through these roles. Role-plays tend to be more structured than improvisations but less scripted than plays. For example, one student might be given the role of an angry father awaiting the late return of his middle school son from a football game; another student could be given the role of the son. Students would have to prepare a dialogue prior to making their presentations.

Simulations provide a context or situation in which students need to interact in order to solve a problem or make a decision together. Simulations have also been referred to as *joint discussion/decision-making activities* (Underhill 1987) and *sociodrama* (Scarcella 1987). Sociodrama is a type of simulation that involves a solution to a social problem but allows more than one solution to be enacted and matches students to roles they can relate to (Scarcella 1987). Students are allowed time to prepare their simulation and present it to the class. In an example taken from local news, students could be asked to take the role of residents, land developers, and representatives of Disney World as they discuss the pros and cons of building a theme park near a historic local landmark.

Use of dramatic techniques is recommended for pairs or groups of students at all levels of proficiency and requires some preparation on the part of students. Simulations, in particular, may be most appropriate for secondary school students because they call for group problem solving in hypothetical situations. Forrest (1992) suggests that improvisations in pairs are more productive than those in groups. Because of the wide range of topics that can be addressed through these techniques, the types of language functions that may be elicited will depend on the topic and the context. However, improvisations, role-plays, and simulations lend themselves quite well to the following language functions: greetings/leave-takings, asking for/giving information, requesting assistance, agreeing/disagreeing, giving or evaluating an opinion, giving advice, giving directions, suggesting, persuading, and encouraging.

To prepare for using dramatic techniques, identify the context and purpose for language use and allow students time to prepare for role-plays and simulations. All written directions for improvisations, role-plays, or simulations should be at the reading level of the students. For beginning students, you can limit the use of language to accomplishing basic survival tasks such as asking for information or requesting assistance. For intermediate level students, you may want to engage students in agreeing/disagreeing or giving an opinion, advice, or directions. Decide whether students will perform before the whole class or in pairs before you alone while the rest of the class works independently.

Be sure students have had a number of opportunities to use oral language in dramatic activities before these activities are used for assessment. Gonzalez Pino (1988) suggests preparing five situations per lesson for students to practice before they are assessed through improvisation. Situations or scenarios should relate to students' everyday lives, such as having to work while going to school, communicating with parents, or getting along with others. For assessment, students can be asked to perform one or more improvisations in pairs. To elicit enough oral language to assign a rating, give enough cues so that each speaker produces from five to seven utterances.

Topics for role-plays should be taken from students' current interests and anticipated experiences (Donahue and Parsons 1982). Possible topics may include discussing a grade with a teacher, refusing an invitation, or clarifying a misunderstanding. Advanced beginners can also participate in role-play through the use of cue cards with incomplete lines for each role. For intermediate and advanced students, cue cards can be used which describe situations and call for creation of dialogue.

To do simulations, present students with a context in which they have to interact in order to reach a decision or conclusion. Cooperative learning activities for team building can be used as simulations. For example, "Survival in the Desert" presents students with a scenario of a small plane crash in a desert and asks them to decide whether to remain or leave the crash site and to determine which are the most important items to salvage for survival (such as a flashlight, a topcoat, or a bottle of salt tablets) (Kagan 1993). Audio and video clips can also be used to provide a context for simulations, for example, a news clip related to a topic of interest to students.

Provide students with a brief written description of the context and task for a simulation. Let students know that they will be evaluated on the quality of the interaction, not on the decision or conclusion reached. For example, Underhill (1987) suggests telling students that they will be evaluated based on the way they justify their opinions and evaluate those of others, not just the way they express facts. There is typically no single right answer to a simulation. Some examples of the types of tasks that can be used with simulations are:

- deciding whether or not to get into a car with a stranger

- choosing between working part-time and using the time to study

- deciding whether or not to report a crime one has witnessed

- deciding whether or not to report a student for using drugs

To rate improvisations, role-plays, or simulations, modify or adapt rubrics for oral language to suit the task and your students' level of proficiency. For example, assessment may include language functions, vocabulary, grammar, discourse strategies, clarity of facts presented, and nonverbal gestures if these have all been part of class instruction. In any task of this nature, some students may tend to talk more than others. You can allow for this in your rating by giving credit for both quantity and quality of talk. Videotaping dramatic presentations is an excellent way to get students to do self-assessment of their performance as well as to get peer feedback.

Oral Reports   Students may occasionally be called upon to present a research or other project in the form of an oral report. Oral reports offer a real-life listening comprehension opportunity which can provide new and interesting information to the listeners (Meloni and Thompson 1980). Oral reports can be used to develop the public speaking skills of the speaker as well as to provide practice to listeners in asking questions, agreeing and disagreeing, discussing, taking notes, and listening for specific purposes. Because of this, they can be used to prepare students to participate in grade-level content classes where they may be required to give oral reports, discuss issues, and take notes on lectures and discussions.

An oral report is presented not by reading aloud but by referring to notes or cue cards created by the student. Oral reports require thorough preparation by students and can be designed at all levels of proficiency. If research is required, oral reports may be more appropriate for intermediate and advanced levels of proficiency. Students at beginning levels of proficiency can make oral reports using realia or describing objects, posters, displays, or other support materials.

To prepare students for an oral report, give them guidelines on how long to speak, how to choose topics, what areas to address on a topic, and how their report will be evaluated. This can include a demonstration in which you conduct a mini-lecture and discuss the scoring rubric to be used for evaluation. The content of the report will necessarily be related to a topic students in your class may be researching, a project they are creating, or a topic of personal interest.

To present an oral report, students must prepare in advance. Each student should be prepared to speak for about five to ten minutes. To assess all students in one class during a one- or two-week period, you could ask one or several students to report each day. Meloni and Thompson (1980) suggest giving students a worksheet to complete in preparation for their oral report. The worksheet can ask students to provide information such as the title of the oral report, an outline of main and supporting ideas, and several comprehension questions for listeners. After the teacher provides feedback on the worksheet and outline, students can tape-record their oral report in a draft form. If

time allows, the teacher may want to critique the recorded version using a scoring rubric before the student's actual presentation. During the oral report, the teacher may either record the presentation for later rating or assign a rating immediately upon completion of the report.

To rate the oral report, begin with a rating scale or holistic rubric that reflects the major focus of instruction and revise it based on students' actual performance. For example, if you have provided students with ample time, guidance, resources for content and preparation, organization guidelines, and presentation techniques (such as eye contact), these should be included in the assessment criteria. Since the primary function of an oral report is to convey information, pronunciation and grammar should count only inasmuch as they detract from this function. An example of a self-assessment format for an oral report is provided in Figure 4.15.

You might also want to provide peers with listening reaction forms based on the scoring rubric. For example, questions such as *What was the main idea of this report?* and *How can the speaker improve the report?* can provide effective feedback to the speaker but should not in any way contribute to the overall rating or grade received by the student (Meloni and Thompson 1980).

Debates   Debates can present opportunities for students to engage in using extended chunks of language for a purpose: to convincingly defend one side of an issue. A debate is a type of role-play where students are asked to take sides on an issue and defend their positions. The debate is probably more often used in content area classrooms than in ESL classrooms. Debates are most appropriate for intermediate and advanced learners who have been guided in how to prepare for them. Debates require extensive preparation by learners, call for interaction in groups, and make use of at least the following language functions: describing, explaining, giving and asking for information, persuading, agreeing, and disagreeing.

To prepare students for the debate, teachers need to make sure that students have been given all the necessary resources and information in order to research and present their side of the

Figure 4.15   **Self-Assessment for an Oral Report**

Name _____   Date _____

Check (√) the box that best describes your oral report. Add comments.

Activity	Always	Sometimes	Rarely	Comments
1. I researched, outlined, and practiced my oral report.				
2. I spoke slowly and clearly.				
3. I glanced at my notes while talking.				
4. I used gestures to help express meaning.				
5. I used my face to express feelings.				
6. I answered questions on my report.				
7. I summarized the main points.				
8. I gave details to support my main points.				

Adapted from Clemmons et al. (1993).

issue. For example, students in a history class might be asked to take the roles of famous historical figures from different points in history to debate a current topic. Richard-Amato (1988) suggests putting the character of Henry VIII in a debate on divorce or Joan of Arc on a panel of women's issues. To prepare, students would have to become thoroughly familiar with each of these character's perspectives on the issue addressed.

To rate student performance on debates, decide whether to rate students as a team, as individuals, or both. In either case, you will need to use a rating scale or checklist to evaluate their performances with regard to specific criteria. As with all other approaches to oral language assessment, students should not only have been introduced to the criteria before engaging in the debate, they should also have been given the opportunity to actually observe a debate (perhaps a video) and rate it according to the specified criteria.

RECORDING TEACHER OBSERVATIONS

In the previous section we described the potential use of specific instructional activities for assessment. In each case we suggested using criteria to evaluate student performance. In this section we discuss the importance of documenting teacher observations by using rating scales, rubrics, or checklists or by keeping anecdotal records.

Teacher Observation   Teachers are not strangers to assessment by observation. What may be relatively new, however, is documenting the results of observations for assessment purposes. Documentation can take the form of checklists, rubrics, rating scales, or anecdotal records and can be done on an individual basis, in pairs, or in groups. The basic difference between checklists and rating scales is that whereas checklists only allow noting the presence or absence of a particular feature, rubrics or rating scales allow for documenting the degree of oral language proficiency exhibited by providing a range of performance levels. Anecdotal records allow for more qualitative descriptions of student performance.

When observing individuals, try to use checklists or rating scales in as unobtrusive a manner as possible so as not to intimidate students. Alternatively, we know some teachers who prefer to explain scoring rubrics to students and be quite explicit about what they are looking for during observations. You should use an approach both you and your students are comfortable with. For pairs of students, you will need to be extra careful to match students of similar proficiency levels and compatible personalities so that one does not dominate the other (Hughes 1989; Underhill 1987). When assessing small groups of three or four students at a time, you will have an opportunity to assess authentic language in action because learners tend to be less inhibited and more spontaneous in their speech when interacting with peers (Underhill 1987). Structured cooperative learning tasks, which provide for positive interdependence and individual accountability, will increase the chances of every student getting a chance to speak (Kagan 1993). A group assessment checklist can be used to rate students simultaneously. Groups can be assessed on the group process, such as participation, and on accuracy in accomplishing a task.

To increase the reliability of your assessment, use a rating scale or checklist and attempt to engage other teachers in your assessment through a program of inter-rater training. This will help make your own ratings more accurate. Although you may be tempted to compare students to one another or to give students higher ratings based on their perceived level of effort, we strongly encourage you to limit your ratings to the criteria on the scoring rubric in order to maintain the reliability and validity of your assessment. Each student's performance should be matched to specified criterion levels. These levels can be determined by examining the characteristics of high levels of oral language proficiency.

Anecdotal Records   Teachers who prefer to keep written notes on their observations may want to use anecdotal records. Anecdotal records have been most typically used to assess progress in literacy in the elementary school (Rhodes and Nathenson-Mejia 1992). Anecdotal records consist of brief notes made shortly after a student has been observed making progress in a key area. Teachers have told us that they keep anecdotal records on yellow sticky notes or on adhesive labels that they later organize by individual student names. Other ways to organize anecdotal records are by keeping a notebook with a section on each student, keeping file folders or file cards for each student, and using computer files (Hill and Ruptic 1994). By selecting a few students to observe each week, it is possible to maintain anecdotal records on all students in a class at least twice in a marking period.

A necessary prerequisite to keeping anecdotal records is the establishment of a classroom environment that allows teachers the time to record their observations. Such a classroom encourages student independence and responsibility and frees the teacher to spend time with individuals or groups as needed.

One of the advantages of using anecdotal records is that they can provide the teacher with a history of the process through which the learner's oral language skills have evolved. This includes documenting the student's use of listening and learning strategies. The open-ended nature of anecdotal records may make them particularly appropriate for use with young children. Anecdotal records allow the teacher to determine what information is important to record in a specific situation, given a student's strengths and needs in relation to instructional goals.

To write anecdotal records, you need to follow three steps (Thorndike and Hagen 1977):

1. Describe a specific event or product.

2. Report rather than evaluate or interpret.

3. Relate the material to other facts known about the student.

Providing an example of the student's work is preferable to making a general conclusion about it. Rhodes and Nathenson-Mejia (1992) suggest that it is acceptable to evaluate or interpret a student's work by commenting on the student's needs and recommending instructional activities.

To analyze anecdotal records, you will need to make inferences from your observations, look for patterns of growth for individuals, groups, and the class, and identify strengths and needs in learning and teaching (Rhodes and Nathenson-Mejia

1992). For example, patterns of oral language use from the native language to English can be documented in different contexts as can use of oral language in group and whole class activities. Make time to analyze anecdotal records during planning periods and meetings with other teachers.

Anecdotal records provide opportunities to corroborate information obtained using a checklist or rating scale through descriptions of specific student performance. The information obtained from anecdotal records can be used not only to inform instruction and assessment but also to communicate with students and their parents on how students are doing. It can also provide feedback to the teacher on the effectiveness of teaching materials and activities.

ORAL LANGUAGE PORTFOLIOS

Although much has been written on using portfolios for assessing reading and writing, there is virtually no published information on their use in assessing oral language development in native or second languages. The reasons for using portfolios to assess oral language are the same as those for assessing literacy: they provide continuous information on student growth over time; they are authentic in that they are directly linked to classroom instruction; they are multidimensional because they provide information on different aspects of student language proficiency; and they call for student reflection in the form of self-assessment. To get started using oral language portfolios, see Chapter 3, where we introduce a seven-step process for implementing portfolios.

Using Oral Language Assessment in Instruction

• • • • • • • • • • • • • • • •

Once oral language assessment results are available, teachers need to make decisions regarding grades, placement, and modifications in instruction. With regard to grading, we refer you to Chapter 2 for suggestions on how to convert performance ratings into grades. Because local grading policies vary from teacher to teacher and school to school, teachers will need to be guided by feedback obtained from colleagues and by trial and error in assigning grades. With regard to placement, local program guidelines can provide specific implications relating to different levels of language proficiency. In lieu of these, teachers can work with colleagues to determine what student performance levels imply for curriculum and instruction.

For making decisions at the classroom level, results of oral language assessment can be used in several ways: for adapting instruction to student needs, for grouping students, and for communicating progress to students and parents. In the classroom, if students are not demonstrating the ability to apply what has been presented through instruction, teachers might want to review and revise their instructional activities and goals. If several students are found to share the same need in oral language (using language to give specific descriptions, for example) they can be grouped together for instruction on this area. For students whose oral language, while comprehensible, reflects pronunciation that impairs effective communication or is a cause for potential embarrassment or ridicule from other students, teachers can provide individual assistance (Carruthers 1987). Parents should be informed of assessment results, especially if students appear to be making little or no progress.

Conclusion

. . . .

In this chapter we described the nature of oral language, with a specific focus on oral language in school, and implications for the assessment of English language learners. We emphasized the need to base assessment of oral language in instruction and provided examples of how to use specific instructional activities for assessment. We proposed steps for assessing oral language as well as guidelines for developing performance tasks and scoring rubrics, setting standards, involving students in self- and peer assessment, selecting assessment activities, and recording teacher observations. We also made suggestions for developing and using oral language portfolios as part of ongoing assessment. Finally, we described ways assessment results can be used for instruction.

In assessing the oral language of English language learners, teachers should keep in mind the following points:

1. Activities for assessing oral language should come from instructional activities.

2. Assessment of oral language, like instruction, requires planning, time, and experience.

3. Assessment activities should be appropriate to students' level of oral language proficiency.

4. Assessment of oral language should focus on both communicative and academic language functions.

5. Authentic assessment of oral language should focus on a student's ability to interpret and convey meaning in interactive contexts which are as authentic as possible.

6. Assessment of oral language should be conducted regularly and be ongoing.

7. Students should be actively involved in their own assessment, whether in setting criteria, engaging in self-assessment, or evaluating peers.

8. Teacher observations of oral language use should be recorded systematically.

9. Results of oral language assessment should be used to inform students, parents, and teachers of needed changes in student performance and in instruction.

APPLICATION ACTIVITIES

. . . .

1. Identify three examples of communicative and academic language used in an ESL/bilingual classroom. Give examples of both oral and written language. Do the same for at least one grade-level classroom for the students you teach or are planning to teach.

2. Classify the examples of communicative and academic language which you have identified in an ESL/bilingual classroom. Classify the language functions in the classroom of a grade-level teacher and compare the two. Use Figures 4.1 and 4.2 to assist in your classification. What conclusions can you reach from the comparison?

3. With a partner, discuss whether your school district assesses the oral language proficiency of ELL students. How do they do this? What use can you make of this information for instruction, if any?

4. With a partner who works or expects to work at the same grade level, plan a process to assess oral language proficiency. What language functions do you want to assess? Will you assess students individually, in pairs, or in small groups? What type of rating scale or rubric do you want to use? When and how often will you assess students? Use Figures 4.3 and 4.4 to help you plan.

5. Work with another teacher to develop a scoring rubric for an oral language interview. Use the oral language scoring rubrics in Figures 4.4 and 4.5 as examples. How many levels do you want on the rubric? How is each level defined? What standard of performance do you want your students to attain on this rubric?

6. Identify an oral language activity, such as role-play or simulation, appropriate for the students you teach or expect to teach. Develop a rating scale for self-assessment and peer assessment of oral language proficiency. Use the examples in Figures 4.6 through 4.10.

7. Plan portfolio entries for oral language assessment based on your instructional goals. Share them with a partner.

READING
ASSESSMENT

· ·

In this chapter we identify and describe practical approaches to the authentic assessment of reading. We begin by examining the nature of reading and the relationship between reading in the first language and reading in a second language. This is followed by a description of new directions in reading instruction with implications for assessment. We then provide step-by-step procedures for assessing reading with English language learners (ELLs), including identifying the purpose of reading assessments, planning for assessment, involving students in self- and peer assessment, developing scoring rubrics and procedures, and setting standards. We elaborate on a number of instructional activities for reading that can be particularly useful for assessment. Sample assessment formats are provided as models for teachers to adapt for their own and their students' needs. Finally, we suggest ways for documenting teacher observations of reading, developing reading/writing portfolios, and using reading assessment results for instruction.

Nature of Reading in School

· · · · · · · · · · · · · · · · ·

READING IN THE NATIVE LANGUAGE

Although reading was once assumed to be a combination of decoding and oral language, it is now acknowledged that reading comprehension depends heavily on knowledge about the world as well as on knowledge of language and print (Fielding and Pearson 1994). In addition to producing literal comprehension, reading entails making inferences and evaluating what is read. Readers construct new knowledge from the interaction between texts and their own background knowledge. We also know that reading and writing are mutually supportive language processes; reading activities may have as great an effect on writing performance as does direct instruction in grammar and mechanics (Farnan, Flood, and Lapp 1994).

READING IN A SECOND LANGUAGE

Reading processes in a second language are similar to those acquired in the first language in that they call for knowledge of sound/symbol relationships, syntax, grammar, and semantics to predict and confirm meaning (Peregoy and Boyle 1993). As they do in their first language, second language readers use their background knowledge regarding the topic, text structure, their knowledge of the world, and their knowledge of print to interact with the printed page and to make predictions about it.

Two important differences between first and second language reading can be found in the language proficiency and experiences of the students. Students reading in a second language have varied levels of language proficiency in that language. The second language learner may be in the process of acquiring oral language while also developing literacy skills in English. Limited proficiency in a second language may cause a reader literate in the native language to "short circuit" and revert to poor reader strategies (such as reading word by word) (Clarke 1988). Also, students may not have the native language literacy skills to transfer concepts or strategies about reading to the second language. Those who do have native language literacy skills may not know how to transfer their skills to the second language without specific strategy instruction. No empirical evidence exists to show that readers do in fact transfer reading strategies automatically from their first to a second language (Grabe 1988; McLeod and McLaughlin 1986).

Another difference between first and second language reading is that second language readers may have more varied levels of background knowledge and educational experiences (Peregoy and Boyle 1993). Students with a limited range of personal or educational experiences on a reading topic will have little to draw on in constructing meaning from text. In fact, the biggest single challenge to teachers of ELL readers may be the range of educational experiences presented by their students (Chamot and O'Malley 1994b).

Models of Reading   Theories of reading in a second language have changed since the mid-1970s from exclusively bottom-up models to models that describe reading as an interaction between bottom-up and top-down processes (Carrell, Devine, and Eskey 1988; Grabe 1988; Samuels and Kamil 1988). *Bottom-up models* refer to the decoding of individual linguistic units on the printed page, working one's way up from smaller to larger units to obtain meaning and to modify one's prior knowledge (Carrell 1988). *Top-down models* begin with the reader's hypotheses and predictions about the text and his or her attempts to confirm them by working down to the smallest units of the printed text. Readers weak in one reading strategy might rely on other processes to compensate for this weakness (Stanovich 1980).

For second language learners, top-down models do not appear to fit the process of reading in the second language unless the learners are already proficient readers (Eskey 1988). The limitation of top-down models is that they emphasize higher-level skills, such as predicting meaning with contextual clues or background knowledge, at the expense of lower-level skills such as rapid and accurate identification of vocabulary and syntactical forms. In contrast, interactive models suggest that fluent reading comprehension depends on mastery of grammar and a large vocabulary, and that automatic word recognition is even more important than the use of context clues. The reader needs to access lower-level skills, such as word recognition and knowledge of cohesive devices and syntax, in order to read with automaticity (Grabe 1988). In fact, research evidence suggests that poor readers can use the context but have not yet acquired automatic decoding skills (Eskey and Grabe 1988). Interactive models of reading are proposed for second language learners to give balanced emphasis to these top-down and bottom-up processes. In these models, the term *interactive* has three meanings: (1) the interaction between the reader and the text, (2) the interplay between lower- and higher-level reading processes (decoding and using prior knowledge), and (3) the relationship between form *(text structure)* and function *(genre)* in texts (Grabe 1988).

For second language learners, because word meanings are context-sensitive, reading comprehension depends on specific examples in memory as well as on abstract and general schemata (Anderson and Pearson 1988). *Schemata* refer to knowledge already stored in memory, while *abstract* and *general schemata* refer to distinctive features that make up generic categories, such as *bird, bachelor,* and *door.* Readers' background knowledge is often culture-bound and may not match the schemata needed for a given reading text. Reading instruction needs to acknowledge the life experiences and cultural assumptions that second language learners bring to school (Au 1993). Reading skills should, therefore, be taught in the context of reading and writing activities that build on students' prior knowledge and experience.

WHAT WORKS IN READING INSTRUCTION

In addition to having new knowledge about the reading process, we also know what works in reading instruction. In particular, reading programs having the following four components can lead to student success: (1) extensive amounts of time in class for reading, (2) direct strategy instruction in reading comprehension, (3) opportunities for collaboration, and (4) opportunities for discussions on responses to reading (Fielding and Pearson 1994). We briefly discuss each of these compo-

nents below and follow with an update on the phonics versus whole language debate.

Spending time reading in class is important because students benefit from the time to apply reading skills and strategies and also because time spent reading results in acquisition of new knowledge (Fielding and Pearson 1994). In turn, knowledge aids comprehension, vocabulary acquisition, and concept formation. Research has shown a consistent positive and mutually supportive relationship between prior knowledge and reading comprehension. However, providing time for sustained silent reading is not enough. To improve reading comprehension, teachers must: (1) provide a choice of reading selections, (2) ensure that students are reading texts of optimal difficulty which challenge but do not discourage them, (3) encourage rereading of texts, and (4) allow students to discuss what they read with others to encourage social negotiation of meaning.

One of the more important findings to emerge from research on reading instruction over the last fifteen years is that reading comprehension can be increased by teaching comprehension strategies directly (Fielding and Pearson 1994). Many reading strategies can be taught directly, including: using background knowledge to make inferences; finding the main idea; identifying sources of information needed to answer a question; and using story or text structure to aid comprehension. The most promising result of the comprehension strategy research is that instruction is especially effective with "poor comprehenders." In fact, Fielding and Pearson found that.

> In some studies, less able readers who had been taught a comprehension strategy were indistinguishable from more able readers who had not been taught the strategy directly. (p. 65)

In addition to class time for reading and direct strategy instruction, peer and collaborative learning also contribute to reading acquisition (Fielding and Pearson 1994). By working collaboratively, students gain access to each other's thinking processes and teach one another effective reading strategies. In particular, cooperative learning and reciprocal teaching, when implemented correctly, appear to promote reading comprehension. (See the discussion below on reciprocal teaching.) These approaches acknowledge the social nature of learning and the role of the reader as a negotiator of meaning.

Traditionally, teachers have led discussions of reading texts by posing a question for student response and then evaluating that response. However, current trends in reading instruction indicate a move away from primarily teacher-directed discussions to student-driven discussions, allowing for acceptance of personal interpretations and reactions to literature (Fielding and Pearson 1994). These discussions are most effective when they incorporate reading strategy instruction. Changing teacher/student interaction patterns is challenging, however, since many teachers feel the need to maintain control while also "covering" the curriculum.

Similar to reading programs for native speakers of English, reading instruction for English language learners should include at least five important components: a large quantity of reading; time in class for reading; appropriate materials that encourage students to read; direct teaching of reading strategies; and a teacher skilled in matching materials and reading strategies to the students' level of interest and language proficiency (Devine 1988; Eskey and Grabe 1988). Such programs result in improved reading ability only when approaches to reading are holistic or integrative rather than skills-based, and when teacher feedback is a core element. In addition, reading instruction for English language learners should tap students' prior knowledge and experiences, focus on comprehension of meaning while teaching skills in context, teach text organization, and allow for collaborative discussions of reading.

Whole Language and Phonics   With regard to the long-standing debate between advocates of whole language and phonics-based approaches to teaching reading, there is evidence that phonemic awareness is a necessary but not sufficient condition for becoming an efficient reader (Pearson 1993). Skills are useful only to the extent that they "can be strategically applied to an authentic reading context" (Routman 1994, p. 298). Routman points out that it is no longer a question of whether phonics should be taught but how to teach phon-

ics in a meaningful context. Whether teaching word skills and phonemic awareness through direct phonics instruction is more or less effective than learning these skills through reading authentic texts remains unclear. What is clear, however, is that low-achieving readers in English (and this probably includes most students in need of language support programs) have typically been provided with phonics instruction and basic skills instead of authentic reading texts. It is also highly probable that students who are poor readers in first grade will still be poor readers in fourth grade. Perhaps for these reasons, Pearson suggests future research on reading focus on the reading acquisition of at-risk students, reasons why some students fail and others succeed in both student-centered and curriculum-based approaches to reading, and how linguistic and cultural conflicts relate to reading failure.

Reading in the Content Areas   Students read for many purposes. One of the most important of these is reading to learn in the content areas. When moving from literature or trade books to content area texts, the purpose of reading changes from learning to read to reading to obtain information. Both the content and organization of the text are likely to be new to readers. This shift occurs in the middle grades, but it is highly unlikely that teachers in middle grades or high school will familiarize students with the reading strategies needed for making sense of content area texts (Alvermann and Phelps 1994; Lapp, Flood, and Farnan 1989).

For English language learners, it is important to make content area topics relevant by involving students in how they learn and by providing opportunities for them to negotiate meaning through both oral and written language (Peregoy and Boyle 1993). By their very nature, content area texts pose special challenges to second language learners. Among these are: schema activation, text structure, and active use of reading and learning strategies (Alvermann and Phelps 1994; Lapp, Flood, and Farnan 1989; Peregoy and Boyle 1993; Vacca and Vacca 1993).

Schema activation is the process by which students access prior knowledge and match it to information in the text (Vacca and Vacca 1993). Research studies have shown that inappropriate or missing schema can limit learning from texts (Alvermann and Phelps 1994). Students need to be familiar with the language as well as the concepts of the content area. Schema help reading comprehension in three ways: (1) by providing the framework for reading selectively and purposefully, (2) by helping readers better organize and retain information, and (3) by enabling students to elaborate information and ask questions of the text.

A second challenge in reading comprehension in the content areas is *text structure.* The content and structure of the text together influence reading comprehension. Content area texts are written to inform, primarily by describing and explaining. Written in expository prose, most content area texts reflect one of the following five text patterns to express logical connections: description, sequence, comparison-contrast, cause-effect, and problem-solution (Vacca and Vacca 1993). Each of these patterns has specific transition words (e.g., *because, however, first, second*) that signal a particular type of organization. Students who are more familiar with these patterns will comprehend texts much better than those who are not.

The third aspect affecting comprehension of reading in the content areas is *active use of reading and learning strategies.* As discussed earlier in this chapter, more skilled readers have a higher awareness of reading strategies and are better able to match them appropriately to text than less skilled readers. Good readers read with a purpose, summarize main ideas, organize information, and monitor comprehension as they read. If a breakdown in comprehension occurs, good readers may apply one or more of the following learning strategies: ignore the word or phrase and read on; think of an example; produce a visual image; read ahead and connect information; and use text patterns, transition words, and pronouns to make connections (Vacca and Vacca 1993). The question of whether reading skills and strategies are generic to all content areas or content-specific remains unresolved (Lapp, Flood, and Farnan 1989).

In summary, to help students learn to read in the content areas, teachers can: (1) activate and assess prior knowledge as well as teach necessary background knowledge, (2) teach students how texts are organized and how to use text structure to increase comprehension, and (3) teach reading strategies that will help students bring meaning to the text. Suggestions for assessment of content area knowledge are provided in Chapter 7.

IMPLICATIONS FOR ASSESSMENT

A number of implications for assessment can be drawn from the foregoing description of the nature of reading in first and second languages and effective instructional practices for increasing reading comprehension. These include the importance of determining students' prior knowledge, making students accountable for how they use reading time in class, assessing students' progress in acquiring both decoding skills and reading comprehension strategies, observing how students collaborate in groups as well as how they work individually, and reviewing students' personal responses to reading.

Garcia (1994) and Routman (1994) suggest that, in tying instruction to assessment, the key questions become: What do I as a teacher need to know about each student's literacy and language development in order to plan instruction? and What instructional activities and tasks can I use to find this out and document it? Information resulting from literacy assessment should help teachers identify students' needs and plan for the most suitable instructional activities. Activities discussed in this chapter that correspond to specific reading assessment purposes are described in Figure 5.1.

In order for reading assessment to become useful in student evaluation, teachers should consider the following (Routman 1994):

- Be thoroughly familiar with developmental learning processes and curriculum.

- Articulate a philosophy of assessment and evaluation.

- Know about and have experience collecting, recording, interpreting, and analyzing multiple sources of data.

- Be flexible and willing to try out multiple assessment procedures.

Figure 5.1   **Reading Assessment: Matching Purpose to Task**

What Do I Want to Know?	How Will I Find Out?
Reading comprehension	• Retellings • Literature response journals • Anecdotal records • Literature discussion groups • Texts with comprehension questions
Reading strategies	• Reading strategies checklists • Reciprocal teaching • Think-alouds • Anecdotal records • Miscue analysis • Running records
Reading skills	• Cloze passages • Miscue analysis • Running records
Reading attitudes	• Reading logs • Interviews • Literature discussion groups • Anecdotal records
Self-assessment	• Interviews • Rubrics/rating scales • Portfolio selections

Adapted from Routman (1994).

• Be committed to understanding and implementing an approach to evaluation that informs students and directs instruction.

Authentic Assessment of Reading

· · · · · · · · · · · · · · · ·

As discussed in Chapter 4, assessment requires planning and organization. The key lies in identifying the purpose of reading assessment and matching instructional activities to that purpose. After identification of assessment purpose, it is important to plan time for assessment, involve students in self- and peer assessment, develop rubrics and/or scoring procedures, set standards, select

assessment activities, and record teacher observations. In this section we discuss each of these steps. We follow this with suggestions for bringing all of the information together in reading/writing portfolios and using reading assessment in instruction.

IDENTIFY PURPOSE

Any assessment of reading must begin with the purpose of the assessment. At least four major purposes for classroom-based assessment of reading have been identified (Johns 1982):

• studying, evaluating, or diagnosing reading behavior

• monitoring student progress

- supplementing and confirming information gained from standardized and criterion-referenced tests
- obtaining information not available from other sources

For second language learners, other purposes of reading assessment are:

- initial identification and placement of students in need of a language-based program, such as ESL or bilingual education
- movement from one level to another within a given program, (e.g., intermediate to advanced levels of ESL)
- placement out of an ESL/bilingual program and into a grade-level classroom
- placement in a Chapter 1 (Title I) or special education classroom
- graduation from high school

In assessing reading skills and strategies, teachers can begin by identifying learners' needs with regard to the local curriculum. At the beginning of each school year and as new students enter throughout the school year, a baseline assessment of reading ability should be conducted to plan instructional goals and activities. For the classroom teacher, the purpose of reading assessment will most often be monitoring growth in reading. For this purpose, you will need to assess both *process* (strategies) and *product* (reading skills and comprehension levels) (Herman, Aschbacher, and Winters 1992).

PLAN FOR ASSESSMENT

Once you have identified your purposes for assessment, you can begin to *outline your major instructional goals or learning outcomes* and match these to your learning activities. However, you may find it easier to identify instructional objectives after naming different kinds of assignments or tasks students find most interesting and challenging (Herman, Aschbacher, and Winters 1992). By *identifying instructional activities or tasks* currently used in the classroom that can also serve for assessment, you will be making the direct link between assessment and instruction and saving yourself the time

involved in planning separate activities for assessment. You will also want to plan for individual, pair, and group assessment activities. A planning matrix similar to the one used in Chapter 4 could be useful for assessment of reading as well (see Figure 5.2).

If you are considering assessing oral reading, be sure to determine the purpose of the assessment and whether it reflects instruction. All too frequently, teachers tell us they assess oral reading for "expression." However, unless students have been trained in oral reading, they will have difficulty performing to meet teacher expectations. Some teachers have told us they ask students to read aloud to determine the difficulty level of a text. Based on what we know about oral reading, unless you have specific goals to assess, keep a running record, or conduct a miscue analysis, reading aloud by students may not be as informative as a student interview or group discussion.

In deciding *how often to collect information* on reading progress, take into consideration the number of students you teach, whether or not they need to be closely monitored for reading growth, and how you will make time during or beyond class time for assessment. You can make time for meeting with individual students and groups during class by having a collaborative classroom where students are used to working individually or in small groups and monitoring their own learning (Routman 1994). To monitor student progress in reading, you may want to consider collecting and documenting information at least twice and preferably several times during each quarter or semester. The more frequently you collect this information, the better you will be able to adjust your instructional goals to meet your students' needs.

Be sure to *provide students with feedback* periodically and each time you conduct an assessment of work for possible inclusion in students' reading portfolios. As in the assessment of oral language, you want to provide feedback as soon as possible after students have been assessed, but this does not mean that you have to assess everything a student does in your classroom. Remember, students can also assess themselves as well as each other, thereby freeing up your time to work with others.

Figure 5.2 **Reading Assessment Planning Matrix**

Reading Assessment Activity	Skills/Behaviors Assessed	Proficiency Level	Individual/ Pair/Group	Age/Grade Level
Retellings	• Reading comprehension	All	Individual, pair	All
Checklists	• Reading skills • Reading comprehension strategies	All	Individual, group	All
Anecdotal records	• Reading skills • Reading comprehension strategies	All	Individual	All
Cloze tests	• Reading skills	Intermediate, advanced	Individual, group	MS, HS, adult
Reading logs	• Reading comprehension • Response to literature • Choice in reading	All	Individual	All

INVOLVE STUDENTS

Students become partners in the assessment process when they are encouraged to engage in self-assessment and peer assessment. Student reflection is a vital element of authentic assessment.

Self-Assessment Self-assessment, while not graded by the teacher, helps both teachers and students become aware of students' attitudes, strengths, and weaknesses in reading (Routman 1994). It also encourages students to become independent learners. Self-assessment questions need to be modeled by the teacher before students can be expected to engage in self-assessment activities. Demonstrate the kinds of questions to be asked with the whole class, then let peers select a few questions to ask each other. Some questions might be:

• *What have you learned about reading in this class?*

• *How do you feel about reading?*

• *What three things do good readers do?*

• *What do you need to improve in reading?*

• *What do you do when you come to words you don't know?*

In the case of young children or low literacy students, teachers can provide short sentences and pictorial responses (e.g., smiling faces) for students to circle to indicate their reading habits. Figure 5.3 provides an example of such a format produced by an elementary school ESL teacher. For pre-readers, teachers can read questions aloud and note students' responses.

Self-assessment of reading can take various formats. Among these are: checklists, rating scales, scoring rubrics, question/answer, sentence completion, learning logs, and reflection logs. In keeping reflection logs, students are asked to express in writing what they feel they have or have not learned (Routman 1994). Students clarify for themselves what progress they have made in reading while teachers get feedback on what students have actually learned or still need to learn. Reflection logs can be written during the last ten

Figure 5.3   **Self-Assessment of Emergent Reading**

Name _____ Date _____

How do you read? Circle one of the faces.

Usually   Sometimes   Not much

1. I read every day for 30 minutes.

2. I read many different types of books.

3. I look at the pictures for new words.

4. I pay attention when the teacher reads a story.

5. I read during free time.

6. I like to read.

7. I tell others about books I read.

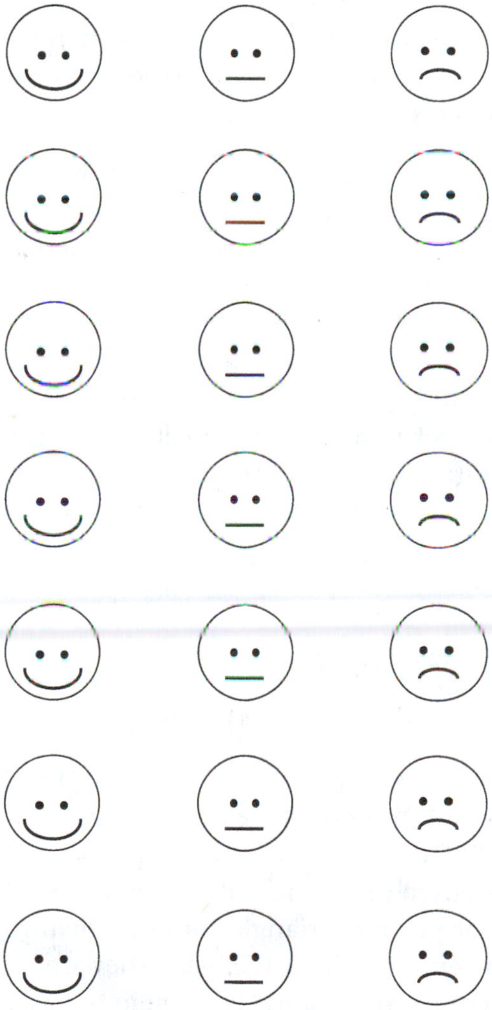

Adapted from a form developed by elementary ESL teacher J. Eury (1994), Fairfax County Public Schools, Virginia.

minutes of class once a week. Some guiding questions might be:

• What did I learn about reading this week?

• What did I have trouble with?

• What would I like to know more about?

To format a self-assessment, be sure to use language at students' reading levels, or ask students to work in pairs to write their own self-assessment questions after you have modeled the kinds of questions that could be asked. You might want to work with a colleague to develop and share various formats; one version could be designed for beginning readers, and others might be developed for intermediate- and advanced-level readers. If the format consists of statements to be rated, be sure to begin by first stating what each student can do and put this in the first person (e.g., "I can..."). For an example of self-assessment of reading practices and strategies, see Figures 5.4–5.6.

Peer Assessment   To involve students in peer assessment, teachers can ask them to rate their peers' reading comprehension levels and attitudes toward reading in reading discussion groups. Teachers will have to model for ELL students how to use guiding questions or statements. The following questions might be used to get students to provide peer feedback to a partner or group during story retelling (adapted from Tierney, Carter, and Desai 1991):

• *What did you like best about your partner's story?*

• *What could your partner have done better?*

• *Suggest one thing for your partner to work on for his or her next story retelling.*

One ESL teacher[1] suggests writing the beginnings of three statements (such as "I like...," "I want to know...," "You can make it better by...") to be completed by each student in a group. Each statement is written on a different side of a construction paper prism or triangle (or other manipulative). This reminds students of what they are supposed to comment on and keeps them on task.

Portfolio partners can provide each other with feedback on their portfolios (see also Chapter 3). Using 3" x 5" index cards, portfolio partners can respond to several guiding questions about their partner's portfolio (Clemmons et al. 1993; Hill and Ruptic 1994). Some sample questions/statements might be:

• What does your partner's portfolio tell you about him or her as a reader?

• Write one positive thing about your partner's portfolio.

• Write one thing your partner needs to work on in reading.

DEVELOP RUBRICS/SCORING PROCEDURES

Develop initial criteria by which students' reading progress will be measured *before* using instructional activities for assessment. Criteria should be stated in terms of what students can do rather than what they cannot do. The best way to develop scoring procedures and rubrics or rating scales is with student input (see Chapter 3). Get students involved by asking them what good readers do. Use a model scoring rubric that you can adapt later or ask colleagues for feedback on. You will probably need to modify the criteria periodically, based on actual student performance. Areas to be assessed in reading should include reading comprehension, use of reading strategies, decoding skills, response to reading, and student choice in reading, depending on students' level of literacy in English. Criteria can take the form of a checklist or a scoring rubric. Because teachers we have worked with seem to prefer a rubric, we have provided one based on a developmental model of reading, as shown in Figure 5.7.

As suggested in Chapter 4, when using a holistic scoring rubric you will be assigning a rating for each student's performance, whether or not that performance meets all of the criteria at a specific level. Many students will be difficult to place in one distinct category or another, but by assigning a rating you will have something to compare to similar performances by the same student. This is also where multiple assessors and assessments come in;

1. Thanks to Mary Lou Kulsick of Fairfax County Public Schools, Virginia, for her idea on the discussion group manipulative.

Figure 5.4   **Self-Assessment Reading Survey**

Name _____ Date _____

1. Do you like to read? Why or why not?

2. What kinds of stories/books do you like to read?

3. What book are you reading now?

4. How do good readers read?

5. What do you need to do to be a better reader?

Figure 5.5 Self-Assessment of Reading Activities

Name _____ Date _____

Read each statement. Put a check (√) in the box that is most true for you.

Statement	Most of the Time	Sometimes	Not Very Often
1. I like to read.			
2. I read at home.			
3. I read different kinds of books.			
4. I read easy books.			
5. I read difficult books.			
6. I read books that are just right.			
7. I talk with my friends about books I have read.			
8. I write about books I have read (literature response log).			

Adapted from a self-assessment developed by ESL teacher K. Harrison (1994) and based on Sharp (1989) and Fairfax County Public Schools, Virginia (1989).

Figure 5.6   **Self-Assessment of Reading Strategies**

Name _____ Date _____

Check (√) the box that indicates how you read.

Reading Strategies	Often	Sometimes	Almost Never
1. I think about what I already know on the topic.			
2. I make predictions and read to find out if I was right.			
3. I reread the sentences before and after a word I do not know.			
4. I ask another student for help.			
5. I look for the main idea.			
6. I take notes.			
7. I discuss what I read with others.			
8. I stop and summarize.			
9. I choose books from the library on my own.			
10. I make outlines of what I read.			

Adapted from Applebee, Langer, and Jullis (1988) and Rhodes (1993).

they provide other sources of information on what you have determined a student's reading level to be.

Between three and six levels of student performance are all that are necessary when designing a scoring rubric. More than that will not yield useful information. We recommend using analytic and weighted rating scales for diagnostic purposes rather than for monitoring student progress (see Chapter 2). These types of rating scales are more time-consuming to use and may require rater training before an acceptable level of inter-rater reliability is reached. It is desirable to use more than one rater on occasion to check for inter-rater reliability. By beginning with identification of at least two categories of reading performance, high- and low-level readers, you can proceed to identify cases that fall along the continuum of reading performance.

SET STANDARDS

Standards for reading comprehension can be set by establishing cut-off scores on a scoring rubric or rating scale. For example, at least three levels of reading performance could be described as novice, intermediate, and advanced. If most of the students you teach are in the intermediate category, you may want to establish several levels within that category in order to show students they are making progress while still at an intermediate level. These sub-categories might be called beginning, expanding, and bridging (see Figure 5.7), terms borrowed from Hill and Ruptic (1994) . Each category or level needs to be defined by criteria to be clearly distinct from the next level (see Figure 5.7). An example of a reading rubric drafted jointly by elementary and secondary ESL teachers is presented in Figure 5.8.

SELECT ASSESSMENT ACTIVITIES

Assessment of reading should be embedded in activities for teaching reading. In this section we describe instructional activities that can also serve for assessment of reading in a second language. These include: retellings, reading logs, literature response logs/journals, literature discussion groups, cloze tests, texts with comprehension questions, and reciprocal teaching (Garcia 1994; Pikulski and Shanahan 1982; Routman 1994).

Retellings   Students can be asked to retell a story or text they have read or that has been read to them. Teachers can use story maps (see Figure 5.9), checklists (see Figure 5.10), or rating scales to evaluate students as they retell the story. You can ask probe questions to elicit information which is not forthcoming from the student. Some examples of probe questions for fiction are:

- *Who was the main character of the story?*
- *What happened to the main character?*
- *Which character did you like best and why?*

Some examples for non-fiction are:

- *What was the main point of the text?*
- *What examples or details were provided to support this point?*
- *What else would you like to know about this topic?*

Retelling gives students an opportunity to speak at length, if they can, without teacher interruption in an informal setting. Teachers can ask students to tell a story as if they were telling it to someone who is not familiar with it. For English language learners, retelling helps develop oral language proficiency as well as reading comprehension (Routman 1994).

Retelling what one has read is a much more powerful tool for assessing reading comprehension than having students read aloud. This is because when students read aloud teachers may focus on pronunciation and intonation instead of reading comprehension. Also, reading aloud is not an authentic reading activity in that when good readers read, they read silently and quickly without reading every word; in fact, reading every word aloud only slows them down. Further, students may use quite different strategies when reading silently than when reading aloud.

To guide students' retelling, teachers can provide students with story maps. *Story maps* outline the structure of a story with specific headings (such as "Setting," "Main Characters," "Events," etc.). Students fill in the story map with single

Figure 5.7   Developmental Reading Rubric

Emergent	• Pretends to read • Uses illustrations to tell story • Participates in reading of familiar books • Knows some letter sounds • Recognizes names/words in context • Memorizes pattern books and familiar books • Rhymes and plays with words
Developing	• Sees self as reader • Reads books with word patterns • Knows most letter sounds • Retells main idea of text • Recognizes simple words • Relies on print and illustrations
Beginning	• Relies more on print than illustrations • Recognizes names/words by sight • Uses sentence structure clues • Uses phonetic clues • Retells beginning, middle, and end • Begins to read silently • Uses basic punctuation
Expanding	• Begins to read short stories and books • Reads and finishes a variety of materials with guidance • Uses reading strategies • Retells plot, characters, and events • Recognizes different types of books • Reads silently for short periods of time
Bridging	• Begins to read chapter books of moderate difficulty • Reads and finishes a variety of materials with guidance • Reads and understands most new words • Uses reference materials to locate information with guidance • Increases knowledge of literary elements and genres • Reads silently for extended periods
Fluent	• Reads most literature appropriate to grade-level • Selects, reads, and finishes a wide variety of materials • Uses reference materials independently • Recognizes and uses literary elements and genres • Begins to interpret and expand meaning from literature • Participates in literary discussions

Adapted from Hill and Ruptic (1994).

Figure 5.8 **ESL Reading Rubric**

Pre-Reader	• Listens to read-alouds
	• Repeats words and phrases
	• Uses pictures to comprehend text
	• May recognize some sound/symbol relationships
Emerging Reader	• Participates in choral reading
	• Begins to retell familiar, predictable text
	• Uses visuals to facilitate meaning
	• Uses phonics and word structure to decode
Developing Reader	• Begins to make predictions
	• Retells beginning, middle, and end of story
	• Recognizes plot, characters, and events
	• Begins to rely more on print than illustrations
	• May need assistance in choosing appropriate texts
Expanding Reader	• Begins to read independently
	• Responds to literature
	• Begins to use a variety of reading strategies
	• Usually chooses appropriate texts
Proficient Reader	• Reads independently
	• Relates reading to personal experience
	• Uses a wide variety of reading strategies
	• Recognizes literary elements and genres
	• Usually chooses appropriate texts
Independent Reader	• Reads for enjoyment
	• Reads and completes a wide variety of texts
	• Responds personally and critically to texts
	• Matches a wide variety of reading strategies to purpose
	• Chooses appropriate or challenging texts

Adapted from a draft compiled by the ESL Portfolio Teachers Group, Fairfax County Public Schools, Virginia (1995).

Figure 5.9 **Story Map**

Name Tomás   Date 3/7

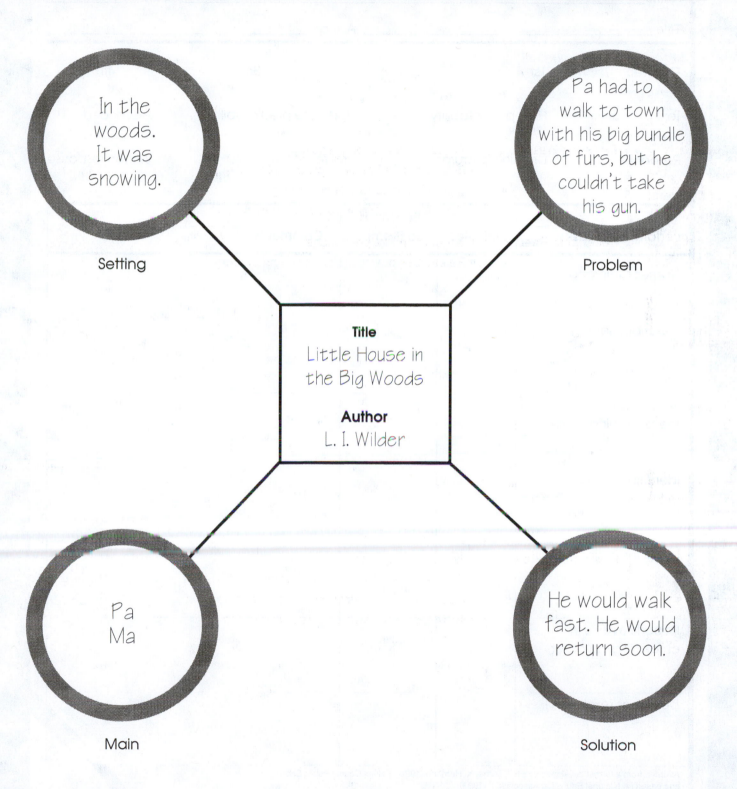

Setting — In the woods. It was snowing.

Problem — Pa had to walk to town with his big bundle of furs, but he couldn't take his gun.

Title
Little House in the Big Woods

Author
L. I. Wilder

Main — Pa Ma

Solution — He would walk fast. He would return soon.

Figure 5.10   **Story Retelling Checklist**

Name_____ Date _____

Title _____ Author _____

Quarter: 1st   2nd   3rd   4th

Text Difficulty: High predictability   Moderate predictability   Advanced

Response: Drawing/pictures   Oral response   Written response

Performance Tasks	Initiates	Responds to Prompt	Comments
Names main characters			
Describes setting			
Starts retelling at the beginning			
Identifies problem or issues			
Identifies major events			
Reports events in chronological order			
Describes resolution			

Adapted from a format developed by ESL teacher K. Harrison (1994), Fairfax County Public Schools, and based on National Education Association (1993).

words or phrases under each heading. Story maps (see Figure 5.9) are particularly appropriate for ESL and bilingual students, who may not be familiar with the discourse structure of a text or who simply may need to sketch their ideas out in writing before beginning to talk about a story or text. Story maps also help second language learners internalize story and text structure so that they become better readers by being able to anticipate the structure of different texts. Students not yet proficient enough to tell the story through oral or written language can draw pictures to tell the story, what Routman (1994) calls *picture mapping*.

English language learners are likely to be able to tell more if allowed to use their native language. Allowing students to respond in the native language can provide opportunities for them to demonstrate their comprehension while oral and written language skills in English are still developing (Au 1993).

Retellings can be conducted in pairs after you have taught students how to engage in peer assessment using story and text maps. *Text maps* differ from story maps by representing expository prose, as in readings in science or history. Each student gets a different story or text to read and retell while his or her partner conducts a peer assessment using a completed story or text map and checking off elements of the text the student describes (Garcia 1994).

Reading Logs   One way to hold students accountable for their progress in reading is to ask them to document the type and quantity of reading they do through *reading logs* (Atwell 1987; Garcia 1994; Hill and Ruptic 1994; Routman 1994). Students are given a chart for entering a story or book's author and title, the date completed, perhaps the number of pages read, and a brief impression or critique of the reading. By reviewing reading logs for reading interest levels as well as for the quantity of materials read independently, teachers can provide feedback to students on their reading progress and on additional materials which may interest them. Teachers can encourage bilingual students to record materials read in each language. Whatever students are reading in or out

of class can be entered in a reading log (Garcia 1994). An example of a reading log is provided in Figure 5.11.

Students can use their reading log to graph the quantity of their reading over time. For example, students can create a bar graph with the number of books or other texts read during each grading period. This gives students a visual representation of how many texts they have read over a specific period of time. Students can also graph the genre or topic of their reading. Teachers first ask students to classify their reading by genre (fiction, non-fiction, biography, poetry, content area reading, etc.). Then students review their reading log to determine the number books or other texts read in each genre. The bar graph is created by entering the number of texts on the Y-axis and the different genres on the X-axis. Teachers have indicated to us that students enjoy the graphing because it shows them how much they have accomplished and if they have neglected one or more genres in their reading.

Literature Response Logs/Journals   Research shows that responding to literature helps students become better readers. With literature response logs, students respond in writing to materials they have read (Atwell 1987; Garcia 1994; Hill and Ruptic 1994; Routman 1994). *Literature response logs*, also called *reading response logs*, are basically journals about what a student is reading. As with journal writing, teachers and students dialogue about the reading material, with students providing a personal reaction to the material and the teacher commenting on the students' observations. If students only summarize what they have read without making a personal response, teachers can respond with questions that call for students' personal reflection. In other cases, teachers may have to talk individually with students to clarify the procedure. Literature response logs, like dialogue journals, can be reviewed on a staggered basis, a few each week. Figure 5.12 shows a rubric developed by an elementary ESL teacher for rating a literature response log.

Some guiding questions for literature response logs that might be asked of students for self-assess-

Figure 5.11   **Reading Log: Books I Have Read**

My Name ___Sergio_____   Grade ___1st/2nd____   Date __12/15___

Title	Author	Date I Began Reading:	Date I Finished Reading:	How I Feel About It:
Gorilla		4/16/95	4/18/95	this book is abat a litto gile that wats to se a rel garela then her Fader bot her a toy garila That he gu and gu and gu an to a ril gorila o wel I lob the store
Matthews Dream	Leo Leone	6/8/95	6/9/95	I likd the part wen Matthews was in hes drean I lik ol of the ameizen pekchers and Matthews paiten in to. thes book is abat a moos tha waders what he wat to be and he does no want he wats to be. a paiter

Adapted from a reading log developed by elementary ESL teacher J. Eury (1994) and a sample from first/second grade ESL teacher L. Morse (1995), Fairfax County Public Schools, Virginia.

ment purposes include (adapted from Tierney, Carter, and Desai 1991):

- *What did you like about this story/book?*
- *How was this the same or different from other things you have read?*
- *Explain why you would or would not read other things by this author.*
- *What kinds of stories do you like to read most?*
- *What type of story/book do you want to read next?*
- *In what ways are you a good reader?*

Literature Discussion Groups   *Literature discussion groups* are heterogeneous small group (five to eight students), student-directed, and teacher-guided discussions that occur while students are in the process of reading a book (Hill and Ruptic 1994; Routman 1994). All students can be asked to read a single book or story, or students can read different books on a similar theme or topic. Shorter books and stories can be discussed in one session upon completion of the reading. Discussion groups (also called *literature circles* and *book clubs*) can last from a day to several weeks, depending on the length of the book. Students can use teacher- or student-made questions from their literature response logs to begin the discussion. While the literature discussion group has many advantages, some benefits for second language learners and language minority students include: increased comprehension levels; opportunities to improve listening skills and develop spoken language proficiency; increased participation of quiet and shy students (with subsequent increases in self-esteem of at-risk students); increased respect for low-achieving students; and more time for teacher observation of student learning. The discussion group is based on critical analysis of the text, with students' opinions being accepted if they can be supported with evidence from the text. Oral reading occurs only to cite evidence for an individual's observations. Students draw on prior experiences and background knowledge to make inferences and arrive at conclusions.

While some students are meeting in discussion groups, others can be working independently.

Weaker readers can listen to a tape of the reading or pair up with a stronger partner in order to follow the text. Even if the student cannot read every word of a book, as long as he or she has the opportunity to listen to and understand it, the student can participate in a literature discussion group (Routman 1994).

Several types of assessment can be used in conjunction with literature discussion groups. These

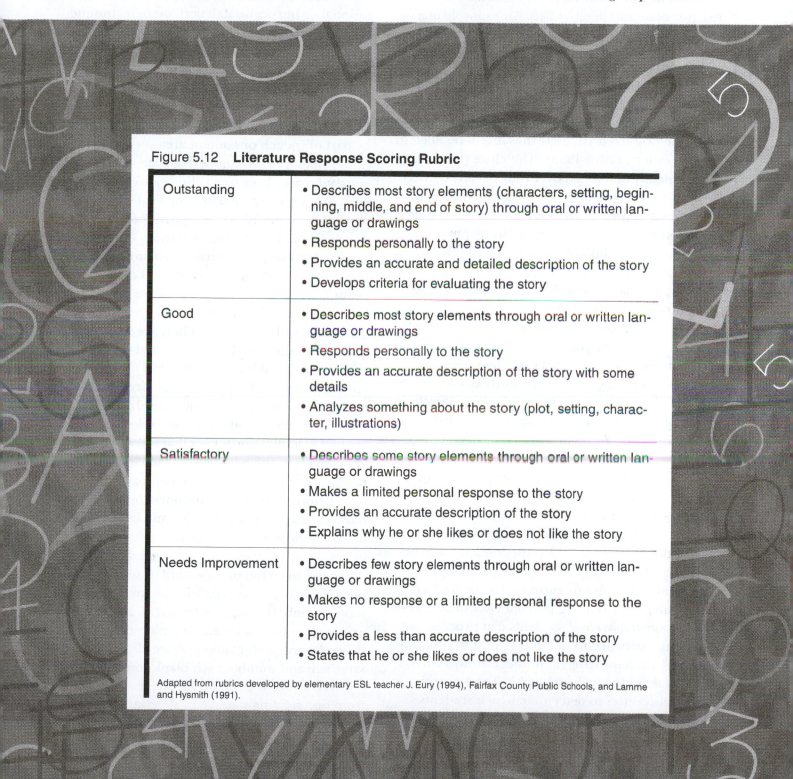

Figure 5.12 Literature Response Scoring Rubric

Outstanding	• Describes most story elements (characters, setting, beginning, middle, and end of story) through oral or written language or drawings • Responds personally to the story • Provides an accurate and detailed description of the story • Develops criteria for evaluating the story
Good	• Describes most story elements through oral or written language or drawings • Responds personally to the story • Provides an accurate description of the story with some details • Analyzes something about the story (plot, setting, character, illustrations)
Satisfactory	• Describes some story elements through oral or written language or drawings • Makes a limited personal response to the story • Provides an accurate description of the story • Explains why he or she likes or does not like the story
Needs Improvement	• Describes few story elements through oral or written language or drawings • Makes no response or a limited personal response to the story • Provides a less than accurate description of the story • States that he or she likes or does not like the story

Adapted from rubrics developed by elementary ESL teacher J. Eury (1994), Fairfax County Public Schools, and Lamme and Hysmith (1991).

include self-assessment, anecdotal records, and teacher observation checklists. In particular, because literature discussion groups result in a change in student attitudes toward themselves and others as well as toward reading, some form of self-assessment might be a strong indicator of the effectiveness of the literature discussion group. Reading strategies can be recorded through self-assessment, anecdotal records, think-alouds, or teacher observation checklists. An example of a self-assessment for a literature discussion group is provided in Figure 5.13, while a teacher observation checklist is provided in Figure 5.14.

Cloze Tests   *Cloze tests* are reading passages with blanks representing words that have been deleted from the original text; the blanks are to be filled in by the reader (Taylor 1953). The cloze procedure was originally developed over four decades ago to determine the readability of texts. Since then, the cloze has emerged in various forms to determine a reader's ability to use context to predict missing words from text (Pikulski and Tobin 1982). The term *cloze* comes from *closure*, a term used in Gestalt psychology to explain the tendency to see the whole picture or fill in gaps in less than complete objects. Readers rely upon syntactic, lexical, and semantic knowledge as well as cultural knowledge and prior background experiences or schemata to predict the omitted words. Cloze tests "reflect overall comprehension of a text" by requiring use of syntactic and discourse level constraints (Oller 1979, pp. 346-7).

Teachers can create cloze passages from instructional materials they currently use; this is more authentic than using commercially-produced cloze passages. Cloze passages are best used as screening devices that quickly and efficiently estimate instructional reading level (independent, instructional, or frustration). At the *independent reading level*, students recognize most of the vocabulary and content in a reading passage (Routman 1994). At the *instructional level*, students can proceed but only with assistance from a teacher. At the *frustration level*, students struggle unsuccessfully with a reading text even with assistance. Teachers can use cloze procedures to determine which students

need extra help or easier material, but the information provided by a cloze passage should be confirmed with other authentic assessments over time. Cloze tests are appropriate for intermediate- and advanced-level readers. They typically involve silent reading in a group or whole class setting, require students to fill in missing words from a passage, and have pre-established standards.

Different types of cloze tests are: fixed ratio, rational or purposive deletion, maze technique, and limited or multiple-choice cloze (Oller, 1979; Pikulski and Tobin 1982). In a *fixed ratio* cloze, words are deleted systematically by counting off, regardless of the part of speech. Every fifth, seventh, or ninth word may be deleted. In a *rational/purposive deletion* cloze, words are deleted by part of speech or content area vocabulary rather than in a set numbering pattern. Using a *maze technique*, three word choices are provided at each missing word interval. For *limited* cloze, word choices (one per blank) are provided all together in a word bank at the top or bottom of the page. For English language learners, you may want to use cloze formats that provide word choices before putting students in a situation where they have to provide the words for themselves. Only the fixed ratio cloze will be described here, because it is the most commonly used technique and also the one that has been subjected to the kind of rigorous analysis needed to produce reliability figures for establishing functional reading level.

To construct a fixed ratio cloze, select a passage about 250 to 300 words long that is representative of the content of the book. Be sure to check that the passage does not rely too much on passages that went before it (possible indicators are words such as *this* and *these*). Keeping the first and last sentences intact, randomly choose one of the first five words in the second sentence and proceed to delete every fifth word from the passage until 50 words have been deleted. A *word* is defined as any group of letters or numbers separated by spaces. Hyphenated words are generally considered two words. Replace deleted words with blanks that are all about the same size and number each blank consecutively.

Three levels of difficulty can be constructed from one reading passage by deleting every fifth,

Figure 5.13   **Self-Assessment: Literature Discussion Group**

Name _____ Date _____

Book/Story _____

1. How much did you participate in today's discussion group? (Circle one.)

   a lot   about the right amount   too little

2. What did you do well in group discussion? (Check what is true for you.)

❏ I finished the reading assignment and came prepared to discuss it.

❏ I wrote in my journal.

❏ I listened to others.

❏ I responded to others.

3. What was an important idea expressed by someone in your group?
(Name the person and describe what he or she said.)

Adapted from Hill and Ruptic (1994) and Rhodes (1993).

Figure 5.14   Literature Discussion Group: Teacher Observation Checklist

Book/Story Discussed _____   Author(s) _____

Theme/Focus _____   Date _____

Names of Students:							
Preparation							
Brought book and other materials							
Read the assigned pages							
Noted excerpts to share							
Participation							
Contributed to discussion							
Used higher-level thinking skills							
Used text to support comments							
Elicited responses from others							
Listened to alternative points of view							
Inferred relationships not stated in text							
Referred to story elements (plot, characters, conflict, theme)							

Adapted from Hill and Ruptic (1994).

Figure 5.15 **Sample Cloze Passage**

Intermediate level text for middle and high school students

The Dream Keeper

Once, long ago, there was a girl who could talk to the birds. When she was little, she _____ happy. She walked in _____ forest and played by _____ stream and never thought _____ her purpose in life. _____ as she grew older, _____ asked: Why am I _____? Where am I going? _____ am I? But no _____ could answer these questions, _____ one day she walked _____ the forest. Maybe the _____ will know, she thought. _____ are my friends and _____ will talk to them. _____ at how they live. _____ is no hesitation in _____ flight. There is no _____ in their song. Surely _____ know their purpose. Maybe _____ know mine, too.

She _____ until she saw a _____ eagle. "Eagle," she asked, "_____ is your purpose?" "To _____ above the earth," the _____ replied. "From there I _____ see all things. Here _____ my feather. Fly with _____." Next she saw a _____. "Hawk," she asked, "What _____ your purpose?" "To be _____ messenger," the hawk replied. "_____ bring news of things _____ come. Here is my _____. Listen for my call."

_____ girl sat down next _____ a river. The sunlight _____ the water and it _____ beautiful, but she was _____. "I know the purpose _____ all the birds," she _____, "but what is my _____?" Then a dragonfly with _____ like paper flew by. _____ dragonfly saw the girl _____ sad and wanted to _____ her. "And you, dragonfly," _____ girl finally asked, "What _____ your purpose?" "To help _____ find their dreams," the _____ replied. "Help me, then," the girl said.

Adapted from "The Dream Keeper," in *Tales of Courage, Tales of Dreams: A Multicultural Reader* by J. Mundahl. Reading, Mass.: Addison-Wesley, 1993.

seventh or ninth word. For example, passages with every fifth word omitted will be more challenging than those with only every ninth word deleted. A sample cloze passage with every fifth word deleted is shown in Figure 5.15. However, longer passages need to be used with seventh and ninth word deletions in order to obtain 50 blanks (250 words for deleting every fifth word, 350 words for deleting every seventh word, and 450 words for deleting every ninth word). The greater the number of blanks, the more reliable the cloze becomes as an indicator of functional reading ability.

Throughout this book, we encourage you to use your instructional activities for assessment. This applies as much to the cloze procedure as to any other technique. Students need practice with the cloze in whole class and group settings before being asked to work individually. To practice with the cloze, select an easy passage for most students and leave only ten to 25 blanks. Instruct students that only one word goes in each blank, and that they should read the entire passage before going back to fill in the blanks. Provide flexible time limits for completion of the cloze.

To score a cloze, count all words that are semantically and syntactically correct or contextually appropriate. Spelling is not counted. Although some specialists recommend counting only exact word replacements (Pikulski and Tobin 1982), we agree with Oller (1979) that for second language learners, accepting any word that is contextually appropriate may have instructional advantages (such as providing diagnostic information). In addition, all scoring methods used with cloze tests are highly intercorrelated (Oller 1979; Pikulski and Tobin 1982). Based on comparisons with other measures of reading comprehension, criterion scores have been determined which relate to a reader's ability to read independently, with instruction, or at a frustration level. However, these scores were established based on exact word replacements. Criterion scores should be higher where synonyms are accepted. Although there is no exact cut score, a range of scores can be used (Alverman and Phelps 1994; Pikulski and Tobin 1982). A rough guide to interpretation of cloze scores is as follows:

- more than 50-60% correct = independent level

- 35-50% = instructional level

- below 35% = frustration level

Teachers need to establish their own standards based on experience with both native speakers of English and English language learners. A rough estimate of grade level could be established by taking a group of native or proficient speakers of English in the fifth grade and administering a cloze. If the scores average out to be on the instructional level, then the text can be said to be at approximately the fifth-grade level. Due to the amount of work involved in estimating grade-level reading equivalents, you may want to save this step for when you are ready to determine student ability to read grade-level texts.

Texts with Comprehension Questions   Most teachers are familiar with asking questions to determine comprehension of reading passages. An idea shared with us by an ESL Resource Teacher[2] at the middle school level allows immediate identification of a student's comprehension level with specific texts. The teacher makes a copy of one page from a short reading passage or story students have been asked to read. On the reverse side of this page, the student responds independently to several comprehension questions posed by the teacher (see Figure 5.16). Students can also create their own questions if teachers have prepared them to do so. After checking students' responses, the teacher has a record of each student's comprehension level with a known text. When the teacher knows the relative difficulty level of specific texts, he or she can make an assessment of how each student is doing with a text at that level. By conducting this type of assessment at least twice during a quarter or semester, students, parents, and teachers can obtain concrete evidence of a student's ability to tackle increasingly difficult passages. This type of activity can be quite informative when passed along to the next teacher in a student's reading portfolio.

Reciprocal Teaching   *Reciprocal teaching* is an instructional approach designed to increase reading comprehension by encouraging students to use reading strategies (Palincsar and Brown 1984). In small groups of four to five, students begin by all reading the first paragraph or passage of the same text silently. Based on the teacher's modeling, one student begins the session by summarizing the paragraph in his or her own words. Then

2. Thanks to Barbara Fagan of Arlington County Public Schools, Virginia, for sharing her text with comprehension questions activity with us.

Figure 5.16 Sample Reading Text with Comprehension Questions

One day Pa said that spring was coming.

In the Big Woods the snow was beginning to thaw. Bits of it dropped from the branches of the trees and made little holes in the softening snowbanks below. At noon all the big icicles along the eaves of the little house quivered and sparkled in the sunshine, and drops of water hung trembling at their tips.

Pa said he must go to town to trade the furs of the wild animals he had been trapping all winter. So one evening he made a big bundle of them. There were so many furs that when they were packed tightly and tied together they made a bundle almost as big as Pa.

Very early one morning Pa strapped the bundle of furs on his shoulders and started to walk to town. There were so many furs to carry that he could not take his gun.

Ma was worried, but Pa said that by starting before sun-up and walking very fast all day he could get home again before dark.

Questions (on reverse side of text page)

1. Who is telling this story? _____

_____

_____

2. Why is Pa taking furs to town? _____

_____

_____

3. Why is Ma worried about Pa? _____

_____

_____

4. What do you think will happen next? _____

_____

_____

Excerpted from *Little House in the Big Woods* by L. I. Wilder. New York: Harper Collins, 1991.

he or she asks the group one question about the content and identifies a comprehension problem or something that was difficult to comprehend about the passage. Finally, the student predicts what will come in the next paragraph or section. After much teacher modeling, students pose questions that elicit both literal comprehension and critical analysis. Each student gets a turn to repeat these steps. Reading comprehension strategies typically used in reciprocal teaching include summarizing, questioning, and predicting. With a good teacher model and sufficient practice, students should be able to formulate higher-order comprehension questions that go beyond factual recall.

Teachers can combine reciprocal teaching and assessment by observing each student's participation as students take their turns. You can make anecdotal notes either during or after the reciprocal teaching session or use a checklist for registering the success with which students use various strategies and higher-order questions. You can follow up reciprocal teaching sessions by asking students to report on their success in using summarizing, questioning, and predicting in their independent reading.

RECORD TEACHER OBSERVATIONS

One of the most effective ways for a teacher to assess a student's reading comprehension is through teacher observation (Routman 1994). This assumes that the teacher knows what to look for and how to document student progress through observational methods. Some types of teacher observation to be described here are: think-alouds, probes, and interviews; reading strategies checklists and rating scales; miscue analysis and running records; and anecdotal records.

Think-Alouds, Probes, and Interviews   To assess use of reading comprehension strategies, teachers can use think-alouds. *Think-alouds* are interactive and focus on active construction of meaning that emphasizes the use of prior knowledge. Because the think-aloud process may be new or difficult for students, teachers should model the process before expecting them to do think-alouds independently (Garcia 1994). In a think-aloud, you can ask students to look at the title of a story or book and ask themselves what the title means, what they expect the story or book to be about, how to guess at the meanings of words, and how to self-correct for errors in comprehension. Once students do this as a class various times, they will be ready to go through think-alouds in groups and individually. You can record strategies used in think-alouds with a checklist similar to the one shown in Figure 5.17, and take notes on each student's strengths and needs as they think aloud. Think-alouds could be used once or twice each quarter or semester to assess English language learners' use of reading strategies.

Probes and individual student *interviews* allow the teacher to discuss reading attitudes with students, ask questions, and obtain information on reading strategies (Routman 1994). Interviews also provide more information than written surveys, especially with ELL students, who may respond to questions with only a few words. Interviews are useful at the beginning of the school year so that teachers can come to know students' needs and interests. Some guiding questions to use in student interviews are (adapted from Routman, 1994):

- *Do you like to read? Why or why not?*
- *What do you like to read?*
- *Do you read at home? Where? How often?*
- *Who reads to you at home?*
- *What do you do when you are reading and you come to a word you don't know?*
- *What do you like to do in your free time?*
- *What can you do well?*
- *What do you need to work on?*
- *Tell me about the last story or book you read.*

Strategies Checklists or Rating Scales

Checklists and rating scales are good for documenting reading skills as well as reading comprehension strategies (Cunningham 1982; Routman 1994). *Checklists* are lists of characteristics or behaviors that are scored as *yes/no* ratings (Herman, Aschbacher, and Winters 1992). Based on observation of student performance, teachers indicate the presence of a behavior with a check mark. For example, a reading skills/strategies checklist indicates which skills essential to reading a student has exhibited (see Figures 5.18 and 5.19). A process checklist might be used to assess whether students have engaged in various processes such as those required for working in small groups, conducting a science experiment, or conducting a research report. Students can use a self-assessment checklist to indicate that they have completed all tasks or steps before submitting assigned work. Because checklists limit the nature of the teacher's observations, they should probably be used judiciously and only after they have been adapted for your own students' needs (Routman 1994). When working

Figure 5.17   **Think-Aloud Checklist**

Student _____ Date _____

Story/Text _____ Grade/Teacher _____

Place a check (√) or write examples in the spaces.

Reading Strategy	Frequently	Sometimes	Rarely
1. Uses prior knowledge			
2. Self-corrects words and sentences			
3. Rereads			
4. Makes predictions			
5. Forms opinions			
6. Paraphrases			
7. Summarizes			
8. Adds ideas			
9. Other:			

Adapted from Glazer and Brown (1993).

Figure 5.18 **Reading Skills/Strategies Checklist** (for Emerging Readers)

Student _____ Date _____

Skill/Strategy	1st 9 Weeks	2nd 9 Weeks	3rd 9 Weeks	4th 9 Weeks
Pre-Reader				
1. Tracks left/right, up/down				
2. Distinguishes upper/lower case				
3. Associates sound/symbol				
4. Begins to sound out words				
5. Can locate words in text				
6. Can read a few words				
Developing				
7. Begins to self-correct				
8. Begins using reading strategies				
9. Locates details in simple text				
10. Reads short, predictable text				
Reader				
11. Uses several reading strategies				
12. Identifies main idea				
13. Recognizes logical order				
14. Recognizes cause/effect				
15. Reads short, simple texts				
Expanding				
16. Draws inferences				
17. Predicts outcomes				
18. Draws conclusions				
19. Recognizes paraphrasing				
20. Chooses to read				
21. Reads chapter books				

Adapted from a checklist developed by middle school ESL teacher D. O'Neill (1994), Fairfax County Public Schools, Virginia.

Figure 5.19　Emergent Literacy Checklist

Student _____ Date _____

Rating Code

U = Usually evident　　S = Sometimes evident

NY = Not yet evident　　N/A = Not applicable

Performance Observed	Date	Date	Date	Date
1. Identifies environmental print				
2. Exhibits pretend reading				
3. Listens with interest to read-alouds				
4. Participates in discussions following class read-aloud				
5. Reads from left to right				
6. Identifies a letter and a word				
7. Attempts to sound out words				
8. Reads during free time				
9. Reads a variety of genres				

Adapted from a checklist created by elementary ESL teacher J. Eury (1994), Fairfax County Public Schools, Virginia.

with individuals or small groups, you can use a reading strategies or decoding checklist and document students' instructional needs over time.

Miscue Analysis and Running Records   One way to reveal reading strategies is to conduct a miscue analysis with individual students (Goodman, Watson, and Burke 1987; Hill and Ruptic 1994; Rhodes 1993; Routman 1994; Watson and Henson 1993). *Miscue analysis* can reveal students' strengths in using graphophonemic, syntactic, semantic, and discourse knowledge. Miscue analysis provides information of at least three types: (1) the reader's ability to use language and the reading process, (2) the reader's approaches to reading and reading comprehension, and (3) information for revising instructional approaches and materials. Miscue analysis involves listening to a student read aloud as well as having the student retell the story or answer comprehension questions. While the student reads aloud, the teacher marks the miscues on a copy of the text. Miscues may include repetitions, substitutions, insertions, omissions, and self-corrections (Goodman, Watson, and Burke 1987). For English language learners, pronunciation and intonation errors are not counted (Garcia 1994).

Four different types of miscue analysis have been developed by Goodman, Watson, and Burke (1987). Procedure I is the most complex and time-consuming. Procedures II and III have a similar focus and provide in-depth information about a student's reading. Procedure IV is an informal analysis to be used with students during individual reading conferences. We limit our discussion here to Procedure III.

To conduct Procedure III, the teacher identifies a story that is beyond the grade level indicated by the student's test scores by at least two or three years. The story should be new to the student and present a complete text with a beginning, a middle, and an end. The length of the story depends on the age and language proficiency of the reader. At least 25 miscues need to be generated in order to profile students' reading strategies. All miscues are not equal; the most serious miscues are those that change both syntax and semantics.

Procedure III consists of four parts: (1) initial interview, (2) oral reading, (3) retelling, and (4) reflection on reading. To begin the miscue analysis, the teacher conducts an initial interview to find out how the student feels about him or herself as a reader and about the reading process. Typical questions include *What do you like to read?* and *What do you do when you come to a word you don't know?* (See the previous section on probes and interviews.) In the second part of Procedure III, the teacher asks students to read the story aloud. Students should be told whether they will be receiving any help as they read (as in cued questions) or will be expected to read entirely on their own. Tell students that they should be prepared to retell the story in their own words when they finish reading aloud. Using a typescript of the text with three spaces between each line, the teacher records miscues on each line and makes brief notes in the margins.

Once the student has completed the oral reading, the teacher asks the student to retell the story. Rate the retelling for main story elements (see the above section on retelling). After the retelling, lead students in a reflection on the reading, with self-assessment questions such as: *How do you think you did?* or *Where did you have trouble reading?* Analysis of miscues will reveal how students decode and use reading strategies (Watson and Henson 1993).

Running records are a type of miscue analysis developed by Marie Clay through her work with young children (Clay 1993a; Hill and Ruptic 1994; Routman 1994). Unlike miscue analysis, running records require little preparation. They can be marked on any piece of paper and are more easily used in daily routines. Like miscue analysis, taking running records requires training. Using a blank sheet of paper, the teacher places a check mark for every word that is read correctly and records words the student reads that do not appear in the text. Each blank line corresponds to a line of the text. Analysis of a running record reveals use of reading strategies and miscue patterns and can inform decisions about text difficulty, individual reading progress, and specific reading difficulties. Running records can be conducted on texts of varying difficulty (both familiar and unfamiliar to the students) in order to determine how the reader reads easy texts and what he or she does when problem solving or processing more difficult texts.

To take running records, allow about ten minutes for a sample text of 100 to 200 words. Indicate word substitutions, self-corrections, and hesitations, and just about everything else the reader does while reading. Analysis of the running record does not penalize the reader for miscues that are eventually corrected. Each word that is not read aloud correctly is counted as an error. More than ten percent of errors in the reading rate indicate that the text is a hard one for the reader (Clay 1993a).

Both miscue analysis and running records require attention to detail, take time to conduct, and benefit from training and practice. They may be most useful when a student is just beginning to read or is having difficulty reading. Teachers may want to seek out a Reading Recovery teacher for training on how to conduct running records (see Clay 1993b). In combination with retellings or comprehension questions, both of these observational approaches can provide useful diagnostic information on student reading growth.

One study of miscue analysis with ESL students indicated the benefits of having students read a whole story (ranging in length from five to 30 pages, approximately) without interruption from the teacher (Rigg 1988). By allowing students to read at length, the teacher encourages the reader to develop essential reading strategies, such as predicting, confirming, and correcting. This is in contrast to emphasizing perfect oral reading performance in the form of "beautiful expression," by which teachers may be emphasizing pronunciation and intonation at the expense of comprehension (Rigg 1988). On the other hand, elementary ESL teachers tell us that when readers read with expression they tend to have good comprehension, but when they read in a monotone or ignore punctuation marks they tend to have minimal comprehension. Clay (1993b) suggests having beginning readers read orally only until it is clear that they can decode successfully; this is to avoid the habit of word-by-word reading.

Anecdotal Records   *Anecdotal records* are observational notations describing language and social development at a specific point in time (Routman 1994). As described in Chapter 4, anecdotal records are typically brief comments specific to how a student is performing and what he or she needs to improve. Anecdotal records can be taken in different situations (e.g., discussion groups or individual interviews or conferences). Anecdotal records are useful for documenting a student's progress in reading. Each teacher determines what to record for each student, but three general rules are (Rhodes and Nathenson-Mejia 1992; Thorndike and Hagen 1977):

- describe a specific event
- report what you see
- interpret what you see based on what you know about the student

Having a collaborative classroom where students are trusted to work independently or in groups will facilitate the teacher's note-taking. To evaluate students, look for patterns of growth by relating anecdotal records to other observations and actual student work.

If you are new to anecdotal records, you might want to begin with a student interview, where you sit with a student to talk about reading (Routman 1994). Ask the student to bring a book or story he or she has read and to either read from the book or to talk about favorite parts of the book. You can take anecdotal records during the interview by noting the title and type of book selected, the student's attitude toward or enjoyment of the text, comprehension of main ideas and details, and strategies used in reading, such as predicting or summarizing. A sample form for anecdotal records is presented in Figure 5.20. Be sure to provide positive feedback on what the student can do upon completion of the interview.

Taking anecdotal records can be time-consuming, challenging, and risky (Routman 1994). The risk lies in the beginning, when a teacher's notes may not be very informative. However, with practice, the records get better. You will find the records useful for informing students, parents, and school staff about student progress, especially if

Figure 5.20   **Anecdotal Record**

Student _____   Date _____

Teacher _____   Grade _____

---

1. Reading Selection

Title _____

Type (circle as many as apply):

fiction   non-fiction   poetry

biography   content text   other:_____

2. Reading Comprehension (understanding of main ideas and details):

3. Strategies (e.g., using prior knowledge, skimming, predicting, summarizing):

4. Response to Reading (attitude and enjoyment):

Adapted from Routman (1994).

you keep them organized and accessible in a notebook or file. Routman suggests color coding student pages in a notebook by day of the week and each day focusing on several students who share the same color. Using this approach, the teacher takes anecdotal records on each student on a weekly basis. While walking around with a clipboard, some teachers take notes on yellow sticky notes or mailing labels and later place these in the student's record.

READING/WRITING PORTFOLIOS

One way to get English language learners to monitor their own progress in reading over time and in a wide variety of contexts is to teach them how to develop and maintain reading/writing portfolios (Valdez Pierce and O'Malley 1992; Tierney, Carter, and Desai 1991). Portfolios can contain samples of student writing (from drafts to revisions to final copy), reading logs and reading response journals, anecdotal records, and any of the other instructional/assessment activities described in this chapter. To ensure that portfolios go beyond a simple collection of student work, select a purpose and required contents as described in Chapter 3. Teachers tell us they have too little time to use portfolios, that they don't know how to decide what goes inside, or that they don't know how to begin to evaluate portfolios. In Chapter 3 we discussed possible approaches to answering these concerns. Here we will focus on the possible purposes and contents of reading portfolios for ELL students.

Portfolios have most typically been used in English language arts classrooms to monitor the development of reading and writing (Tierney, Carter, and Desai 1991). In ESL/ bilingual classrooms, they are beginning to be used for similar purposes. Should you choose to assess only reading, a portfolio can be compiled which documents each student's growth in reading across time. Although portfolios have been the focus of many training sessions and publications, they are being used in only a limited manner with ELL students. Based on our experience with ESL/bilingual teachers, those using portfolios seem to be using them for what we referred to in Chapter 3 as *collections*.

Portfolio assessment means purposeful selection of specific samples of student work based on student reflection and teacher observations that represent classroom activities and document student progress. Routman (1994) notes that portfolio assessment at present "seems to overemphasize collections of things" (p. 330). Collections may be a first step toward portfolio assessment, but they need to be followed by teaching students how to evaluate their own work (see Chapter 3). In the case of reading assessment portfolios, students need to know the basis for selecting entries. Teachers can provide guidelines for required and optional entries, and these can be negotiated with students. Teacher guidance can also be provided in the form of assisting students in the selection of portfolio entries; this might be particularly appropriate for low-level proficiency students and for those new to the process. Examples of literacy portfolios designed by ESL teachers for use on a program-wide basis are provided in their portfolio cover sheets, as seen in Figures 5.21 to 5.24.

Using Reading Assessment in Instruction

. . . .

Results of authentic assessments of reading can be used in a number of ways, including informing program placement, determining grades, and improving instruction. For program placement purposes, you will need to determine whether or not student performance meets standards for moving on to the next level of your ESL/bilingual program or out of it completely. These standards are typically set by teachers within the program. To assign grades, ask colleagues about local grading policies in order to arrive at your own. When assigning grades, be sure that students know what each letter grade means by specifying the criteria upon which each one is based (see Chapter 2).

Assessment results can also be used to improve instruction. By improving instruction, we mean making it more meaningful and useful for the stu-

Figure 5.21 **Emergent Literacy Portfolio**

Student _____ Teacher _____

School Year _____ Grade _____

Proficiency/Program Level _____ School _____

Native Language _____

Required Entries	1st Quarter	2nd Quarter	3rd Quarter	4th Quarter
Emergent Literacy Checklist				
Dialogue journal				
Reading log				
Literature response journal				
Self-assessment of reading				
Optional Entries				
Fiction story				
Anecdotal records				
Revised writing				
Letters				

Comments

Adapted by elementary ESL teacher J. Eury, Fairfax County Public Schools, Virginia, from an ESL Portfolio Cover Sheet developed by Prince William County Public School ESL Teachers, Virginia (1994).

Figure 5.22   Elementary Reading/Writing Portfolio Cover Sheet

Student _____	School Year _____
Teacher _____	Grade _____
Level _____	Base School _____
	ESL Center _____

Required Contents	1st Quarter	2nd Quarter	3rd Quarter	4th Quarter
1. Oral summary				
2. Story summary (writing or drawing)				
3. Writing sample (teacher choice)				
4. Student choice of writing (any type)				
5. Student self-evaluation				

Optional Contents

	1st Quarter	2nd Quarter	3rd Quarter	4th Quarter
1. List of books/stories read in class				
2. List of books/stories read independently				
3. Reading interest inventory				
4. Literacy development checklist				
5. Content-sample (e.g., reading comprehension sample, project, report)				
6. Student choice (any type)				

Test	Initial Testing			Final Testing		
IPT	_____Date	_____Score	_____Level	_____Date	_____Score	_____Level
Reading	_____Date	_____Score	_____Level	_____Date	_____Score	_____Level
Writing	_____Date	_____Score	_____Level	_____Date	_____Score	_____Level
Placement						

Comments

Making progress?

Developed by elementary school ESL teachers, Prince William County Public Schools, Virginia.

Figure 5.23   **Middle School Reading/Writing Portfolio Cover Sheet**

Student _____ Grade _____

Teacher _____ School _____

Level _____ School Year _____

Required Contents	1st Quarter	2nd Quarter	3rd Quarter	4th Quarter
1. Cloze sample				
2. Writing sample				
3. Self-rating strategies checklist				
4. List of books read				
5. Reading passage with comprehension questions				

Optional Contents				
1. Content area samples				
2. Audio/video performances				
3. Illustrations				
4. Other				

Teacher Observations

1st Quarter	2nd Quarter	3rd Quarter	4th Quarter

Parent Comments

Signature	Signature	Signature	Signature

Developed by middle school ESL teachers, Prince William County Public Schools, Virginia.

Figure 5.24   High School Reading/Writing Portfolio Cover Sheet

Student _____   Grade _____

Teacher _____   School _____

Level _____   School Year _____

Date of Entry _____

Required Contents	1st Quarter	2nd Quarter	3rd Quarter	4th Quarter
1. Reading passage with comprehension questions				
2. Cloze sample				
3. Writing sample				
4. Written response to oral stimulus				
5. Written response to prompt/literature				
6. Self-rating strategies checklist				
7. Student choice				

Optional Contents

	1st Quarter	2nd Quarter	3rd Quarter	4th Quarter
1. Content area samples				
2. Audio performances				
3. List readings with short synopsis				
4. Oral language sample (including native language)				
5. Other				

1st Quarter	2nd Quarter	3rd Quarter	4th Quarter
Test scores LPT _____ _____ Signature	 _____ Signature	 _____ Signature	 _____ Signature

Developed by high school ESL teachers, Prince William County Public Schools, Virginia.

How do I rate?

dent. How can we use assessment results to motivate students to read and write more, to promote responsibility for self-monitoring, to communicate to students what they need to improve? We can begin by using multiple assessments in diverse contexts across time. Because individuals may vary widely in their performance across tasks and settings, we need to collect information on which conditions best support the development of each student's literacy (Wolf 1993). The informed teacher observes students, keeping information on what students read, the contexts in which reading activity takes place, and the tasks that students engage in related to reading (Afflerbach 1995). For example, if students seem highly motivated to read about a specific topic and then seem to lose interest, try having students read in different contexts, from individual silent reading to literature discussion groups. When students lack background knowledge, help them acquire it or show them how to make predictions from cues in a text. If students lack rapid, automatic word recognition skills, you can help them develop those skills by increasing the amount of challenging, interesting material read as well as by increasing the frequency of reading.

In determining how to use assessment results to improve instruction, make hypotheses about what students need and check against various sources of information until you have identified the most beneficial combination of topics, settings, and contexts for students. As an observer of students, notice what students say about reading and writing and how they use literacy in daily tasks. Students who do not use literacy for authentic purposes (their own) or who do not read frequently will need to be observed closely; you will need to try to make out the puzzle each student poses by planning, teaching, observing, and reflecting (Afflerbach 1993) and by talking with students about how they view reading and writing (Siu-Runyan 1993).

Conclusion

This chapter has provided an overview of the processes of reading in a first and a second language, commonalities and important differences between these two processes, and implications from research for the instruction and assessment of English language learners. We described steps to planning and designing valid and reliable teacher-made assessments of reading, including identifying purpose, planning time for assessment, involving students in self- and peer assessment, developing rubrics and scoring procedures, and setting standards. We provided examples of instructional activities that can also be used for assessment of reading. We made suggestions for designing reading/writing portfolios and recording teacher observations. Finally, we discussed instructional uses for results of reading assessments.

Some basic points to remember in the assessment of reading of English language learners include:

1. Activities for assessing reading should be based on activities for teaching reading.

2. Assessment of reading, like instruction, takes planning, time, and experience.

3. Assessment of reading should include both decoding skills and reading comprehension strategies.

4. Assessment of reading should include student attitudes and feelings toward reading.

5. Assessment of reading should hold students accountable for how they use time in class for reading.

6. Assessment of reading should be conducted regularly and be ongoing.

7. Students should be actively involved in their own assessment, whether it be in setting criteria, engaging in self-assessment, or evaluating peers.

8. Teacher observations of reading should be recorded systematically.

9. Assessment of reading should consist of multiple assessments for each student in order to monitor student progress.

10. Results of reading assessment should be used to inform students, parents, and teachers of needed changes in student performance and in instruction.

APPLICATION ACTIVITIES

1. What implications for assessment can you draw from the following instructional activities: (a) direct strategy instruction in reading comprehension, and (b) opportunities for personal responses to reading?

2. Make a plan for completing the following steps: (a) identify a purpose for reading assessment, (b) identify the major instructional goals you want to assess, (c) identify instructional activities or tasks that can also serve for assessment, (d) develop scoring rubrics for these activities, (e) decide how often you want to collect information on reading progress, and (f) decide how often to provide students with feedback on their performance. Get feedback from a colleague on your plan.

3. Develop and carry out a plan for teaching students how to engage in self-assessment and peer assessment in reading.

4. If you currently teach, try one or more of the following forms of assessment with your class: retellings, reading logs, literature response logs/journals, literature discussion groups, cloze tests, texts with comprehension questions, and collaborative reading or reciprocal teaching.

5. Try out one or more of the following forms of assessment: think-alouds/probes/interviews, reading strategies checklists or rating scales, running records, miscue analysis, or anecdotal records. Confirm the results you obtain by comparing different forms of assessment with the same students.

6. Outline a reading/writing portfolio with required and optional entries that reflect instruction.

WRITING
ASSESSMENT

. . . .

This chapter focuses on authentic assessment of writing. We begin with an overview of the nature of writing in schools, including the role of the writer, the purposes of writing, and recent innovations in writing instruction. We then describe the nature of the writing task, identify various types of authentic assessments in writing, and suggest a number of scoring rubrics for writing. Two important parts of this discussion are self- and peer assessment. We conclude by describing instructional uses of assessment results and the interaction between instruc-

tion and writing assessment. As in other chapters, we have included sample assessments that can be used to evaluate student proficiency. We encourage you to use or adapt any of these samples according to the English proficiency of your students or to adapt the samples for native language assessment.

Writing assessment with ELL students meets at least three purposes. First, writing assessment in English and/or in the native language is used for identification and program placement in ESL or bilingual programs. Moreover, ELL students are typically reclassified as English proficient based on writing assessment in English when they are prepared for grade-level instruction. Second, writing assessment can be used to monitor student progress and determine if changes in instruction are required to meet student needs. The ongoing assessment of student writing enables review of student growth over time and a determination of the success of instructional approaches. A third purpose of writing assessment with ELL students is accountability. Writing assessment is often conducted as part of district or statewide accountability assessment programs for all students. In some cases, students must attain a minimum score for grade-level advancement or for high school graduation. These varying uses of assessment results point to the importance of accurate writing assessment with ELL students.

Nature of Writing in School

• • • • • • • • • • • • • • • • • • •

Teacher judgment has always played an important role in the assessment of writing. Teachers ask students to write on any number of topics and then assess the substantive information contained in the message, the clarity of the message conveyed, and the mechanics of writing (spelling, capitalization, and punctuation). Teachers typically define the topics for writing, establish the criteria for evaluating the writing, and grade the writing themselves. This teacher-centered approach is not surprising given that many teachers have origins in a transmission model of learning and instruction, in which teachers provide the basic knowledge to be imparted to students. The transmission model isolates content areas in teaching and emphasizes mastery of component skills in sequential order. One by-product of this model has been that students have learned to write in isolation from reading and other activities related to literacy. Another by-product has been that teachers have tended to over-emphasize mechanics (spelling, capitalization, and punctuation) and grammar in their evaluations at the expense of content and meaning in writing (Glazer and Brown 1993).

We can get a broad picture of the emergence of new views on writing by looking more closely at the writer, the purposes for writing, and the nature of writing instruction.

THE WRITER

Writing is a personal act in which writers take ideas or prompts and transform them into "self-initiated" topics (Hamp-Lyons 1990). The writer draws on background knowledge and complex mental processes in developing new insights. To write well, students need to incorporate the purpose or prompt into their own unique approach to writing. How do they do this? By calling on several different kinds of knowledge. Let's assume that you have asked a student to write an essay on an experience the class shared together, perhaps watching a demonstration on home fire safety conducted in the classroom by local firefighters. The purpose of the essay is to convey to other students precautions they can follow in fire safety.

In writing the essay, your students will rely on at least four types of knowledge: knowledge of the content, procedural knowledge to organize the content, knowledge of conventions of writing, and procedural knowledge required to apply the three other types of knowledge in composing a written product (Hillocks 1987). In expressing *knowledge of the content,* students conduct a memory search and call on prior knowledge and experience. What did students see and hear (i.e., what images and concepts did they retain from the safety demonstration)? Generating ideas is one of the important sub-processes that contributes to planning in writing (Flower and Hayes 1981). Brainstorming, making lists or semantic maps, collaborating with peers, and elaborating on key ideas with personal information are useful retrieval strategies.

Second, students need the *procedural knowledge to organize the content,* to group ideas, and to sequence the ideas in ways that match the purposes of the writing. That is, once students have retrieved the information, they can begin to manipulate and organize it. They must also formulate goals and plans for creating an organized structure for their compositions. Thus, more is required in writing than just prior knowledge about a topic. Students must be able to manipulate this content in responding to a writing prompt or in generating a written composition suitable to the topic.

The third type of knowledge students use in writing is *knowledge of discourse structures, syntactic forms, and conventions* of writing. Discourse structures are evident in the ways that various types of writing are organized. For example, persuasive essays often introduce a problem or question, state a position, present arguments in support of the position or against other alternatives, and draw some implications of the position taken. Fables and autobiographical compositions have different structures altogether. Writers must be familiar with the various ways of organizing different types of writing and in expressing meaning through syntactic constructions and writing conventions (e.g., formatting and mechanics).

The fourth type of knowledge students rely on is *procedural knowledge for integrating all the other types of knowledge.* This is the basis for composition. Quality writing does not automatically result from simple knowledge of formal grammar (Gebhard 1983) or even the ability to recognize "good" paragraphs (Hillocks 1987). Rather, students must use procedures that combine the three types of knowledge just indicated in composing a written piece that responds to the original purpose. Students writing on fire safety in the home who can remember the procedures or who can recall the rules for grammar have only the beginnings of writing. Students need extensive opportunities for writing in which all of the types of knowledge are combined as they compose a message for a purpose with a particular audience.

These four types of knowledge used in writing have at least two implications for writing assessment with ELL students. First, writing assessment should evaluate more aspects of writing than just mechanics and grammar. The types of knowledge required in writing go far beyond these familiar elements. Second, writing assessment should capture some of the processes and complexity involved in writing so that teachers can know in which aspects of the writing process students are having difficulty. In addition, writing assessment

should look at the context in which the writing occurs.

PURPOSES AND TYPES OF WRITING

Students write to accomplish a variety of purposes and use a number of different genres to do so. Purpose in writing determines the nature of the writing. Students need clear specification of the purpose in order to plan and compose a piece that responds to the task. The genre defines the style the writer will use and suggests choices about the language and structure of the composition (NAEP 1987). Writers who gain control over various genres have a broader repertoire of writing abilities and an increased understanding of the value of writing for interpersonal communication, for documenting important ideas, and for achieving their own ends than those who do not.

Purpose   For what purposes can students be asked to write? There are at least three purposes in writing: informative writing, expressive/narrative writing, and persuasive writing. The three purposes described are similar to the purposes used in national assessments (NAEP 1987) and encompass the major types of writing in programs for ELL students as well as in many state writing assessments (e.g., California Assessment Program 1990; Maryland State Department of Education 1987; Vermont Department of Education 1990).

Writers use *expository* or *informative writing* to share knowledge and give information, directions, or ideas. Examples of informative writing include describing events or experiences, analyzing concepts, speculating on causes and effects, and developing new ideas or relationships. This type of writing could include a biography about a well-known person or someone from the writer's life. The writer can rely on existing knowledge or new sources of information and can cover a range of thinking skills from simple recall to analysis and synthesis. Informative writing helps writers integrate new ideas and examine existing knowledge.

Expressive/narrative writing is a personal or imaginative expression in which the writer produces stories or essays. This type of writing is often based on observations of people, objects, and places and may include creative speculations and interpretations. It may include an autobiographical incident or a reflection in which a writer describes an occurrence in her or his own life. This type of writing is often used for entertainment, pleasure, discovery or, simply, as "fun" writing and can include poems and short plays.

In *persuasive writing*, writers attempt to influence others and initiate action or change. This type of writing is often based on background information, facts, and examples the writer uses to support the view expressed. Writers use higher-level cognitive skills in this type of writing, such as analysis and evaluation, to argue a particular point of view in a convincing way. This type of writing might include evaluation of a book, a movie, a consumer product, or a controversial issue or problem. Writers can also use personal experience or emotional appeals to argue in support of their view. The three purposes of writing described here can overlap, as when students write an informative, persuasive essay.

The three purposes of writing describe the kinds of writing students do in second language classrooms as well as in grade-level classrooms. ELL students, for example, write expressive narratives describing personal experiences and write to inform using biographies of people they have known. Many teachers also ask ELL students to write persuasive essays in which they analyze a point of view or a book they have read.

An important point to remember is that student writing ability may vary considerably depending on the purpose (Herman 1991). That is, students who write excellent informative essays may not write good expressive essays. Even within a particular purpose, students' writing may vary depending on the topic or prompt, which may match conveniently with prior knowledge in some cases and less so in others. Assessment across a variety of purposes and prompts is therefore necessary to obtain generalizable information about student performance and progress in writing.

Genre   Students can use a variety of genres or types of writing to accomplish writing tasks. Examples of different genres are biographies, essays, stories, journal entries, letters, newspaper reports, manuals, and research papers. The writer's selection of genre depends on the purpose and often determines the style, or decisions about language and organization (NAEP 1987). For example, a newspaper report will have a different style and organization than a research paper. With beginning-level ELL students, the genre may include correspondence to friends, descriptions of experiences shared with the class, journals or learning logs, brief summaries or notes, and descriptions of various experiences. Two important genre that we will discuss later in describing writing assessment are dialogue journals and learning logs.

WRITING INSTRUCTION

In traditional writing instruction, reading and writing skills were taught independently of the writing process. Teachers "fractioned" the curriculum into a variety of small skills that were taught largely in a teacher-directed manner with little student participation (Calkins 1994; Tchudi 1991). It was assumed that knowledge about writing could be assessed by asking students to respond to multiple-choice items on vocabulary, spelling, punctuation, and grammar. Writing skills were also taught independently of content-area instruction, such as social studies and science, perhaps because writing skills were presumed to transfer once instruction had been completed. Two recent departures from this traditional paradigm are Process Writing and writing across the curriculum. Each of these instructional approaches has strong implications for assessing writing with ELL students.

Process Writing   In Process Writing, students are involved in the construction of narratives on topics in which they have a personal interest (Hudelson 1989). Students share their writing with peers, who comment on the piece and ask questions or offer comments and encouragement. Student-teacher conferences are also an important form of feedback students receive on their writing. Stu -dents use the feedback to edit and revise their work. Process Writing marks a shift from exclusive emphasis on the products of writing to emphasis on the process of writing and interactive learning between teachers and students with a focus on meaning.

To encourage Process Writing, teachers can model the selection of topics or the writing process itself. Three stages of the writing process are: (1) *prewriting*, or motivation, discussion, and concept development; (2) *writing*, which takes place in classrooms or at home so students can rely on both teachers and other students for feedback and support; and (3) *postwriting*, in which students share their writing with others, read aloud what they have written, or exchange writing with other students (Gebhard 1983). In the prewriting stage, students might use graphic organizers as an aid to clarify the concepts they will use in writing. During the writing process, opportunities should be provided for students to edit and revise their work, share ideas with other students on how to improve their writing, or review the criteria against which the work will be evaluated with an eye toward improvement (Peregoy and Boyle 1993).

An important component of Process Writing instruction is conferencing (Church 1993). In *conferencing*, teachers meet with students individually and ask questions about the processes they use in writing. The questions reflect the stages of Process Writing and might focus on how the writer selects the topic, plans the writing, composes the written pieces, and edits or revises the product afterwards. As we will see later in this chapter, conferences can provide varied opportunities for assessment.

Writing Across the Curriculum   The fundamental idea behind writing across the curriculum is quite simple: students who write about topics tend to understand them better (Shuman 1984). Students write to learn rather than learn to write (Newmann 1989). In writing across the curriculum, teachers give students opportunities to write for varied purposes in the content areas, such as note-taking from lectures or from reading assignments, summarizing text, reporting experiments in science, and analyzing or explaining problem-solving methods used in math or science. Students use writing to manipulate information, to consolidate prior learning, to prepare for future learning activities, and to extend or reformulate prior

learning (Newell 1989). Some teachers in the content areas, particularly in math and science, feel that writing instruction should be left to language arts teachers. The writing across the curriculum movement counters this view by extending writing to all content areas. We discuss writing across the curriculum further in Chapter 7.

Authentic Assessment of Writing

In examining the nature of writing, we have looked at the writer and the type of knowledge writers bring to the writing task. We have indicated that the purpose of writing and the genre determine what and how students write. We have highlighted two recent changes in writing instruction to set the stage for describing changes in assessment. These changes have strong implications for what is assessed, for how assessment is conducted, for the teacher's role in aligning assessment with instruction, and for the student's role as a participant in assessment and instruction.

Two important components in the authentic assessment of writing are the nature of the task and the scoring criteria. In what follows, we present some guidelines for constructing writing tasks, or prompts, and some examples of different types of scoring criteria, or rubrics. We also provide a means for reviewing students' developmental level of writing and the processes they use in writing. In addition, we discuss at length some approaches for getting students to rate their own interest in and awareness of writing and the quality of their written work. We also include suggestions for peer assessment of writing.

THE WRITING TASK

A writing prompt defines the task for student writing assignments. The prompt consists of the question or statement students will address in their writing and the conditions under which they will write. The task should specify the amount of time students will have to complete the writing; the resources they will have available (such as a dictionary); if they can plan, write, and revise; and if they will be using paper and pen or pencil, a type-writer, or a computer. We encourage you to ensure that the writing assignment reflects the content of your classroom instruction and to provide ample time for students to complete the writing task. Teachers who use Process Writing provide students with an opportunity to edit and revise as part of any writing assessment in order for the task to be authentic with regard to classroom instruction. An assignment in which students have an opportunity to edit and revise is probably a good idea with ELL students even if you are not using Process Writing.

The prompt can specify a particular purpose in order to elicit narrative, informative, or persuasive writing. For example, a narrative prompt might ask the student to write about an event that was shared by all students in the classroom, such as a classroom activity or field trip. The prompt might also be more personal, asking the student to reflect on a personal experience. The following narrative prompt was adapted from one developed for third grade students by Fairfax County Public Schools in Virginia:

> *Today you will write about something that happened to you or something that interests you. You may choose your own topic. For example, you might want to write about something that happened when you were on a trip, or about someone in your family, or a pet you have known, or a game you like to play.*

With younger students, the prompt could ask students to write about a shared experience in the classroom or on a field trip.

Should you provide students with a single prompt or should each student have an opportunity to select the topic on which they prefer to write? Common sense would suggest that students perform better when they have the opportunity to select the prompt from a variety of topics. When various topics are presented, students should find one that interests them most, on which they have background knowledge, and on which they can write a coherent passage. However, research results are mixed on whether students write better with single or with multiple prompts (Hamp-Lyons 1990). The performance of students given multiple prompts may be less than expected because

students waste time deliberating over the topic to select when they should be investing effort in planning, writing, and editing.

We suggest that you involve your ELL students in the decision to use single or multiple prompts. Ask if the students would prefer to have options during a writing assessment. Students might brainstorm a variety of prompts that you can use in subsequent writing assessments. If you decide to use multiple prompts, be sure that they all elicit the same processes and are in the same genre in order for the writing task to be comparable and fair. We also suggest checking the type of prompt required in grade-level classrooms in your school and in any formal accountability assessment conducted by the district or the state. ELL students should have experience with the types of prompts expected in these settings.

Criteria for Writing Prompts Whether you use single or multiple prompts, each prompt used in the writing assessment should meet the following criteria (California Assessment Program 1990):

- invite the desired type of writing or genre
- engage the thinking, problem-solving, composing, and text-making processes central to the type of writing
- be challenging for many students and accessible to all
- provide equitable opportunities for all students to respond
- produce interesting, not just proficient writing
- be liked by many students

The last part of the prompt should tell the students what will be valued in the writing. That is, the students should know in advance on what criteria their papers will be evaluated. One way to do this is to present a checklist of criteria at the end of the prompt that students can use to edit and revise their writing. The following is one example of such a checklist intended for students in analyzing their own narrative writing (adapted from materials developed by the Maryland State Department of Education 1987):

Writer's Checklist

- Did you write on the assigned topic?
- Did you write for the assigned audience?
- Did you identify a central theme?
- Did you explain the key ideas or events for the theme?
- Did you use complete sentences?
- Did you correct errors in spelling, capitalization, punctuation, and usage?

The items included in the checklist should mirror the components of the scoring rubric used in rating student papers. When this checklist is placed at the end of the prompt, students can review their own writing to determine if it meets the criteria against which it will be evaluated.

Integrated Language Assessment   In assessment of Process Writing, you have the opportunity to use prompts that allow you to observe and assess integrated language skills including reading, speaking, and writing. Language arts teachers in Prince William County, Virginia, recently designed an assessment of persuasive writing for seventh and tenth grade students on the topic of television violence. Students were provided with readings on the topic, including a newspaper and other articles discussing evidence related to the influence of television violence on violent behavior in society. Students were asked to write a persuasive piece taking a position for or against public control of violence on TV. The topic and the readings can easily be adjusted to the level of English proficiency of the students. The writing task had the following components, each of which was presented in a single class period on successive days:

Day	Activity	Description
1	Reading	Students read background materials on topic/take notes.
2	Discussion	Students discuss readings in small groups/modify notes
3	Draft 1	Students write first draft.
4	Review Rubric	Students are given the rubric and discuss its applications.
5	Edit and Revise	Students edit and revise to produce the final product.

In this example of integrated language assessment, there are varied opportunities to monitor student learning in all language skills. On Day 1, students read background materials and take notes. This is the first opportunity for assessment. Teachers can collect the notes and review the way students record their impressions as well as their success in capturing the central ideas and details of the readings. On Day 2, students discuss their ideas with peers in small groups. This gives the students an opportunity to review their ideas and test out the reasoning they expect to use in their writing. This is the second opportunity for assessment. Teachers can move about the room with an observation checklist containing categories for participation, oral language, and thinking skills. Students might be rated on language comprehensibility, level and type of interaction, use of the reading, use of personal background experiences, and use of analytic or evaluative statements in their discussion. On Day 3, students write a first draft of their paper from their notes. Day 4 is an opportunity to review the scoring rubric that will be used in grading the papers. Students should have been exposed to this or similar rubrics during previous instruction. On the final day, students edit and revise their paper to produce the final version that is scored. There is an opportunity for teachers to review the draft from Day 3 and compare it with the final version from Day 5 in order to determine how successfully the student edits and revises following the steps in Process Writing. Thus, there are multiple opportunities throughout this evaluation for integrated assessment of reading, oral language, and writing.

Note the similarity of this assessment process to classroom instruction and the varied opportunities teachers have to assess all four language skills. These varied opportunities for combining assessment with instruction across the settings in which students are observed give this approach a high payoff for the time invested. Also, because the assessment opportunities are embedded in literacy instruction, the assessment need not detract from instructional time.

TYPES OF SCORING

The scoring of authentic assessments should always be defined before the exercises and assessment procedures are developed. Three types of rating scales generally used in scoring writing are holistic, primary trait, and analytic scoring (Cohen 1994; Herman, Aschbacher, and Winters 1992; Perkins 1983). Each of these types has a different purpose and focus in instruction and will provide different types of information to teachers and students. Holistic and analytic scoring were introduced in Chapter 2 and will be described in more detail here.

Holistic Scoring   *Holistic scoring* uses a variety of criteria to produce a single score. The specific criteria selected depend on local instructional programs and language arts objectives. The rationale for using a holistic scoring system is that the total quality of written text is more than the sum of its components. Writing is viewed as an integrated whole. We have provided an example of a holistic scoring rubric developed by ESL teachers in Figure 2.5 of Chapter 2 that contains the following four dimensions:

- *Idea development/organization:* focuses on central idea with appropriate elaboration and conclusion.
- *Fluency/structure:* appropriate verb tense used with a variety of grammatical and syntactic structures.
- *Word Choice:* uses varied and precise vocabulary appropriate for purpose.
- *Mechanics:* absence of errors in spelling, capitalization, and punctuation.

The rater selects a score on a 1-6 holistic scale that best describes the writing sample. A student's paper need not meet every condition in each of the four dimensions but is rated on overall consistency within one of the six levels.

Another holistic scoring rubric, developed by ESL teachers in Prince William County, Virginia, focuses on the type of writing typically found among ELL students. These teachers reviewed various scoring rubrics and reflected on actual writing samples in developing this holistic scoring system. The rubric has six levels, as shown in Figure 6.1, a Holistic Scoring Rubric for Writing Assessment with ELL Students. The criteria for which ratings are assigned fall along five dimensions: meaning, organization, use of transitions, vocabulary, and grammatical/mechanical usage. Criteria appropriate to each level vary depending on the developmental nature of the writing. For example, at Level 1 writing may be characterized by copying from a model, using diagrams or drawings, and using single words or simple phrases. In contrast, at the highest level students may show evidence of the complex writing that is characteristic of native English speakers, including elements of style, composition, sentence construction, and grammar.

In reviewing this and other scoring rubrics, you can use sample papers from your own students to define the levels on the rubric more precisely. Select papers representing each level of the rubric and determine if you need to change the rubric to capture more accurately the writing of your own students. In this way, you can individualize the scoring scales for your own classroom objectives in language arts.

Primary Trait   A variation on holistic scoring that lends itself to classroom use is *primary trait scoring*. This type of scoring focuses on whether or not each paper shows evidence of the particular trait or feature you want students to demonstrate in writing. The trait could be a language-based feature emphasizing any one or more of the criteria for holistic scoring indicated above, such as Idea Development/Organization or Sentence Fluency/Structure. The advantage of this approach is in focusing on specific aspects of instruction that most reflect the objectives being covered when the writing assignment is given. Alternatively, the scoring could be based on a content-based feature, such as accurate content or use of concepts in the subject area. Pearce (1983) provides an interesting example:

> *Write a time capsule document analyzing Martin Luther King's approach to civil rights during the 1960s. Compare this approach to one taken by other Black leaders.*

Figure 6.1   Holistic Scoring Rubric for Writing Assessment with ELL Students

Level 6	• Conveys meaning clearly and effectively • Presents multi-paragraph organization, with clear introductions, development of ideas, and conclusion • Shows evidence of smooth transitions • Uses varied, vivid, precise vocabulary consistently • Writes with few grammatical/mechanical errors
Level 5	• Conveys meaning clearly • Presents multi-paragraph organization logically, though some parts may not be fully developed • Shows some evidence of effective transitions • Uses varied and vivid vocabulary appropriate for audience and purpose • Writes with some grammatical/mechanical errors without affecting meaning
Level 4	• Expresses ideas coherently most of the time • Develops a logical paragraph • Writes with a variety of sentence structures with a limited use of transitions • Chooses vocabulary that is (often) adequate to purpose • Writes with grammatical/mechanical errors that seldom diminish communication
Level 3	• Attempts to express ideas coherently • Begins to write a paragraph by organizing ideas • Writes primarily simple sentences • Uses high frequency vocabulary • Writes with grammatical/mechanical errors that sometimes diminish communication
Level 2	• Begins to convey meaning • Writes simple sentences/phrases • Uses limited or repetitious vocabulary • Spells inventively • Uses little or no mechanics, which often diminishes meaning
Level 1	• Draws pictures to convey meaning • Uses single words, phrases • Copies from a model

Developed by ESL teachers, Prince William County Public Schools, Virginia.

A student's paper could be evaluated for (1) accurate and sufficient content about civil disobedience, (2) comparisons of civil disobedience with at least one other approach to civil rights, and (3) coherent presentation of ideas supported by evidence. The scoring contains elements that focus on the content, comparisons with other approaches, and the coherence of the overall paper. In primary trait scoring, the paper is scored *only* on these features, and other features of the paper are ignored.

Analytic Scoring   The third type of rating scale uses *analytic scoring*. Analytic scales separate the features of a composition into components that are each scored separately. The separate components are sometimes given different weights to reflect their importance in instruction. Two advantages of this type of rubric are in providing feedback to students on specific aspects of their writing and in giving teachers diagnostic information for planning instruction (Perkins 1983). Another special advantage of analytic scoring with ELL students is in providing positive feedback on components of writing on which they have progressed most rapidly (Hamp-Lyons 1991). We have heard more than one teacher indicate that students ask for more specific detail on scoring than is provided in a holistic scale. Two limitations of analytic scoring are that teachers sometimes do not agree with the weights given to the separate components and that they may have to spend more time completing the scoring. Analytic scoring rubrics are used at the state level in Kentucky, Vermont, Virginia, California, and other states. Many of these rubrics contain similar elements with variations suited to local emphases.

An example of an analytic scoring rubric used for statewide assessment in Virginia is shown in Figure 6.2 (adapted from Self, n.d.). The major differences between the analytic scoring rubric shown in Figure 6.2 and the holistic scoring rubric in Figure 6.1 are that individual scores are assigned to each component of the scoring, weights are sometimes assigned to the components, and the total score is a sum of the weighted component scores. Scoring for each component is based on the degree of control the student's paper exhibits for that component. Separate scores on a scale of 1 (little or no control of the component) to 4 (consistent control) are assigned to each of the five components. In Virginia, Composing is weighted 3, Style is weighted 2, and the other components are weighted 1 in deriving the total score.

Notice that the differentiated scoring for Sentence Formation, Usage, and Mechanics (each is weighted 1) gives a balanced emphasis to these dimensions relative to the weight given to Composing (which is weighted 3). We expect that you will decide to weight the components of your analytic scoring rubric consistent with local language arts programs and objectives.

STAGES OF WRITING DEVELOPMENT

How do students become good writers? They progress through a number of stages as they gain competency in writing. We describe seven stages of writing development in Figure 6.3. The stages range from Pre-Emergent to Proficient. The form shown in Figure 6.3 was originally developed for a native English-speaking population (Misencik, Briggs, and the DMES Alternative Assessment Committee 1993). Figure 6.3 was adapted from the Misencik et al. approach by rephrasing descriptions to emphasize the presence rather than the absence of characteristics, by simplifying the number of characteristics at each stage, and by deleting developmental age ranges at each stage. Similar scales have been developed by Glazer and Brown (1993) and by Hill and Ruptic (1994). We chose to present the scale shown in Figure 6.3 because the descriptions at each stage are relatively specific, the stages seem relatively sequential, and the number and definitions of levels seems appropriate for ELL students.

We do not show age ranges corresponding to stages on the developmental scale. Age ranges for ELL students on developmental scales are quite fluid and may vary considerably depending on the students and the age at which they began to learn English. The age ranges would be particularly variable for preliterate students. The rate at which these stages emerge depends on each student's

Figure 6.2   Analytic Scoring Rubric for Writing

Domain Score*	Composing	Style	Sentence Formation	Usage	Mechanics
4	Focuses on central ideas with an organized and elaborated text	Purposefully chosen vocabulary, sentence variety, information, and voice to affect reader	Standard word order, no enjambment (run-on sentences), completeness (no sentence fragments), standard modifiers and coordinators, and effective transitions	Standard inflections (e.g., plurals, possessives, -ed, -ing with verbs, and -ly with adverbs), subject-verb agreement (we were vs. we was), standard word meaning	Effective use of capitalization, punctuation, spelling, and formatting (paragraphs noted by indenting)
3	Central idea, but not as evenly elaborated and some digressions	Vocabulary less precise and information chosen less purposeful	Mostly standard word order, some enjambment or sentence fragments	Mostly standard inflections, agreement, and word meaning	Mostly effective use of mechanics; errors do not detract from meaning
2	Not a focused idea or more than one idea, sketchy elaboration, and many digressions	Vocabulary basic and not purposefully selected; tone flat or inconsistent	Some non-standard word order, enjambment, and word omissions (e.g., verbs)	Some errors with inflections, agreement, and word meaning	Some errors with spelling and punctuation that detract from meaning
1	No clear idea, little or no elaboration, many digressions	Not controlled, tone flat, sentences halted or choppy	Frequent non-standard word order, enjambment, and word omissions	Shifts from one tense to another; errors in conventions (them/those, good/well, double negatives, etc.)	Misspells even simple words; little formatting evident

*4 = Consistent control
3 = Reasonable control
2 = Inconsistent control
1 = Little or no control

Adapted from Self (n.d.).

Figure 6.3   **Developmental Descriptors of Writing**

Student _____ Date _____

Stage/Characteristics	Teacher Comments
Stage 1: Pre-Emergent • Scribbles or draws to communicate • Shows interest in letters and words	
Stage 2: Emergent • May recognize/name letters or simple words • Uses letter forms to label drawings • Sometimes writes with left-to-right progression • Sometimes writes with sound/symbol relation-ships • May be able to explain writing	
Stage 3: Dependent • Uses inventive spelling with beginning and ending sounds • Uses print from the environment • Uses simple vocabulary • Sometimes leaves spaces between words • Develops a sense of story. • Writer may forget meaning after time • Meaning sometimes evident to reader	
Stage 4: Developing • Begins to use vowels in inventive spelling • Begins to write simple sentences • Uses elaborations from personal experience • Can read back to an audience • Rereads to check meaning	
Stage 5: Independent • Matches oral language to writing • Writes for variety of purposes • Begins to use an organizing plan when writing • Makes corrections while writing • Develops authorship and voice	

Adapted from Misencik, Briggs, and the DMES Alternative Assessment Committee (1993).

Figure 6.3 **Developmental Descriptors of Writing** (continued)

Student _____ Date _____

Stage/Characteristics	Teacher Comments
Stage 6: Fluent • Uses story structure (beginning, middle, end) • Shows clear organization • Takes risks with writing styles and language • Initiates independent writing • Uses editing/revising process • Recognizes need for standard spelling • Uses a variety of genre and styles	_____ _____ _____ _____ _____ _____ _____
Stage 7: Proficient • Writes for a variety of purposes (narrative, informative, persuasive, creative, etc.) • Communicates main idea with elaboration • Uses distinct voice • Uses language structures appropriately • Uses word selection appropriate to purpose • Has effective control of mechanics of writing	 _____ _____ _____ _____ _____

Summary Comments

_____

_____

_____

_____

_____

_____

_____

_____

_____

_____

_____

_____

Adapted from Misencik, Briggs, and the
DMES Alternative Assessment Committee (1993).

prior educational background, the student's proficiency in English, and the type of instructional support provided, among other variables.

Teachers can use the scale in Figure 6.3 by noting the characteristics of each student's writing and the developmental stage to which the writing has progressed. The scale may be most useful in classrooms for ELL students at the primary, elementary, and middle grades.

The level of writing shown by a student will depend in part on the prompt. Students who customarily write at the developing stage may exhibit characteristics of independent writers with familiar topics or genres, particularly when the prompt has a high interest level or is self-selected (Glazer and Brown 1993). Thus, teachers should not expect that a scale of the type shown in Figure 6.3 will uncover a consistent level of writing for each piece of work that a student produces. Appropriate use of the form should nevertheless enable a teacher to see developmental trends occurring over time for various pieces of writing for each student.

MONITORING STUDENT PROGRESS IN PROCESS WRITING

With the shift from the products of writing to the processes by which effective writing is generated, many teachers have attempted to monitor what students actually do while writing. For example, you may want to know how students function in the pre-writing and post-writing stages of writing as well as in the writing stage. Direct observation of writing is one way to collect this type of information. Conferencing with students is also a good way to collect information about student writing processes, progress, and response to instruction.

Strategies for Process Writing   To monitor the prewriting and postwriting stages, you can use the Process Writing Checklist, as shown in Figure 6.4. During each stage of the writing process, students can learn strategies that will assist them in accomplishing the work for that stage. For example, in the prewriting stage, students can formulate the topic before writing, consider various approaches to the topic, and decide on a way to organize the information. During the writing process, students

can monitor their writing by rereading and reviewing what they have written while the product is still being developed. When students are uncertain of a word or spelling, they can convey messages through drawings, invented spellings, or word substitutions. Postwriting strategies include editing or making word-level changes, revising or making sentence-level changes, and rewriting or recomposing the passage or perhaps writing in a different genre, as in changing from a narrative to a persuasive mode. In addition to the three phases of the writing process, Figure 6.4 provides opportunities for teachers to observe the applications and interests of students, two other important components of writing. The end result of the writing process should include the ability to write for pleasure, to write in other subject areas, to write in a variety of genres, and to participate in discussions about writing. One of the most important applications of writing is in editing and commenting on the written work of other students.

In reviewing the Process Writing Checklist, you will notice markings for "Usually," "Sometimes," and "Rarely" that can be entered during the school quarter. In order for the checklist to work for you, you will need to define these terms for the type of writing students do in your classroom. Three ways to define these terms include: (1) observing students as they write, (2) conferencing with individuals or small groups of students, and (3) collecting samples of student work that represent different levels of effective writing. For example, you can discuss students' prewriting strategies with small groups and make anecdotal records for yourself as a reminder of what each student said. This will help you build a collection of effective prewriting strategies to share with other students.

You can rate the writing progress of individual students using Figure 6.4 based on conferences or your familiarity with their written work. The students' use of a strategy may be evident from writing samples, particularly if you ask students to give you the version of their writing on which they have made editing comments. While the Process Writing Checklist has columns for recording each quarter, you can define the columns in terms of school months or weeks if you feel that more fre-

Figure 6.4 **Process Writing Checklist**

Student _____ Date _____

Mark: X = Usually / = Sometimes — = Rarely

Writing Process Quarter:	1	2	3	4
I. Prewriting Strategies				
▪ Formulates topics before writing	____	____	____	____
▪ Considers approach to topic	____	____	____	____
▪ Discusses topic for writing	____	____	____	____
▪ Outlines or makes schematic organizer	____	____	____	____
II. Writing Strategies				
▪ Monitors writing (rereads, reviews, backtracks)	____	____	____	____
▪ Uses adaptive techniques (e.g., skips word, makes substitutions)	____	____	____	____
III. Postwriting Strategies				
▪ Edits (word-level changes)	____	____	____	____
▪ Revises (sentence-level changes)	____	____	____	____
▪ Rewrites (composition-level changes)	____	____	____	____
▪ Gets feedback from others	____	____	____	____
IV. Applications and Interests				
▪ Writes for pleasure	____	____	____	____
▪ Uses writing to communicate (letters, notes, etc.)	____	____	____	____
▪ Actively seeks guidance in writing activities	____	____	____	____
▪ Writes in subjects other than language arts	____	____	____	____
▪ Participates in discussions about writing	____	____	____	____
▪ Shares writing with others	____	____	____	____
▪ Edits writing of others	____	____	____	____

Comments

Adapted from materials produced by the Georgetown University Evaluation Assistance Center (EAC) East (1990), Washington, D.C.

quent recording is necessary for the class or for individual students. The comments section can be used to record any impressions that are significant about a particular student's writing, special interests, instructional approaches you plan to use with this student, or specific materials you have used and the student's response to them. The Process Writing Checklist can serve as a reminder of some of the key components of Process Writing as well as point the way for adapting instruction to the needs of individual students. You can maintain the checklist for individual students in a folder or student portfolio.

Writing Conferences   Another important assessment opportunity occurs in the questions asked during conferencing. Your selection of questions to ask will depend on the writer, the purpose of the writing, and your instructional focus for any particular student. Among the questions teachers might ask students are:

- *How did you choose the topic?*

- *Did you write about something you did or something you read?*

- *Before you wrote, did you talk about the topic with someone?*

- *Before you wrote, did you make a plan? Write an outline?*

- *When you have a problem writing or get stuck, what do you do?*

- *Did you write a draft?*

- *Did you edit what you wrote and then rewrite it?*

- *What do you look for when you edit?*

- *What was hard in writing? What was easy?*

- *What do you want to do better in writing?*

One assumption in asking these types of questions is that students will later internalize them (Kritt 1993). Students should be able to ask themselves questions like these as a guide to their own writing as they develop constructive methods to improve their writing over time. It is for this reason that conferencing should be done in a positive and supportive manner and rely on the student's perceptions of the written work. The same assumption, from a social to an internalized standard, applies to peer assessment.

Teachers using writing conferences will need to find a system for recording the discussion held with each student. The system should be efficient and easy to use and maintain (Church 1993). Some possibilities are tape recordings, anecdotal records jotted on a notebook with the student's name at the top, index cards, and adhesive address labels on which you can make brief notes to be inserted in a folder for each student. We have also seen teachers keep notes on a single sheet of paper divided into 3″ x 3″ cells, which they reproduce and on which they write individual student's names as the students are interviewed. You may need to experiment with various approaches until you find the technique that is most effective for you.

How often should these conferences occur? The answer is up to you and what you find most useful for each student. However, a mid-quarter and end-of-quarter conference should provide you with information enabling you to see progress in the student's writing processes over the school year. How do you schedule conferences along with teaching? You conference with only a small number of students at any one time or day. A flexible schedule of conferencing with about two to three students a day over a few weeks should enable you to have conferences with all students in your class for a school quarter. Collaborative learning assignments can be used to engage students not participating in the conferences.

WRITTEN SUMMARIES

One of the most important types of writing students use in school is writing to summarize. You will probably need to provide support for your students as they learn how to summarize. Summarizing involves (1) deleting minor details and redundant information, (2) combining similar details, and (3) selecting or composing main idea sentences (Casazza 1992). Students may need some cognitive maturity to perform these steps independently. With younger students, you may need to model and teach these steps using explicit instruction. You can provide opportunities for students to read a text, summarize it, and then compare their summary with a model. Students can edit and evaluate summaries provided by their peers. Summarizing procedures that may be appropriate for younger students include T-Lists, in which students write main ideas on the left side of a page and corresponding details on the right, and graphic organizers, such as semantic maps (Chamot and O'Malley 1994a; Hamp-Lyons 1983; Peregoy and Boyle 1993). Examples of these types of summarizing procedures are presented in Chapter 7. Students who have difficulty summarizing without copying text exactly should work from a T-List or a semantic map as they write.

Students can write summaries in both dialogue journals and learning logs. Students can keep journals in reading or in each content area in which they summarize briefly their observations about the day's class, what they want to remember, what they found difficult, what they will seek assistance on to understand better, and what attitudes they have about learning in this subject area. This type of summary is extremely useful in assisting students retain critical information they learned and in probing for further information on which they need assistance. Writing a summary provides excellent practice for note-taking in content-area classrooms, while aiding students in self-assessment and control of their own learning activities.

You can provide students with feedback on their summaries by scoring the accuracy of the main ideas and important supporting information represented. Students who have seen the rules for summarizing modeled and have had extensive practice with them will begin to apply them independently. The guide shown in Figure 6.5 will enable you to monitor student summaries and provide meaningful feedback to students. You can modify the guide to emphasize the parts of summarizing that are most important in the subject area students are learning in your classroom.

SELF-ASSESSMENT IN WRITING

Self-assessment in writing encourages the type of reflection needed to gain increased control as a writer. Self-assessment encourages students to think about their purpose in writing and to reflect on what and how much they are learning. Four ways in which you can encourage self-assessment are through dialogue journals, learning logs, self-assessment of interests and writing awareness, and checklists of writing skills.

Dialogue Journals   In *dialogue journals*, students regularly make entries addressed to the teacher on topics of their choice. The topics may be on a book they particularly liked, their interests, or their attitudes toward learning in different classes or content areas. The teacher writes back, modeling appropriate language use but not correcting the student's language. Dialogue journals maintain a non-threatening context in which students write at their own proficiency level on self-selected topics of interest to them (Hamayan 1989). Journals can be maintained in a notebook or on a computer disk. Students typically write in class for five to ten minutes at the end of a class period or at any convenient time during the day (Peyton and Reed 1990). Beginning writers should be permitted the opportunity to write on a self-selected topic and to communicate through pictures. You can also focus the writing on certain topics and specify the amount of writing expected.

Dialogue journals provide numerous opportunities for students to see growth in their own writing ability. While the teacher's evaluation of dialogue journals should not result in corrections of student writing, you can examine the student's writing for topic initiation, elaboration, variety, use of different genres, expression of interests and attitudes, and awareness about the process of writing (Peyton and Reed 1990). You can keep anecdotal notes on improvements or variations in each student's writing in your record book.

Learning Logs   Another form of self-assessment in writing is provided through a learning log (Atwell 1990; Chamot, O'Malley, and Küpper 1992; Jan 1992; Pradle and Mayher 1985). In one type of learning log, students make entries during the last five minutes of each period, responding to the following types of questions:

Figure 6.5 **Summary Evaluation Guidelines**

Student _____ Date _____

This Student:	Never	Sometimes	Often	Always
• identifies the topic	1	2	3	4
• identifies the main idea	1	2	3	4
• combines/chunks similar ideas	1	2	3	4
• paraphrases accurately	1	2	3	4
• deletes minor details	1	2	3	4
• reflects author's emphasis	1	2	3	4
• recognizes author's purpose	1	2	3	4
• stays within appropriate length	1	2	3	4

Comments

Adapted from Casazza (1992).

- What did I learn today?
- What strategies or approaches worked best for me in learning?
- What was hard to understand?
- What will I do to understand better?

A learning log is especially useful for students who are hesitant to raise their hand in class and ask questions. Teachers can review learning logs from time to time or review the logs of a few students during or at the end of each class to keep track of students' learning needs. Questions to answer as you review the logs are as follows:

- Does the student define and/or use new vocabulary from the lesson?
- Does the student use content vocabulary appropriately?
- Does the student illustrate and label drawings correctly?
- Does the student identify a range of strategies that worked in learning?
- Does the student have reasonable plans for improving her or his learning?

As with dialogue journals, teachers should avoid correcting student language in the learning log. However, you may wish to write comments in the student's log to encourage writing and provide language models. Both dialogue journals and learning logs can help students' self-evaluation in documenting the progress they are making in learning, in writing or understanding new concepts, and in identifying plans to improve learning.

Surveys of Interest and Awareness   To determine student attitudes toward writing, you can assess their interest in and awareness of writing through surveys or rating scales (Hill and Ruptic 1994). A sample self-assessment is shown in Figure 6.6. Students are asked to indicate their attitudes toward writing and to gauge their improvement as writers. Students can complete a self-assessment like this once they have sufficient command over English to be able to respond to the questions. By occasionally reviewing the Survey of Writing Interest and Awareness, you can keep in touch with your students' experiences during the writing process. You may want to modify this sample assessment by selecting only the parts that are relevant to the developmental level of your students or their level of English proficiency.

Writing Strategies   One of the most important components of writing is the strategies students use while writing, as discussed earlier in the section on Process Writing. A form for self-assessment of writing strategies is shown in Figure 6.7. Strategies may be used before writing, during writing, and after writing. The pre-writing strategies emphasize topic review and organization. Strategies used during writing advance the writing toward meeting the original purpose. These strategies are used to overcome obstacles or enhance communication through examples, clarification, and drawings. After writing, students should reread, edit, and revise their writing to ensure it meets the original purpose. You should not expect students to use all of these strategies with every piece of writing they produce. Nevertheless, over a number of written products with varying purposes and genres, students should use many of these strategies.

You can assist your students in becoming aware of their own strategy use by modeling strategies aloud as you produce a written product for the class, by asking students to talk about their strategies in cooperative learning groups, and by giving students positive and constructive feedback on their strategy selections as they write independently (Chamot and O'Malley 1994a; Harris and Graham 1992).

Writing Checklist   In order for students to make progress in learning, they should understand (1) the activity and what proficiency it requires, (2) the steps needed to attain proficiency, and (3) how they are progressing (Hayward 1993). Self-assessment is a key element in Process Writing as students review, edit, and revise their own work. An important part of self-assessment is for students to check their own writing with respect to the types of standards typically contained in holistic and analyt-

Figure 6.6 **Survey of Writing Interest and Awareness**

Name _____ Date _____

Check one box for each statement.

	A Lot	Some	A Little	Not at All
1. I like to write stories.	❑	❑	❑	❑
2. I am a good writer.	❑	❑	❑	❑
3. Writing stories is easy for me.	❑	❑	❑	❑
4. Writing to friends is fun.	❑	❑	❑	❑
5. Writing helps me in school.	❑	❑	❑	❑
6. I like to share my writing with others.	❑	❑	❑	❑
7. I write at home.	❑	❑	❑	❑

8. What kinds of things do you like to write about?_____

_____

_____

_____

9. How have you improved as a writer? What can you do well?_____

_____

_____

10. What else do you want to improve in your writing? _____

_____

_____

_____

Adapted from materials developed by the Georgetown University Evaluation Assistance Center (EAC) East (1990), Washington, D.C.

Figure 6.7   **Self-Assessment of Writing Strategies**

Name _____ Date _____

Check one box for each statement.

	Yes	No
Before writing:		
1. I talked to a friend or partner about the topic.	❏	❏
2. I made a list of ideas on the topic.	❏	❏
3. I made an outline or semantic map.	❏	❏
During writing:		
4. I skipped words I didn't know and went back to them later.	❏	❏
5. I substituted a word from my own language.	❏	❏
6. I used drawings or pictures in my writing.	❏	❏
After writing:		
7. I checked to see if the writing met my purpose.	❏	❏
8. I reread to see if it made sense.	❏	❏
9. I added information or took out information.	❏	❏
10. I edited for spelling, punctuation, capitals, and grammar.	❏	❏

Other strategies I used:

Adapted from materials produced by the Georgetown University Evaluation Assistance Center (EAC) East (1990), Washington, D.C.

ic scoring rubrics. That is, writers should review the quality of each written piece for dimensions such as composition, style, sentence formation, usage, and mechanics. These specific terms will have little meaning for most ELL students unless they are rephrased as questions or statements that assist students in reviewing the quality of their writing. A sample of this type of assessment is shown in Figure 6.8, the Self-Assessment of Writing Dimensions.

Figure 6.8 is divided into two sections because the types of questions used in rating may differ depending on the genre. The top part can be used to rate informative, narrative, and persuasive writing using terms that have meaning for students (fiction, non-fiction, biography, autobiography), while the bottom part is reserved for poetry. Self-ratings in the top part focus on organization, word usage, mechanics, and format. Ratings in the bottom part concentrate on specific elements that are important in writing poetry. In self-assessment, students should focus on how effectively they have crafted sentences and paragraphs to communicate a meaningful message in addition to correcting technical errors.

PEER ASSESSMENT IN WRITING

Students can evaluate each other's writing through *peer assessment* as they participate in student writing conferences (Cramer 1982; Pearce 1983). This involves the students in evaluation of writing and eases the burden on you for evaluating every paper that each student produces. You don't have to rate or grade everything each student produces, but you may want to ensure that students receive some form of regular feedback. You can evaluate papers selectively for different students on a rotating basis, enabling you to gain an understanding of each student's progress while allowing students opportunities to apply performance standards to the work of others. Students are sometimes reluctant to share impressions with their peers for fear of hurting the other persons' feelings. One way to overcome this reluctance is to make the student whose paper is being assessed responsible for finding out how the paper can be improved. Another way is to have students pair up and read their

papers to each other (Pearce 1983). Each student is encouraged to respond to the other student's paper by answering three questions:

• What did you like about the paper?

• What facts or ideas could be added to the paper?

• What changes could be made to improve the paper?

Students easily become acquainted with these procedures and gain skill in being able to discuss each other's work. One possible follow-up to this procedure is to have students exchange papers and use a scoring rubric to rate them. Students should then be given an opportunity to edit and rewrite their papers. Whatever the procedure selected, you should vary it from time to time so that students treat the evaluation in a serious manner.

One process for peer editing is contained in the form shown in Figure 6.9. The peer evaluator using this form would write her or his own name at the top, the name of the writer, the title, and the type of writing. The remainder of the form is used to communicate with the writer both the strengths of the work and the aspects of the writing that need improvement. When students learn to evaluate the work of their peers, they are extending their own opportunities to learn how to write (Cramer, 1982).

Using Writing Assessment in Instruction

Writing assessment can be used most effectively with instruction when the criteria for scoring written products are clear to the students and when the students see an obvious relationship between what they have written and the scores they received. As we have noted, students and teachers see the connection between their writing and the scores more clearly with analytic scoring rubrics than with holistic scoring. This is not to suggest that analytic rubrics must be used at all times, but merely to indicate that writers sometimes need specific feedback at certain stages of their writing development.

Figure 6.8 **Self-Assessment of Writing Dimensions**

Author's Name _____ Date _____

Title of Work: _____

Genre:	Fiction	Non-Fiction	Biography	Autobiography

Purpose and Organization   Yes   No

1. I stated my purpose clearly.   ❑   ❑
2. I organized my thoughts.   ❑   ❑
3. My work has a beginning, middle, and end.   ❑   ❑
4. I chose words that helped make my point.   ❑   ❑

Word/Sentence Use

5. I used some new vocabulary.   ❑   ❑
6. I wrote complete sentences.   ❑   ❑
7. I used correct subject-verb agreement.   ❑   ❑
8. I used the past tense correctly.   ❑   ❑

Mechanics/Format

9. I spelled words correctly.   ❑   ❑
10. I used capitals to start sentences.   ❑   ❑
11. I used periods and question marks correctly.   ❑   ❑
12. I indented paragraphs.   ❑   ❑

Editing

13. I read my paper aloud to a partner.   ❑   ❑
14. I asked a partner to read my paper.   ❑   ❑

Genre: **Poetry**

1. I used descriptive language in the poem.   ❑   ❑
2. I used the required format (e.g., quatrain).   ❑   ❑
3. I illustrated the poem.   ❑   ❑
4. I used nouns, verbs, and adjectives.   ❑   ❑
5. I presented the poem to the class.   ❑   ❑

Adapted from Claire Waller, ESL Middle School Teacher, Fairfax County Public Schools, Virginia.

Figure 6.9 **Peer Evaluation and Editing Form for Writing**

Reader's Name _____ Date _____

Author's Name _____

Title of Piece _____ Type of Writing _____

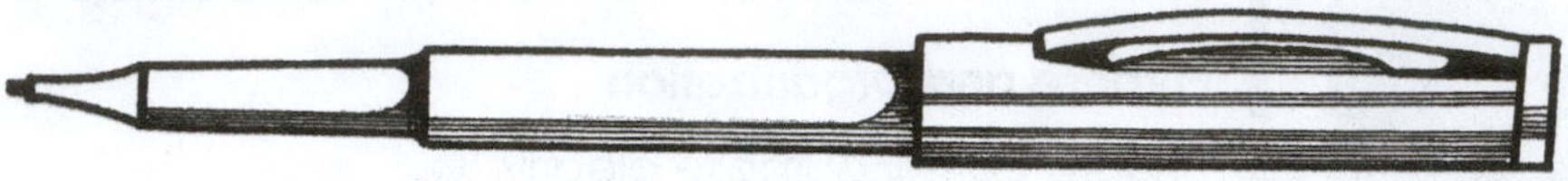

Peer Evaluation

This piece of writing was: _____

_____

_____

The part I liked best was: _____

_____

_____

_____

This piece can be improved by: _____

_____

_____

_____

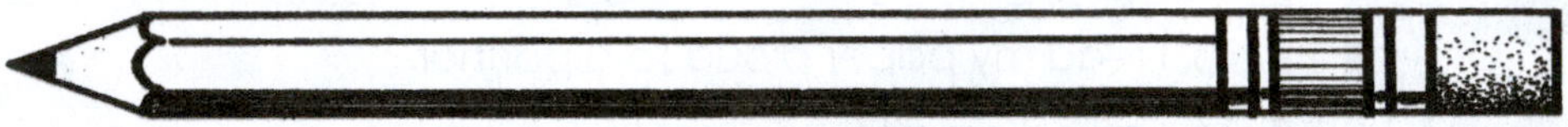

Editing Form

Look for these things when editing someone's paper.

Punctuation:
- periods
- question marks
- capital letters at beginning of sentence
- capital letters for names

Spelling:
- correct spelling

Other:
- neat handwriting

Sentences:
- are complete and have a verb.
- have variety.
- writer uses paragraphs.

Overall Paper:
- has a main idea.
- is logical and makes sense.
- is organized well.

Adapted from C. Waller (1994), ESL Middle School Teacher, Fairfax County Public Schools, Virginia.

One way to use writing assessment in instruction is to share the scoring rubrics with students. We believe that assessment criteria should be public for students and that they should be familiarized with the scoring rubrics so they can plan their writing effectively. Kolls (1992) familiarized students with scoring rubrics in advance of the writing activity and found that those who benefited most were ELL and learning-disabled students. The ELL students in particular became more effective at following the directions for a writing prompt, writing on topic, and responding to on-demand requests to produce writing in response to a prompt. The study was conducted as part of an overall project on portfolio assessment. Teachers in grades 3-12 were provided staff sessions to familiarize them with anchor papers at each of six points on a scoring rubric. The anchor papers were intended to be used by students to assist them in seeing how other students attained high scores for effective writing. Students at any point on the scoring rubric were shown papers for the next highest level and enabled to rewrite their own paper following the example. They were able to discuss the scoring rubrics in small groups and were provided numerous opportunities to improve their writing. Scores on a six-point scoring rubric increased by two points for the ELL students from the pretest to the posttest in one school year, more than for any other group.

From this study and from our own experience working with teachers, we suggest the following guidelines to maximize the interaction between writing assessment and instruction:

1. *Select prompts that are appropriate for the students.* Ensure that the prompts you select invite the desired type of writing, engage the type of thinking and problem solving you want to assess, and are both challenging and accessible to all students. Furthermore, the prompts should be sensitive to the cultural background of the students, produce interesting writing, and be enjoyed by the students. Discuss with students whether they would prefer to select the topic for the prompt from a list of options or to suggest prompts themselves.

2. *Select rubrics students can use.* Select or develop rubrics that students can use to improve their writing. Keep the rubric uncomplicated so that students can use it. Try using both analytic and holistic rubrics with your students and elicit their comments on the usefulness of each scoring system. Ask students which type of rubric provides the most meaningful information and gives them the type of feedback they can use to improve their own writing. You may also want to try out primary trait scoring. The rubric used will vary depending on the type of writing and student input.

3. *Share the rubrics with students.* Share the rubric with students, and give them opportunities to use the rubric with their own writing and to evaluate the writing of their peers. Students need repeated opportunities to internalize the rubric so that it becomes a natural part of their editing process as they review their own work.

4. *Identify benchmark papers.* One of the ways to communicate to students what good writing looks like is to select benchmark papers, (i.e., papers that you have rated high on the components of your scoring rubric). Share these papers with students as models they can emulate. For each student, use a model that is rated slightly higher than the current writing level of the student so the target is within reach to them. Use models from both ELL students and native English speakers, if possible.

5. *Review how students write not just what they write.* Checklists that focus on Process Writing and students' writing strategies should be particularly useful in gaining an understanding of how students write. Both you and your students will profit from a better understanding of writing processes. This is not to suggest, however, that you should ignore essential elements of good writing, such as composition, style, sentence formation, word usage, and mechanics in your ratings.

6. *Provide time and instructional support for self-assessment and peer assessment.* Students will profit considerably from rating their own writing and from

rating the writings of their peers. Teachers need to make time and provide guidance on self- and peer assessment. These can support instructional goals by enabling students to refine their understanding of the scoring rubrics, of effective writing, and of the strategies that work in producing good writing. When students gain familiarity with the scoring rubrics, teachers can rate student writing selectively and not feel compelled to rate every paper themselves.

7. *Introduce self-assessment gradually.* Students may need scaffolded support in learning to edit and revise their own work. Beginning ELL writers may take an entire grading period before they have adjusted to the initial challenge of writing. Teachers might model the editing process or introduce the parts of the rubric one at a time. Engage students in generating criteria for good writing (see Chapter 3 on self-assessment). Place criteria charts in key places around the classroom (Cramer 1982). Students will require opportunities to edit numerous writing samples and to edit the writing of peers as they internalize the standards for good writing. Students can listen to their own writing by working with a partner.

8. *Use conferencing to discuss writing with students.* Occasional writing conferences provide excellent opportunities to ask students key questions about their writing processes and to provide students with personalized feedback on their writing. Conferencing is also an excellent opportunity to inquire about the effectiveness of various instructional materials or approaches you have tried.

Students in bilingual classrooms can be familiarized with scoring rubrics in their native language before being introduced to the rubric in English. Students may need to have demonstrations of the way in which the rubric applies to English even though they understand the rubric's applications in their native language. You may need to make special adaptations for preliterate students and monitor their literacy development using a developmental scale such as the one shown in this chapter.

Conclusion

This chapter has provided an overview of the nature of the writing process, the role of the writer, and current directions in writing instruction, including Process Writing and writing across the curriculum. Writing is presented as a process that must be understood and applied rather than simply as a product to be evaluated. We described the different purposes and types of writing, approaches to the design of writing tasks, and various types of scoring rubrics. We emphasized the importance of feedback to students, through familiarity with scoring rubrics, self-assessment, and peer assessment. We concluded by describing instructional uses of writing assessment.

In assessing the writing proficiency of ELL students, we encourage teachers to consider the following:

1. Assess the stages of writing development as students gradually gain control of writing processes, particularly for beginning writers.

2. Assess writing in the context of other language skills, when appropriate, as with integrated language assessment.

3. Assess all domains of writing, especially composition, in addition to sentence construction, word usage, and mechanics.

4. Include self-assessment of writing, share scoring rubrics, and involve students in setting criteria as well as in developing and selecting writing prompts.

5. Assess writing processes and strategies as well as the products of written efforts.

6. Use multiple assessments of writing across various purposes, genres, and content areas, including written summaries and learning logs.

7. Include writing samples in portfolios to illustrate student growth over time and to show accomplishments relative to classroom objectives.

8. Use the results of writing assessments and of your conferences with students to plan instruction. Identify student strengths, educational needs, and interests and determine what works most effectively in instruction for each student.

APPLICATION ACTIVITIES

1. To assess strategies applied in Process Writing, use Figure 6.4. You can obtain this information through observation, in conferences held with each student, or in small group discussions. Carefully define terms used in the checklist—such as *usually, sometimes,* and *rarely*—and develop examples of student work representing student strategies.

2. Hold writing assessment conferences with individual students. Plan in advance the types of questions you will ask, and plan for the way in which you will record student responses. Also plan how often you will hold conferences with students.

3. Design and try out a series of writing prompts for your students. Elicit student comments on the different prompts.

4. Show students a writing sample and ask them to generate criteria for assessing it. List on the chalkboard the criteria that they indicate are associated with good writing. Suggest others as needed. Involve students in self-assessment of their own writing with these criteria.

5. Try out holistic scoring and analytic scoring with different writing samples. Involve students in a discussion of which of these approaches they prefer based on the type of feedback they receive on their writing. Use the rubrics in Figures 6.1 and 6.2 as examples.

6. Encourage self-assessment in writing through the use of at least one of the following approaches: dialogue journals, learning logs, self-ratings of writing interest and awareness (e.g., Figure 6.6), self-assessment of writing strategies (e.g., Figure 6.7), and a self-assessment checklist (e.g., Figure 6.8). Engage students in discussions of what they learned from the form of self-assessment they tried.

7. Encourage students to use peer assessment of their writing, as in Figure 6.9. Have peers discuss the writing sample with the partner whose paper they evaluated.

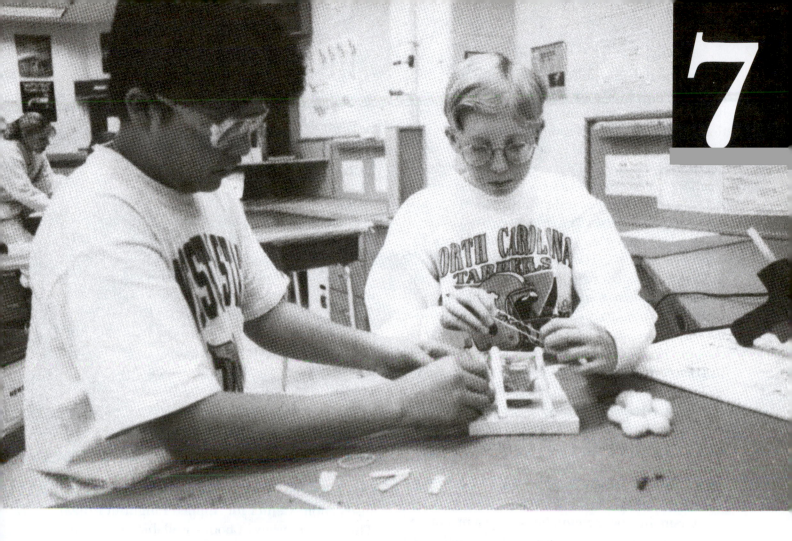

CONTENT AREA
ASSESSMENT

· ·

This chapter describes authentic assessment of English language learning (ELL) students in the content areas. We first identify the purposes of content area assessment with ELL students and the reasons for increased interest in the integration of language and content. We also indicate how content area instruction is changing for native speakers of English in grade-level classrooms. We then introduce approaches to authentic assessment in the content areas, including both basic assessment techniques and those specific to particular content

areas. Among the general techniques are assessment of writing across the curriculum, cloze tests, and assessment of thinking skills. The specific content areas we address are mathematics, science, and social studies. We also identify procedures for self-assessment and peer assessment. The last section of the chapter describes instructional uses of assessment in the content areas. As in other chapters, we include sample formats for assessment and encourage you to use or adapt any of these to meet the needs of your students.

Content area assessment is used for at least three purposes with ELL students. The primary purpose is to monitor student progress in attaining instructional objectives to determine if adaptations to instruction are required to better meet student needs. Assessment in the content areas enables teachers to review student growth over time and to determine the success of their instructional strategies. The second use of content area assessment is for *reclassification* (i.e., to determine if ELL students are ready to advance to a higher level of English language instruction or can benefit from grade-level instruction). In reclassification decisions, ELL students are often assessed in the content areas as well as in language arts. The third purpose of assessment in the content areas with ELL students is for accountability. Many state education agencies and school districts administer minimum competency tests for accountability in reading, writing, and mathematics to all students at benchmark grade levels and, in some cases, require a minimum score for high school graduation (Council of Chief State School Officers 1991; O'Malley and Valdez Pierce 1994).

Assessments for accountability have a profound impact on ELL students, who must eventually meet the same performance standards as all other students. The fact that many states exempt ELL students from testing for up to three years only postpones the requirement (O'Malley and Valdez Pierce 1994). Even if the state does not require a minimum score for a standard high school diploma, ELL students may be called on to participate in the assessment so the state can monitor school-level performance. One unintended consequence of the "high stakes" use of assessment for school-level accountability is that ELL students are sometimes exempted from testing indefinitely by a school or excluded from reporting beyond the period when it is appropriate. The exemption avoids low average test scores for a school or district. However, when schools exclude ELL students from estimates of local performance, they have no way of accounting for their growth in English and the content areas. Also, the scores of these students will not be available to influence the amount of academic or financial support provided to address their needs.

Content Area Instruction in Schools

Content area instruction is undergoing major revisions both in English as a second language (ESL) classrooms and in grade-level classrooms. These reforms have direct implications for assessment by indicating both the form assessment should take and the standards of performance for which students are held accountable. In the following discussion, we describe some of the changes in ESL instruction and then identify changes in content area instruction in grade-level classrooms.

CONTENT AREA ESL INSTRUCTION

In increasing numbers of ESL classrooms throughout the United States, English is being learned through integrated language and content area instruction (Center for Applied Linguistics 1993). There are a variety of books available describing teaching approaches for integrating language and content area instruction (Brinton, Snow, and Wesche 1989; Cantoni-Harvey 1987; Chamot and O'Malley 1994a; Crandall 1987; Mohan 1986; Short 1991) and an expanding number of student materials integrating language and content (Chamot 1987; Chamot and O'Malley 1988; Chamot, O'Malley, and Küpper 1992; Crandall, Dale, Rhodes, and Spanos 1989; Fathman and Quinn 1989; Johnston and Johnston 1990; Kessler et al. 1994; Short, Seufert-Bosco, and Grognet 1991).

Innovative assessment procedures in the content areas are called for to respond to this rapidly expanding interest in the integration of language and content in ESL (Short 1993). New assessments in the content areas are also important for bilingual programs, which have traditionally met the needs of ELL students through native language instruction in the content areas (Crawford 1989; Krashen 1991; Ramirez, Yuen, and Ramey 1991).

We focus on English language assessments but encourage teachers in bilingual classrooms to adapt the techniques for various languages.

Assumptions Practitioners of content-based ESL believe that students need to be introduced gradually and progressively to concepts and language in the content areas (Mohan 1986). More traditional language teaching methods—in which students practice communication skills, grammar rules, and correct linguistic forms—are based on the assumption that students will be able to integrate and apply these linguistic elements in learning content subject matter. However, what second language educators have overtly recognized is that the language of each content area has special concepts, vocabulary, and language functions that require unique forms of instruction in which language and content are integrated (e.g., Chamot and O'Malley 1986, 1994; Crandall 1987; Short 1991). As part of this instruction, students should have opportunities to learn and apply concepts in the content areas through all four language skills rather than learning language elements as a prerequisite to content area instruction. Research has shown that appropriate content instruction facilitates language learning (Kessler and Quinn 1980).

The practice of teaching ESL through the content areas receives direct support in Cummins' (1982, 1983) distinction between academic and communicative language proficiency. Whereas communicative language proficiency, as we have noted earlier, is highly contextualized and places modest cognitive demands on thinking, academic language proficiency has fewer contextual clues for meaning and is more conceptually demanding. Cummins' research, supported by Collier (1989), noted that academic language may take five to seven years or more to master, whereas communicative language skills require a much shorter period of time to acquire. Because academic language takes longer to learn, it makes sense to expose students as early as possible to integrated language and content instruction. To learn only communicative language skills in a traditional ESL classroom is insufficient preparation for the more demanding and specialized academic language

which all ELL students in public schools must eventually be able to use.

Approach In content-based ESL classrooms, teachers use the language of the content area as the foundation for designing instruction. The traditional approach would be to base the curriculum on controlled sequences of grammar and syntax. However, history texts require frequent use of the past tense, so it would be inappropriate to delay use of the past tense as in the typical language-based curriculum. The passive and conditional constructions typical of science texts require earlier exposure than appear in the typical language syllabus. Similarly, specialized vocabulary and concepts in mathematics call for early exposure and use, as evidenced in word problems and in math terms with nonmathematical meanings, like *table, round* and *root*. The demanding new terms and concepts in science, mathematics, and social studies need to be supported by specialized instruction.

Content-ESL teachers are trained in instructional techniques that give scaffolded support for learning content area language and concepts, including use of visuals, demonstrations, realia, graphic organizers, cooperative learning, and learning strategies (e.g., Chamot and O'Malley 1994a; Short 1991). These teachers introduce high priority concepts and language in theme-based content area instruction founded on analyses of content area curriculum frameworks, texts, and especially on collaboration with grade-level teachers. Content-ESL teachers also provide students with in-depth exposure to these concepts so that the basic foundations of learning in mathematics, science, and social studies are firmly established.

Implications for Assessment The integration of language and content presents major challenges in assessment for ESL and content area teachers. Integrated content classes are sometimes taught by ESL teachers and sometimes by content area specialists, depending on local policy and/or grade level. Regardless of who has responsibility for content-ESL classes, ESL and content teachers should work together to plan instruction and assessment. ESL teachers must become acquainted with the language and concepts in each of the content areas and the special instructional methods used in presenting them. They must also become acquainted with assessment procedures appropriate to each subject area. Similarly, content area teachers must become acquainted with special instructional approaches appropriate for ELL students but must also determine how to evaluate the learning of ELL students using classroom-based assessments.

Most classroom assessments in the content areas are heavily language dependent and confound the assessment of language and content (Short 1993). Students are typically required to read content passages in order to respond, or to express their understanding of concepts and procedures through writing. The challenge to ESL teachers in the content areas is to determine if ELL students understand the concepts and procedures integral to the subject area even though they are still learning English. While it might be desirable to isolate the assessment of language from the assessment of subject knowledge (Short 1993), the practical reality is that language and content are highly interdependent in most content areas.

We recommend three general procedures for adapting content area assessments to the needs of ESL students. First, rather than trying to separate language from content, teachers can reduce the language demands whenever necessary by *scaffolding*, (i.e., by providing contextual supports for meaning). This is similar to the kind of scaffolded instruction teachers use when presenting concepts through manipulatives, semantic maps, and other visuals. The scaffolding techniques we suggest for reducing language demands in assessing language and content include:

- *exhibits or projects:* involving students in presenting projects or demonstrations that illustrate concepts or procedures;

- *visual displays:* asking students to use graphic organizers, such as diagrams or semantic maps to show their understanding of vocabulary and concepts;

- *organized lists:* asking students to present lists of concepts or terms and then show understanding of how the concepts are organized or sequenced;

- *tables or graphs:* asking students to complete or construct and label tables and graphs showing they understand how data can be organized and interpreted; and

- *short answers:* asking students to give short answers or explanations that focus on content area concepts.

By reducing the language demands of the assessments, you increase the likelihood that ELL students will successfully reveal their strengths in the content areas. Multiple assessments adapted to the language proficiency of ELL students can assist in cross-checking identified areas of strength and educational need. To allow ELL students the opportunity to understand and process questions in English, we recommend giving flexible time limits to complete assessment tasks.

Other examples of scaffolded assessments that reduce language demands in the content areas are shown in Figure 7.1. Examples of different types of assessment are shown accompanied by a description of a scaffolded assessment and an unscaffolded assessment. The scaffolding techniques are presented in bold text. For example, students might be asked to define/describe an object or concept by giving a written description (unscaffolded) or providing labels for objects in a picture depicting the object or concept (scaffolded). Similarly, students might be asked to summarize textual material by identifying five main ideas and giving examples (unscaffolded) or by completing an outline or a semantic map (scaffolded) of the ideas. In mathematics, students could be asked to create a word problem by writing the numbers, the story, and the question (unscaffolded) or by completing an outline of the word problem using numbers and objects that are provided (scaffolded). In the section on authentic assessment later in this chapter, we give specific examples of these and other scaffolded assessments.

A second approach we recommend to address the needs of ELL students in assessing language and content is to use differentiated scoring. *Differentiated scoring* provides separate scores on written passages for language conventions and for content knowledge. That is, students might be

Figure 7.1 Assessment with/without Scaffolded Prompts

Assessment Examples	Without Scaffolding	With Scaffolding
Define/describe object or concept	Write a description of the object or concept and (if appropriate) label it	Write a **list** of the main features of the concept, or provide labels for objects in a **picture** that is **provided**
Provide examples of a concept and justify them	Provide 3 examples and explain orally or in writing why these are good examples	**Select** 3 examples from a **list provided** and explain **orally** why they were selected
Retell or summarize text	Write 5 main ideas from an article and give examples	Complete an **outline**, a **T-List**, or a **semantic map**
Write a word problem	Create a problem from own numbers; give equation, story, and question	Complete a word problem **given examples and an outline** of a sample problem
Summarize a science experiment	Write a summary of procedures in a science experiment following scientific principles	**Complete** a summary **given a list** of procedures in science experiments, including questions, materials, a plan, observations, and conclusions, or **demonstrate** the steps using actual materials

scored once for grammar and language mechanics and receive a separate score for the content of the written passage. The scoring of grammar might take into consideration sentence formation and word usage. Criteria used in the content scoring might provide ratings for understanding the concept, the accuracy of the response, and the methods students use to derive the answer. These separate scores provide the teacher and the student with information about the student's progress in both language and content and provide the teacher with guidance for planning future instruction.

A third general approach we recommend for meeting the needs of ELL students is to use *visible criteria*, (i.e., to provide students with information on how their work will be scored before the assessment is given). This approach is appropriate for assessment in any of the language skills but is particularly important for assessment in the content

areas when teachers are using differentiated scoring. The separate scores could be initially confusing to ELL students until they have had an opportunity to become acquainted with the scoring criteria. Students should be introduced gradually to the scoring procedures and be shown anchor papers or exhibitions at the different levels of scoring as a way of familiarizing them with the criteria. Students should have an opportunity to review and discuss the scoring criteria over a period of time to ensure that the criteria have become internalized.

INSTRUCTION IN GRADE-LEVEL CLASSROOMS

Before describing specific techniques for assessing content area knowledge and processes, we want to discuss some of the changes that have taken place in content area instruction over the past decade. These changes suggest expected areas of performance for all students in the curriculum areas and influence the type of assessments we need to discuss for ELL students.

Two major trends in grade-level classrooms emerging from educational reform are the thinking curriculum and the development of high standards of performance in the content areas. The need for reform has been indicated by declining scores on standardized tests and poor performance of U.S. students in comparison to their counterparts in other countries (Resnick and Resnick 1991; Stevenson 1993).

The Thinking Curriculum   The *thinking curriculum* specifies the types of higher-order mental processes that students engage in while learning (Resnick and Resnick 1991). These processes include solving routine and nonroutine problems and exercising personal judgment. The complex, technological nature of today's workplace calls for these kinds of higher-order skills. The traditional educational system was designed to ensure that all students were literate and possessed basic skills, but did not anticipate shifting demands in a complex work environment that call for more adaptive skills in addition to fundamental reading and computational literacy. In the past, higher-order thinking skills were reserved for more advanced students or those who mastered the basic skills with ease.

The thinking curriculum is designed for *all* students, not just for advanced students who have shown exceptional performance. As Resnick and Resnick (1991) note,

> It is new to seriously aspire to make thinking and problem solving regular aspects of the school program for the entire population, [for] minorities, non-English speakers, [and] children of the poor. (p. 39)

The reasoning behind this new view of educational reform is straightforward: a considerable body of research has shown that the kinds of reasoning and problem-solving skills advocated in the thinking curriculum are fundamental to learning. These thinking skills are not something reserved for certain types of problem solving encountered by only a few of the most advanced students. The thinking skills that are the subject of this new curriculum are used with activities that *all* students experience. They are the fundamental thinking and reasoning skills used in reading, writing, mathematics, science, and other core subjects. Furthermore, these thinking and reasoning skills are *essential* for successful performance in these core areas (Shepard 1989).

Young children enter school with reasonably sophisticated problem-solving routines for basic mathematical and reasoning tasks (Resnick and Resnick 1991). In both mathematics and science, effective students generate and test personal theories about the way in which the world operates, and either confirm or disconfirm the theories based on information they collect, organize, and interpret. Similarly, good readers have a goal, ask questions as they read, make predictions, make inferences, and summarize the text. Good writers plan and evaluate the progress and quality of their writing and revise as needed to clarify their thoughts.

The way in which literacy and mathematics are taught in traditional educational settings emphasizes memorization of facts and rules rather than use of reasoning and judgment. Many children discontinue effective problem-solving routines altogether or rely only on factual recall, while a few continue to use advanced thinking processes in reading, writing, and computation. According to this view, part of the failure of the education system has been the failure to match instruction to the most effective way that children learn. Thinking must "pervade the entire school curriculum for all students from the earliest grades" (Resnick and Resnick 1991, p. 40). The emphasis on thinking should accompany important concepts and knowledge taught in content area curricula. Too often, thinking has been treated as a special course taught outside the regular curriculum.

Standards of Performance   The second major effort in education reform is a call for higher standards of performance in the content areas for *all* students. The standards require a clear definition of what students should know and be able to do. The call for higher standards emerges in part from international comparisons with students in other countries, in part from analyses of the kinds of skills students will need in the future workplace, and in part from redefinitions of important student outcomes in the content areas (Simmons and Resnick 1993). The standards are important because teachers across the country vary dramatically in what they teach and how they teach. The result is that students have different levels of exposure to fundamental components of the curriculum and, consequently, achieve different types of outcomes. The development of uniform standards in the content areas does not mandate one curriculum or instructional approach, but it does require *all* students to attain designated standards of performance. The standards can be used to guide local emphases in instruction, select text materials, and develop new forms of assessment.

In response to this call for new standards of performance, educators across the disciplines have been preparing formal documents containing what they believe is important for students to learn. The National Council of Teachers of Mathematics (NCTM) (1989) was the first of many professional associations to draw on the expertise of teachers and other professionals in developing new ways of thinking about what students are expected to know and be able to do in their respective disciplines. Most of these professional associations are also developing standards for curriculum, teaching, and assessment. The disciplines working on standards include science, social studies, and language arts (O'Neil 1993).

A representative set of standards in English language arts, geography, history/civics, mathematics, and sciences is presented in Figure 7.2. This figure, adapted from materials developed by the Council for Basic Education (CBE) (1994), is intended to illustrate and provide an update on the various standards being developed in the content areas by professional organizations and associations. The vision statement shown on the figure for each content area represents desired goals that "guide a child's education." The vision is reflected in the various standards presented at grades 4, 8, and 12. CBE selected these grades because they represent key grades in a child's education and because they overlap with the grades used in the National Assessment of Educational Progress (NAEP). Related standards across content areas are cross-referenced by various symbols:

○ English language arts

❏ geography

◗ history/civics

■ mathematics

▼ science

This cross-referencing system shows the connections between the subject areas and provides ideas on how teachers can integrate their curriculum. The original CBE chart is more extensive and contains standards for art and foreign languages as well. We have abbreviated the original chart to focus on standards we thought to be of most interest to teachers of ELL students and to cover only the content areas that we address in this book. CBE cautions that the table is not complete and represents, in some cases, standards in the process of development by the respective professional associations.

You can use Figure 7.2 in at least three ways. First, you can use the table shown in this figure to understand the kinds of standards being discussed for native speakers of English in grade-level classrooms. These standards go far beyond basic skills such as decoding for reading and computation in math. Included among them are standards for listening and speaking as well as for reading and writing, for understanding and using content information, for using learning strategies, for using information obtained from peers to interpret texts, and for self-evaluation of content knowledge and skills. The standards focus on applications of knowledge in a variety of ways that will have practical utility for students in school, at work, and in the community. These standards have implications for the ing of ELL students throughout their participation in ESL and bilingual programs, but especially as these students approach readiness for grade-level instruction.

A second use of the table is as a basis for identifying content area emphases for your own curriculum and assessments. Educators in state agencies and school districts should determine their own standards of performance for students, using standards from the professional associations as a guide. You can compare this or other subject area tables

Figure 7.2 Standards of Performance in the Content Areas

Subject	Vision	Grade 4	Grade 8	Grade 12
○ English Language Arts	• Read and listen interpretively and critically; find pleasure and satisfaction in reading and writing. • Write and speak English effectively and eloquently to various audiences for various purposes. • Understand literature as the written expression of the human imagination and as a transmitter of culture and values. • Analyze, classify, compare and contrast language and literature; make inferences; and draw conclusions from a variety of oral and written texts.	• Decipher unfamiliar words and meanings in texts, employing a variety of strategies (including sound/letter relationships) and resources. • Understand unfamiliar oral or written texts by using prior knowledge. ▼ ◗ • Read and listen critically and interpretively; respond personally to, and comprehend the literal messages of, a variety of texts, including poems, essays, stories, and exposition. ◗ • Recognize and write in a variety of forms, including narratives, journals, stories, poetry, exposition, articles, and instructions, for many purposes and audiences. ◗ ❑ • Read, comprehend, discuss, and interpret literature of various cultures and eras. ◗ ❑ ▼	• Select, summarize, paraphrase, and analyze important passages of texts. • Analyze and construct the meaning of oral discourse delivered for various purposes, including lectures and discussions. • Generate ideas for writing, select and arrange them, express them, and revise what has been written. ❑ ◗ ■ ▼ • Formulate questions and produce information using research tools, such as encyclopedias, almanacs, and computer databases and keep track of sources. ◗ ▼ • Evaluate and make valid inferences from literature of different cultures and eras, including ancient cultures. ◗ ❑	• Analyze the structure, language, and content of oral discourse (lectures, discussions) in other disciplines. ❑ ◗ ■ ▼ • Read critically non-literary documents and articles associated with other disciplines. • Use language effectively to convey knowledge, meaning, and community; evaluate one's own language use; and evaluate how others use language for effect. • Analyze and evaluate world literature, using knowledge of historical eras and of the role of literature as a transmitter of culture and values. ◗ ❑ ▼
❑ Geography	• Understand why people live in certain places for reasons of climate and topography. • Understand the geographic background of local, national, and global events and conditions.	• Compare one's own community with other communities, compare rural and urban environments. ◗ • Use distance, direction, and scale symbols. ■ ▼ • Analyze environmental changes in terms of positive/negative consequences. ◗ ▼	• Use latitude and longitude, maps, charts, graphs, and tables to display data. ■ • Map the physical and cultural areas and regions in North America; describe economic areas and map the relationship between resources and industry. ◗ ○ ▼	• Describe the significance of state and regional geography in terms of economic, historical, and social conditions. ◗ • Describe interrelated global patterns, such as atmospheric and oceanic circulation, land forms, climate, transportation and communication, and cultural diffusion. ▼ ○ ■

Adapted from Council for Basic Education (1994).

Figure 7.2   **Standards of Performance in the Content Areas (continued)**

Subject	Vision	Grade 4	Grade 8	Grade 12
❑Geography (continued)	• Perceive the factors surrounding environmental degradation, the rational use of ocean resources, and nuclear arms and energy. • Understand that relationships between people, places, and environments depend on an understanding of space.	• Locate and describe major geographical features and regions, and compare and contrast them. • Discuss how regions are defined; compare and contrast regions on a state, national, or world basis using case studies of different peoples, cultures, and environments. ■▼	• Identify global problems (e.g., deforestation, pollution, overfishing) and offer suggestions for improvement in both developing and developed nations. ▼▸■ • Plot distributions of population and key resources on regional maps. ▸▼■	• Understand processes shaping the physical environment; how water cycles and tectonic and erosion processes relate to land forms, climate, and oceans. ▼ • Explore the origin and spread of cultures and the human use of the habitat, its resources, and its impact on ecology. ○▸■▼
▸History/ Civics	• Explain the sequence of and connections among events in world history. • Describe the development of the United States and its role in world history. • Offer specific examples of the interplay of change and continuity in history • Recognize the difference between fact and conjecture, evidence and assertion. • Understand the economic problems and institutions of the nation and world; make reasoned decisions as citizens, workers, consumers, and members of civic groups. • Demonstrate a tolerance for ambiguity and understand that not all societal problems have single solutions	• Discuss the main ideas of the basic documents of the United States— Declaration of Independence, Constitution, Bill of Rights. • Understand past events and issues as they occurred at the time. ○❑■▼ • Give examples of the significance of change, location, diversity, justice, power, and compromise in local history. ❑ • Understand the variety of family, work, and government systems of the world and how communities fit into the larger picture. • Recognize the relationships between human activities and various locations, e.g. (work, recreation, shopping, education, and religion). ❑	• Present the story of the U.S. as the creation of a new nation. ○❑■▼ • Present an overview of the economic and political development of the U.S. through World War I and its changing social, economic, and political relationships with the rest of the world. ○▼❑ • Understand the early history of Western and non-Western civilizations, including the Near East and Africa, ancient Hebrew civilizations, Greece, Rome, and the classic civilizations of India and China. ○❑■▼ • Examine social, cultural, and technological changes in early and modern times. ○❑■	• Explain the changing role of the U.S. in WWI and WWII, during the Cold War, and in global economic relations; analyze what has/has not worked and why. ❑ • Act as a responsible citizen within community and state. • Know the basic beliefs of the world's principal religions. • Apply tools such as graphs, statistics, and equations to understand economics. ■▼ • Discuss the distinctively American tensions between liberty and equality, liberty and order, region and nation, individualism and the common welfare, and cultural diversity and civic unity. ❑

Adapted from Council for Basic Education (1994).

Figure 7.2   **Standards of Performance in the Content Areas (continued)**

Subject	Vision	Grade 4	Grade 8	Grade 12
▶History/ Civics (continued)		• Tell the stories of different peoples living under different conditions of work, geography, and tradition. ❑ ○ ▼	• Compare/contrast socialism, capitalism, and communism. ❑ ○ ▼	
■Mathematics	• Understand mathematics as a science of patterns. • Think and reason mathematically and apply mathematics to various situations. • Understand the value of mathematics. • Understand the connections among related mathematical concepts; apply these concepts to other content areas. • Understand algebra and geometry and know how and when to use them. • Use the power of reasoning to explore, make conjectures, and validate solutions. • Read, hear, write, and speak about mathematics in both everyday and mathematical language.	• Add, subtract, multiply, and divide. • Understand and use numbers, place value, fractions, decimals, and estimation. • Use arithmetic to solve problems, use calculators for computation, and explain solutions. • Understand the properties of geometric figures and relationships. • Collect and organize statistical data, begin to understand chance and probability, and recognize patterns. ▼ • Solve and create real-world problems. ▼ ❑ ▶ • Begin to see the connections between mathematics and other content areas. ○ ❑ ▶ ▼ • Understand and apply the basic concepts of measurement, such as length, weight, mass, area, volume, time, temperature, and angle using metric and non-metric systems. ▼	• Use mathematics to reason inductively and deductively with proportions/graphs. • Make connections between related mathematical concepts and apply these concepts to other content areas. ○ ❑ ▶ ▼ • Develop a sense of numbers and operations, estimate for solving problems, and check the reasonableness of results. • Create algorithms; develop and use tables, graphs, and rules; and interpret mathematical representations. ▼ • Use statistical methods to describe, analyze, evaluate, and make decisions. ▼ ○ • Model situations involving probability. ▼ • Use basic geometry to solve problems.	• Explore connections between a problem situation, its model as a function in symbolic form, and the graph of that function. • Use computer-based methods, such as successive approximations and graphing, for solving equations and inequalities. ▼ • Solve real-world problems using algebra. ○ ▼ • Construct and draw statistical inferences from charts, tables, and graphs that summarize data from real-world situations. ▶ ❑ ▼ • Use probability to represent and solve problems involving uncertainty. ▼ ○ • Communicate problem situations and their solutions using oral, written, and graphic forms, including graphs, matrices, sequences, and recurrence relations. ○ ❑ ▼ ▶

Adapted from Council for Basic Education (1994).

Figure 7.2   Standards of Performance in the Content Areas (continued)

Subject	Vision	Grade 4	Grade 8	Grade 12
▼Science	• Know when and how to use scientific knowledge and habits of mind. • Understand measurement and mathematics as essential components of the sciences. • Understand the growth of scientific ideas, the roles played by diverse investigators and commentators, and the interplay between evidence and theory over time. • Know how to use accurately and safely scientific equipment and materials.	• Write and speak with clarity about observations and experiments; understand the importance of keeping records during experiments. • Collect, sort, catalog, and classify; calculate; observe, take notes, and sketch; interview, poll, and survey; and use hand lenses, microscopes, thermometers, cameras, and other common instruments. ○ ■ • Understand cause and effect; that evidence is imperative for the confirmation of theory; and that scientific theories are based on evidence and thought. • Begin to see the relationships between systems and parts. ■ • Begin to understand the concepts of the living environment, including balance, heredity, life cycles, nutrition, and energy. ❑ ■ • Construct models to scale. ■ ❐ • Begin to understand the physical properties of the earth and universe, including light, temperature, weight, and gravity. ■ ❑	• Understand the vastness of the universe and the place of our solar system in it, including the relation of the earth to the sun and other planets, the relation of the moon to the earth, and their orbits. ❑ ❐ ■ • Understand the fragility of the earth's balance and the effect human activity can have on the environment's capacity to support all forms of life. ❑ ❐ • Analyze the composition of matter and how different substances interact; understand the conservation of matter. • Connect the Periodic Table of Elements and its divisions to atomic structure and what that structure means. ■ • Analyze the interdependence of earth systems (i.e., water cycle, carbon cycle, nitrogen cycle, rock cycle) and of organisms within the food web. ❑ ■ • Understand plant and animal reproduction.	• Distinguish between scientific evidence and personal opinion. ○ • Understand the unifying concepts of the life and physical sciences, such as cell theory, geological evolution, organic evolution, atomic structure, chemical bonding, and transformation of energy. ❑ ■ • Draw conclusions and make inferences from data; select and apply mathematical relationships to describe results obtained by observation and experimentation; interpret, in nonmathematical language, relationships shown in mathematical form. ❐ ○ ■ • Understand the central concepts, principles, and basic factual material of chemistry, biology, and physics. ❑ ■ • Understand that scientists assume that the universe is a vast single system in which the same basic rules apply, but that change and continuity are persistent features of science. ❑ ■

Adapted from Council for Basic Education (1994).

with local curriculum specifications in selecting important content for ELL students. The table may give teachers ideas for expanding local curriculum objectives and may signal for ESL teachers the curriculum areas that should be treated in depth during instruction. You can also use the table to verify that the content you have selected for assessment represents important objectives and standards of performance. You will find assessment activities in this book for some of the standards identified in the table.

Third, you can use this chart as the basis for establishing your own standards of performance in ESL. The development of standards across the curriculum areas has promoted interest in standards development among professionals in ESL (Genesee 1994). The Teachers of English to Speakers of Other Languages (TESOL), the major professional association for ESL teachers, has a Task Force on K-12 Policy and Standards for ESL Students that is conducting work on standards. The association sees these types of standards as essential for providing guidance and direction in the education of ELL students. Other groups are also collaborating to set suitable standards for ELL students (Hakuta, August, and Pompa 1994). We encourage all teachers to begin the process of reviewing and developing local standards for ESL, English language arts, and the content areas that will be used with ELL students.

Implications for Assessment   Education reform that embodies a thinking curriculum and higher standards of performance for all students has serious consequences for assessment. Resnick (1987) suggests that traditional forms of assessment may "interfere" with the kinds of higher-order skills being encouraged in the content areas. Analyses of standardized tests have revealed that the tests may contain significant gaps in the kinds of skills being advanced in the thinking curriculum or in the movement toward new standards (e.g., Romberg and Wilson 1992). Two simple principles sometimes used in analyzing and developing new forms of assessment are as follows (Resnick and Resnick 1991):

1. *You get what you assess.* Teachers will teach to the tests if the tests have an impact on them or on their students. If teachers use multiple-choice tests, they will spend time giving students practice on those types of items rather than on constructed responses, discussions, problem solving, and essays.

2. *You do not get what you do not assess.* Information and skills that do not appear on tests will disappear from classrooms over time. Educators must include problem solving and other important thinking skills in their assessments if these processes are expected to survive in the curriculum.

This second principle is illustrated in ESL classrooms by a teacher who told one of the authors she did not teach oral proficiency "because the county doesn't assess that any more." This teacher did not include instructional opportunities to strengthen oral language development simply because it was not tested, even though oral proficiency was part of the county curriculum and was reportedly valued by the teacher. We can use both principles for guidance as we consider the development of new forms of assessment.

Authentic Assessment in Content Areas

. . . .

Assessments of content knowledge and skills should be interpreted in the context of background information collected about students. Teachers of ELL students may have to exercise considerable initiative to obtain this information. The information is particularly important for new ELL students in your school, whether they come directly from other countries or from other U.S. schools. The background information should include answers to the following questions, where available (adapted from Hamayan and Perlman 1990):

1. How much content area instruction has the student received and in which language?

2. What content area textbooks was the student exposed to? In what language?

3. If the student was in a U.S. bilingual program, what content curriculum was covered in the student's native language and what was covered in English?

Answers to these questions will assist you in making initial decisions about the types of assessment each student will be able to respond to. Students who have little exposure to U.S. schools and little familiarity with English may require more scaffolding in their assessment than other students.

In the following sections, we begin with a description of basic assessment techniques that cut across content areas and continue with assessments specific to science, mathematics, and social studies. Assessment information obtained from any of the procedures described should always be interpreted in the light of other information known about the student, including background information and classroom performance.

BASIC ASSESSMENT APPROACHES

In assessing ELL students in the content areas, the first thing you will want to determine is the kind of background knowledge students have when they come to your classroom. As you provide content-ESL instruction to these students, you will be interested in monitoring their conceptual knowledge, reading comprehension, vocabulary skills, thinking skills, and the extent to which they can construct written responses to content area prompts. The sections which follow contain sample assessments that will assist you in collecting this type of information. Many of these general assessment techniques can be used across the content areas, across grade levels, and in the native language of the students.

Prior Knowledge   The assessment of background knowledge is essential because new information in content areas is learned most effectively by building on prior knowledge (Gagné, Yekovich, and Yekovich 1993; Jones et al. 1987). Teachers should determine what students know about new information to be presented, how this information is organized in the student's memory, and how the information can be retrieved effectively for future learning. Too often, ELL students believe that any

information they possess in their native language is irrelevant to what they will be learning in English, when in fact the concepts and the way that the information is organized in memory are critical to facilitate new learning (Gagné et al. 1994; O'Malley and Chamot 1990).

A variety of techniques by which you can determine what your students know about new content information are presented in Figure 7.3. There are six techniques for eliciting prior knowledge in Figure 7.3, accompanied by a specific example and a list of advantages and disadvantages (adapted from Holmes and Roser 1987). The advantages and disadvantages concern the amount of time you must spend in preparing for the assessment, the language demands on the student, the amount of time spent in conducting the assessment, and the type of information you obtain. You can ask questions for eliciting prior knowledge orally or in writing. Many of the procedures are scaffolded so that students can respond even with a minimum of English proficiency. We have tried to list these from top to bottom in terms of increased language demand.

We suggest that you review the different ways of assessing background knowledge in Figure 7.3, identify one or more approaches that are appropriate to your students, and try them out to determine if they accomplish what you need. Because the examples provided are limited to a specific science topic, you will need to generate your own examples in science, social studies, or literature. You may want to try out a number of these approaches until you settle on the one(s) that seem most suitable for your students. The approaches you find most helpful should change as your students acquire increased language skills.

Conceptual Knowledge   Assessing what ELL students know about content area information and procedures can be aided with the use of semantic maps. A *semantic map* enables students to represent the concepts and relationships in texts with geometric shapes (Schmidt 1986). Semantic maps were originally designed to enable students to take notes and to represent information. While the semantic map may be a useful learning device for any student, it may be particularly useful for stu-

Figure 7.3   Procedures for Assessing What Students Know in Science

Technique/Description	Example	Advantage	Disadvantage
Nonverbal: Ss follow directions or act out without speaking.	T: *Make a sound like a snake. Find a picture of a snake. Draw a snake. Do something a snake does.*	Useful with students at beginning level of proficiency	Does not assess oral production or writing
Recognition: T asks specific questions with answer options. Asks Ss to choose the one correct answer.	T: *Cold-blooded means (a) having cold blood, (b) having constant body temperature, (c) changing body temperature to one's surroundings, (d) never being too hot.*	Good for finding out what Ss know, and very efficient to administer	Takes lots of time and skill to prepare items; limits information obtained; may not assess thinking skills as effectively as other techniques
Structured Questions: T asks students probe questions about a topic.	T: (1) *Does a snake keep the same skin all its life?* (2) *What happens to it?* (3) *How does the skin come off?* (4) *How often does it come off?*	Elicits the most information per minute of assessment time	May limit information obtained; requires preparation
Unstructured Discussion: T asks Ss to tell about personal experiences on the topic.	T: *Have you ever seen or touched a snake? What happened? What did it feel like?*	Useful for motivation of Ss; can be used to explore Ss' organization of knowledge	Not very efficient if time is limited
Free Recall: T asks Ss to describe what they know about a given topic.	T: *Let's write a story with everything there is to know about snakes. What should it say?* (Ss respond.) *Are you sure that's everything?*	Takes least T preparation time; requires only one probe	Ss must have adequate language and organization of knowledge to respond
Word Association: T asks Ss to play a word game in which T says a word and Ss say everything they can think of.	T: *Tell me everything you can think of about the way snakes move.*	Easy to use; easy to prepare for; gives more information than free recall	May be time consuming; Ss may get side-tracked

T = Teacher, S = Student

Adapted from Holmes and Roser (1987).

dents who consider themselves to be visual learners or for ELL students.

Four common types of maps are shown in Figure 7.4, Semantic Maps for Instruction and Assessment. The shape of the map communicates the type of information it captures most effectively. The first semantic map is a "spider" diagram, indicated in Figure 7.4(a). The spider map is useful in representing the main idea and supporting details of paragraphs. The spider map may have any number of appendages and the "legs" can go off in any direction, depending on the concepts represented. The second map is a "time ladder" diagram, shown in Figure 7.4(b). The time ladder map is particularly good at showing sequences of events, noted on this version as a descending ladder from top to bottom. The "contrast overlay" map shown in Figure 7.4(c) is a Venn diagram and is useful in making comparison/contrasts between two concepts. The diagram shows the areas of independence and overlap in the concepts illustrated. The last map, a "cause/effect" diagram indicated in Figure 7.4(d), shows relationships in which one concept or event causes another. Sometimes cause/effect maps are used to show multiple causation or chain reactions.

In addition to their uses in note-taking, semantic maps can be used to assess understanding of concepts in the content areas or to assess depth of knowledge for vocabulary. By showing their understanding of the hierarchies and connections between concepts, students demonstrate more than the ability to simply recognize or repeat accurate definitions of terms. Semantic maps are particularly effective in scaffolding the assessment for beginning and intermediate-level ELL students. Give your students prior instruction and experience in this form of note-taking prior to using it for assessment. During the assessment, you can ask students to read or listen to any content area textual information and perform one of the following: (1) draw and label one of the diagrams, (2) label an existing diagram that you have provided, or (3) complete a diagram that you have partially labeled. The scaffolding evident in options (2) and (3) will be useful when the students' limited proficiency in English is an obstacle to constructing their own diagrams.

Reading Comprehension Reading in the content areas for ELL students requires them to overcome numerous challenges. The vocabulary and concepts introduced in the content areas are only the beginning of these challenges. The student is called on to think and reason using the language of the content area. The discourse structure of content area texts differs from the structure of texts in literature and often differs from one content area to another. Diagrams and charts require interpretation and integration with the text information. The simple process of pausing occasionally to paraphrase or summarize the text requires demanding mental processing. Taking notes can require extensive time to think through the language appropriate for expressing the gist of the text. (See Chapter 5 for more information on assessment of reading.)

There are a variety of ways teachers can assess reading comprehension in the content areas. You can ask students to display written notes on the reading, to discuss the reading in small groups, to respond to short-answer or multiple-choice items on the reading, and to summarize their understanding of the reading either orally or in writing. Asking students to display written notes can be particularly effective if the students have been given prior instruction on specific methods of note-taking, such as semantic maps or T-Lists. The *T-List* is a technique in which students draw a large "T" on the page and enumerate main ideas to the left of the vertical line and corresponding details to the right (Chamot and O'Malley 1994a; Hamp-Lyons 1983). The T-List indicated in Figure 7.5 is pre-structured with three main ideas and a few details corresponding to each main idea. You can scaffold T-Lists just like a semantic map by providing a diagram with selected entries completed or a diagram with only the lines completed, or by simply asking students to complete a T-List given only a blank piece of paper. Semantic maps and T-Lists are useful assessment techniques at all levels of English proficiency.

Another way to assess reading comprehension in the content areas is through the cloze test. While we have discussed cloze tests in Chapter 5 on reading assessment, we mention them here again

Figure 7.4   Semantic Maps for Content Area Assessment

(a) The Spider Map: Main Ideas and Details

The Gutierrez family has a favorite vacation place. There is a lake nearby for water skiing and boating. They can also play basketball and go hiking. Tennis courts and a swimming pool are close to their cabin.

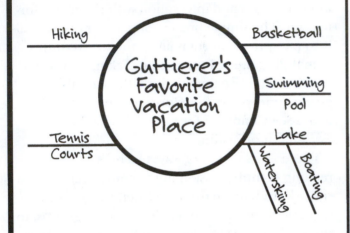

(b) The Time Ladder Map

It was already dark by the time Beth and María left the library. They immediately started walking as quickly as possible to the bus stop. Unfortunately, the bus had already left when they got there. They had to telephone María's mother for a ride home.

(c) Contrast Overlay Map

The computer and the human mind are very much alike. Both can store and recall information. However, the computer must be told what to do with the information. The human mind can invent new and different ways to use information.

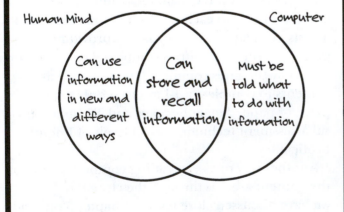

(d) The Cause/Effect Map

Hundreds of years ago a fierce group of people called the Huns attacked China. The Huns wanted to conquer China. The Chinese built a huge wall 1,500 miles long to keep the Huns out of China. The wall is still standing today.

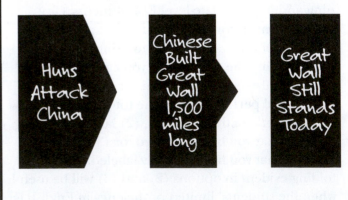

Adapted from Schmidt (1986).

Figure 7.5   Sample T-List

Main Ideas	Details
Different types of clouds	(1) cirrus—they are fluffy
	(2) cumulus—bunch together
	(3) nimbus—gray cloud across the entire sky

Adapted from Chamot and O'Malley (1994) and Hamp-Lyons (1983).

because assessment in the content areas with cloze tests has some unique features. The *cloze* procedure possesses the following characteristics that make it desirable for classroom assessment: (1) teachers can easily construct their own cloze tests, (2) cloze tests can be constructed from any text that is used for instruction, (3) cloze tests can be group administered, (4) standards are established based on a criterion of performance rather than on a normative comparison with other students, and (5) cloze tests are useful in identifying the reading materials that best enable a student to profit from instruction (Pikulski and Tobin 1982). It is this latter feature that makes cloze tests particularly attractive to teachers of ELL students.

In the typical cloze test, every fifth, seventh or ninth word is deleted from a reading passage and the student is asked to fill in the missing word. Called a *fixed ratio cloze*, this is also often referred to as a *random deletion* cloze because the words deleted have no systematic relationship to each other. It is this form of cloze that is typically recommended for either of two purposes: (1) to assist in identifying reading materials and ungraded instructional materials; or (2) to evaluate the appropriateness of a content area text for the reading level of the student. (See Chapter 5 for details on the procedures for constructing random deletion/fixed ratio cloze tests.)

One use of the cloze test is to assess student mastery of content area instruction. In a *rational* or *purposive deletion cloze*, you can delete key content area words that represent important vocabulary or concepts. We suggest that you follow the same guidelines as in constructing a random deletion cloze except that the deletion interval (e.g., every seventh word) can vary somewhat to meet the purpose of deleting key words. The purposive deletion cloze has no empirical evidence to indicate that it can be used to evaluate the effectiveness of instruction, even though it seems reasonable to use it for this purpose (Pikulski and Tobin 1982). Similar guidelines to those used in constructing random deletion cloze tests should be followed concerning passage length and type of passage. However, in scoring, credit should be given for synonyms and other substitutions which indicate that students understand the concepts on which they are being evaluated.

The purposive deletion cloze can be combined with a *limited cloze*, in which you provide students with a list of the words that have been deleted. In this procedure, the deleted words are randomly listto fill in the blanks. In scoring a limited cloze, credit should be given only for exact words rather than synonyms. Neither the purposive deletion nor the limited cloze can be converted directly to yield readability indices (see Chapter 5) as can the random deletion cloze (Pikulski and Tobin 1982).

Vocabulary   Classroom assessments of vocabulary in content areas typically measure knowledge superficially by asking for definitions or, at best, associations. There is also heavy reliance on multiple-choice or matching items to assess vocabulary. The traditional instructional process is that students are given word lists which they look up in a dictionary, followed by practice in a definition or synonym exercise, and then are tested on using a multiple-choice format (Simpson 1987). The problem with this approach is that it assesses rote understanding of the terms rather than full understanding of the concepts underlying them.

A number of alternative ways of assessing vocabulary have been proposed (Simpson 1987). These include the following:

1. *Recognizing and generating attributes, examples, and nonexamples.* In assessing vocabulary, you can ask students to present an example of a concept. In a content area lesson on civics, you might ask students to provide an example of a right guaranteed in the Bill of Rights. In a lesson on magnetism, you can ask students to list examples and nonexamples of objects that are attracted to a magnet or magnetic field. In math, you can ask students to use a geoboard[1] and explain the unique features of a shape they have constructed.

1. A *geoboard* is a board approximately 6″ x 6″ x 1″ with twenty-five one-inch pegs extending perpendicularly from the surface in five rows and five columns. Teachers ask students to make figures of varying shapes (square, triangle, rectangle, etc.) on the pegs using a rubber band. One advantage of the geoboard is that students can easily display their work and, therefore, show their understanding of math concepts. Teachers often ask students to classify their figures, explain why the specific shapes go together, and explain the unique characteristics of each shape.

2. *Sensing and inferring relationships.* Three recommended procedures for assessing vocabulary through inferred relationships are:

- Create *paired-word questions* and ask if two words would ever go together and why or why not. For example, in a social studies lesson on human activities, ask how the terms *work* and *recreation* do or do not go together. In a lesson on physical science, you might ask how the terms *light* and *temperature* do or do not fit with each other.

- Ask students to provide and explain *analogies.* An example in science drawn from a lesson on the five vertebrate groups (fish, amphibians, reptiles, birds, and mammals) is to supply the missing word in the following: Trout is to fish as dog is to (mammal).

- Ask students to *classify* a list of objects or concepts by using category labels, a classification table, a Venn diagram, or a semantic map. In the lesson on vertebrates, you might ask students to classify the members of a list and explain why they go together.

3. *Applying concepts to a variety of contexts.* Students can demonstrate their understanding of the contexts in which vocabulary words can be used by sentence rewriting, as when they are asked to change a sentence so that it includes a specific word. An example might be to change the following sentence to include the word *judgment:* "His decision was based on firm evidence." (His judgment was based on firm evidence.)

4. *Generating novel contexts.* You can ask students to generate a novel sentence in which two words can be used simultaneously. An example from social studies is as follows: "Use the words *citizen* and *democracy* in a sentence." (Citizens in a democracy are able to vote.)

In assessing vocabulary, whatever procedure you select, match the item format to the subject area, the unit objectives, and the instructional strategies you use to introduce and reinforce vocabulary. You should introduce and familiarize students with the various formats before using them on assessments. Also, be sure to vary the formats across units and tests so that students do not become familiar with only one type of question. The procedures above should be reasonably easy to construct and to match with your instructional goals and procedures (Simpson 1987).

Thinking Skills The development of thinking skills in today's curriculum is emphasized both in the thinking curriculum (Resnick and Resnick 1991) and in the new standards of performance advocated by professional associations (CBE 1994). Thinking skills are also emphasized in a variety of publications emerging on instruction and assessment (e.g., Ennis 1993; Marzano, Pickering, and McTighe 1993; Stiggins, Rubel, and Quellmalz 1986). A variety of state curriculum frameworks also emphasize thinking skills, such as those in California, Connecticut, Colorado, and Vermont. As a teacher of ELL students, you can assess these higher-order thinking skills, even among students with beginning-level skills in English, if you use a variety of scaffolded techniques that enable students to respond appropriately.

In the following discussion we focus on an adaptation of the taxonomy used by Stiggins, Rubel, and Quellmalz (1986) in their monograph on measuring thinking skills in the classroom. We show how the assessment of these skills can be made accessible for ELL students at all levels of proficiency through scaffolding and make suggestions concerning assessment in selected content areas. Teachers will benefit from assessment of thinking skills in two important ways: (1) You will be able to determine how students are performing in an important part of the curriculum, and (2) you will be able to provide feedback to students about the types of thinking that will aid them in becoming more effective classroom learners. The guidelines we provide on the assessment of thinking skills also suggest how thinking skills can be integrated with content area instruction.

We begin with a taxonomy of thinking skills derived from Stiggins, Rubel, and Quellmalz (1986) that identifies five levels of thinking in the cognitive domain, as shown in Figure 7.6. We use five basic thinking skills: comprehension, analysis,

Figure 7.6 Definitions and Examples of Thinking Skills in the Content Areas

Thinking Skill	Definition	Reading	Mathematics	Social Studies	Science
Comprehension	• Recall or paraphrase information	• Respond to texts, comprehend the literal meaning, and infer meanings	• Recognize and use numbers in computation with the four operations, recognize place value, and use fractions and decimals	• Understand the variety of systems of government • Understand past events and issues as they occurred • Understand main ideas of basic documents in the United States government	• Understand procedures of scientific inquiry • Begin to understand the physical properties of the earth and universe, including light, temperature, weight, and gravity
Analysis	• Divide a whole into component elements, including part/whole, cause-effect, or elements in a sequence	• Identify components of literary, expository, and persuasive discourse • Analyze the structure, language, and content of oral or written discourse	• Use arithmetic appropriate to solve a problem and explain solutions • Identify the properties of geometric figures and their relationships	• Examine social, cultural, and technological changes in early and modern times • Explain the changing role of the U.S. in WWI, WWII, the cold war, and in global economic relations; analyze what has/has not worked and why	• Understand cause/effect • See the relationships between systems and parts • Analyze the composition of matter, and how different substances interact • Analyze the interdependence of earth systems
Comparison	• Recognize or explain similarities and differences based on one or more attributes	• Make connections both within and among oral and written texts • Make connections between text and prior knowledge	• Make connections between related mathematical concepts and apply these concepts to other content areas • Express a rational number in a variety of forms, including fractions, decimals, percents	• Compare/contrast socialism, capitalism, and communism • Know the basic beliefs of the world's principal religions • Discuss the American tensions between liberty and equality, liberty and order, etc.	• Collect, sort, catalog, and classify objects and materials
Synthesis	• Combine elements to form a unified whole or to form a generalization from knowledge of elements • Use deductive and inductive reasoning	• Draw on literary and non-literary documents in reaching generalizations or conclusions	• Create and solve real-world problems • Apply the basic concepts of measurement in solving problems	• Show relationships among the variety of family, work, and government systems of the world and how communities fit into the larger picture	• Connect the Periodic Table of Elements and its divisions to atomic structure and summarize what the structure means • See the relationship between systems and parts
Evaluation	• Judge the quality, worth, or credibility of information or arguments	• Evaluate believability, significance, form, completeness, clarity • Evaluate one's own language and how others use language for effect	• Use estimation for solving problems, and check the reasonableness of results • Use statistical methods to describe, analyze, evaluate, and make decisions	• Give examples of the significance of change, location, diversity, justice, power, and compromise in local history • Act as a responsible citizen within community and state	• Distinguish between scientific evidence and personal opinion • Show how evidence is needed to confirm a theory

Extracted from Council on Basic Education (1994).

comparison, synthesis, and evaluation. Each of these terms is defined in the table and accompanied by a variety of examples from the content areas. While there are a number of ways of organizing thinking skills (e.g., Bloom et al. 1956; Marzano, Pickering, and McTighe 1993), we have adapted the Stiggins et al. approach because of its simplicity and familiarity to most teachers. The thinking skills we use in the examples are drawn from the standards for language arts, social sciences, mathematics, and science presented in Figure 7.2.

Teachers can use Figure 7.6 in several ways. First, the table can be used to develop an understanding of the various levels of thinking skills that are being emphasized in curricula for grade-level students. The connection between the standards of performance shown in Figure 7.2 and the thinking skills illustrated here confirms that all students are being expected to know and be able to use complex reasoning and thinking in the content areas. A second way that this table can be used is to guide instruction in thinking skills for ELL students. Teachers should begin to introduce their ELL students to these ways of thinking and reasoning as they integrate language and content in their classrooms. While language required to introduce and discuss many of the examples in Figure 7.6 may seem to be beyond most ELL students, a number of ESL instructional guides contain ways that these concepts can be introduced through scaffolded instruction (e.g., Chamot and O'Malley 1994a; Short 1991). The third way Figure 7.6 can be used is to guide assessment. Teachers in content-ESL should ask students questions orally and in writing that build on these levels of thinking.

Examples of questions that elicit specific thinking skills are shown in Figure 7.7 (adapted from materials developed by the Maryland State Department of Education, n.d.). The five levels of thinking illustrated in Figure 7.6 are included along with a Knowledge level for simple identification and recall of information. At each level, specific examples are given indicating how to ask questions of students corresponding to that level of thinking. At the Analysis level, you can ask students to classify or organize materials or concepts. Two simple dimensions for organizing objects might be color

and shape. More abstract dimensions for classifying conceptual knowledge might be a literary theme and the roles of different individuals in an historical event.

Figure 7.7 is formatted like an individual student record for convenience, with a space for student and teacher name. Columns are provided to indicate student performance by week, school quarter, or any other period over which you wish to observe and record an individual student's behavior. The marks placed on the form indicate X = Performs without Assistance, / = Performs with Assistance, and — = Needs Work. The assistance provided can be from the teacher, an aide, or a peer working in a cooperative learning group. This form for rating student performance is based in part on Vygotsky's zone of proximal development, in which performance is evaluated based on the degree to which students can complete tasks independently or with scaffolded assistance (Brown and Ferrara 1985). In Vygotsky's theory, cognitive processes are gradually internalized through shared, interactive processes. Thus, it is extremely important for teachers to record information on what students can do with scaffolded support and without assistance. In order to verify that these ratings of student performance are reliable, teachers will need to compare their criteria, tasks, scaffolding, and ratings with those used by other teachers.

The questions or probes presented in Figure 7.7 vary in terms of the language demand and the scaffolding provided for the student. At any of the levels, you can ask students to indicate agreement with an example of the thinking skill or to produce the example themselves. That is, students can demonstrate Evaluation as a thinking skill by selecting a statement pointing to the significance of the Civil War or by giving three examples why the Civil War is a significant event in U.S. history. To demonstrate Synthesis as a thinking skill, students can be asked to add two concepts to a partially completed semantic map or be asked to provide a solution for a real-world problem, such as pollution. We suggest that you review these various ways of asking questions and ensure that you weave each type of question into your daily instruction with students as well as into your assessments.

Figure 7.7 Thinking Skills Development Questions

Student _____ Teacher_____ Date _____

Mark: X = Without Assistance   / = With Assistance   — = Needs Work

Thinking Skill Quarter _____ Week:	1-3	4-6	7-9	10-12
I. Knowledge (identification and recall of information) Who, what, when, where, how? Describe _____.	___	___	___	___
II. Comprehension (organization and selection of facts and ideas) Retell the story or information in your own words. Tell the main idea of _____.	___	___	___	___
III. Analysis (separation of whole into parts) What are the parts or features of _____? Classify _____ according to _____. Outline/diagram/web _____. How does _____ compare/contrast with _____? What evidence can you present for _____?	___ ___ ___ ___ ___	___ ___ ___ ___ ___	___ ___ ___ ___ ___	___ ___ ___ ___ ___
IV. Comparison (recognize similarities/differences) How is _____ similar to _____? How is _____ different from _____? How is _____ related to _____? How is _____ an example of _____?	___ ___ ___ ___	___ ___ ___ ___	___ ___ ___ ___	___ ___ ___ ___
V. Synthesis (combination of ideas to form a new whole) What would you predict/infer from _____? What ideas can you add to _____? How would you create/design a new _____? What might happen if you combined _____ with ____? What solutions would you suggest for _____?	___ ___ ___ ___ ___	___ ___ ___ ___ ___	___ ___ ___ ___ ___	___ ___ ___ ___ ___
VI. Evaluation (development of opinions, judgments, decisions) Do you agree with the statement that _____? What do you think about _____? What is the most important _____? Prioritize _____ according to _____. How would you decide about _____? What criteria would you use to assess _____?	___ ___ ___ ___ ___ ___	___ ___ ___ ___ ___ ___	___ ___ ___ ___ ___ ___	___ ___ ___ ___ ___ ___

Adapted from *Questioning for Quality Thinking.* Maryland State Department of Education (n.d.).

ELL students will have a much greater likelihood of success in grade-level classrooms if they have been exposed early and often to thinking skills instruction and assessment.

Writing in the Content Areas   One way to assess writing and subject area knowledge is to provide subject area *prompts* (Scott 1989), as shown in Figure 7.8. Two significant values of this type of assessment are that knowledge in virtually any subject area can be assessed, and the prompts can be constructed to mirror the thinking processes students use during instruction. These prompts can be adapted to various levels of language proficiency.

In Figure 7.8, prompts are presented in mathematics, science, and social studies. The first prompt in mathematics uses the phrase *number sentence*, or a numerical "sentence" which contains one or more numerical operations (+, —, x, or ÷) and a series of numbers on which the operations are performed. For example, $5 \times 6 = ?$ is a number sentence, as is $3 + 5 = 8$. The students are asked to write a sentence describing what the number sentence tells them to do, such as "Multiply five times six," or "Three plus five equals eight." The ability to produce the language for simple number sentences like these either orally or in writing is an important skill for ELL students. The second math question asks the student to explain how to solve problems, an important process skill for any student. This type of writing promotes language development and content area learning. The third question contains the prompts for writing a word problem. As a teacher of ELL students, you can provide step-by-step examples of how to develop word problems prior to administering this type of assessment.

You can extend beyond these approaches to the assessment of math word problems by asking students to write a real-life story in which math is used (M. Helman, personal communication, 1995; Winograd and Higgins 1995). Student responses will vary depending on the topics being discussed in class (i.e., whether the topic is fractions, percents, money, or some other topic). Examples of possible responses are adding the price of items at the grocery checkout, deciding what to buy on a

fixed budget, and identifying the percent of students in the class wearing different colored clothes. Students work to solve these problems, discuss the solutions with peers, and revise their problem based on the feedback they receive.

The science prompts in Figure 7.8 ask the student to write procedures that will communicate important information to another student and to explain some of the steps in science experimentation that were followed in a science project. The general outline of a science project shown in Question #2 was based on an approach used by a multi-grade elementary teacher[2] of ELL students in Prince William County, Virginia. The third science prompt asks students to explain a graph they had constructed earlier in a science activity. The graph could involve any science activity, such as taking the pulse rate for different students, a measurement of finger length, or the height of different students.

The social studies prompts ask students to write a complete sentence about selected topics in civics and to explain why any one of the basic rights (freedom of speech, freedom of assembly, etc.) is important to them. Students can also write to describe a graph on a social studies topic, such as an opinion poll or survey questions asked in class concerning preferences for food, sports, or entertainment, that are analyzed to reveal differences between boys and girls.

Integrating Language and Content   With any of the writing prompts noted in Figure 7.8, students can make an oral presentation either independently of or in combination with the written report. The oral presentation can be made to the full class or to a small group. Students can be asked to explain how they solved problems or, if they missed a problem, to explain how they can avoid missing similar problems in the future. Students who discuss math problems in cooperative learning groups gain control over academic language and have an opportunity to review with other students

2. Donna Hankins, former ESL teacher, Prince William County Schools, Virginia.

Figure 7.8 Prompts for Writing Across the Curriculum

Subject Area	Prompts
Mathematics	1. What does the number sentence tell you to do? _____ _____ 2. How did you solve the problem? _____ _____ _____ 3. Write a word problem. Write the numbers _____ Write an operation and make a number sentence. _____ _____ Now make a story to go with the question. _____ _____ _____ _____
Science	1. Tell another student how to find the temperature outside. _____ _____ 2. In your science project, describe the: Question: _____ Materials: _____ Plan: _____ _____ Observations: _____ _____ _____ Conclusion: _____ 3. Today you made a graph in your science activity. What information did you show on the graph? _____ _____
Social Studies	1. Write one complete sentence about each topic in U.S. civics. Voting: _____ Rights: _____ Responsibilities:_____ _____ _____ 2. Choose a right that is most important to you and explain why. _____ _____ 3. Today you made a graph based on your survey. Describe and discuss the difference shown on the graph. _____ _____ _____

Adapted from Scott (1989).

the strategies they used for problem solving (Noddings, Gilbert-MacMillan, and Leitz 1983).

For example, one elementary level ESL teacher[2] with whom we have worked asked her ELL students (high beginning level of proficiency) to solve multiplication problems such as the following:

Luis rode his bike 3 miles round-trip to the library one day. He also rode his bike to soccer practice 4 miles round-trip each day for 4 days. How many miles did he ride his bike?

The teacher then asked students to explain orally how they solved the problem using steps like the following:

1. Read the problem aloud.

2. Identify the question.

3. Tell what strategy to try and why.

4. Solve the problem, explain how, and use correct language.

5. Check the strategy and the calculations.

Students can be asked to complete this type of assignment both orally and in writing. The assignment can also be the basis for cooperative learning in small groups by asking students to take turns completing each step or to complete all steps on alternate problems. The integrated assessment of language proficiency in content areas enables the teacher to observe the students' oral language skills as well as their writing skills.

One of the decisions all teachers make in writing across the curriculum involves whether to rate the student's performance on the content only, on the language used in communicating the content, or both. Some teachers choose to rate both if they feel that students have sufficient English proficiency to benefit from feedback in both areas and if both have been part of classroom instruction. Other teachers may prefer to score only the content, leaving feedback on the grammar and mechanics of language for independent exercises on which they can focus instruction. Sample scoring rubrics for evaluating the language used in writing were provided in Chapter 6. Additional rubrics for scoring content area knowledge are indicated elsewhere in this chapter.

In the following sections we describe authentic assessment in the content areas for science, mathematics, and social studies. Each section contains a description of the instructional context for authentic assessment and discusses assessment procedures teachers that can use to monitor student progress and to support student self-assessment.

SCIENCE

Knowledge in science and other subjects can be classified in terms of declarative or procedural knowledge (Anderson 1983; Gagné, Yekovich, and Yekovich 1993). *Declarative knowledge* consists of the things that you know or can "declare," such as facts. *Procedural knowledge* consists of the things that you know how to do. Examples of declarative knowledge in science include labels for parts of a leaf, the classification of the animal kingdom, the names of the planets in order from the Sun, and theories about the origin of the universe, light, electricity, and the structure of matter. Examples of procedural knowledge include measurement procedures, problem-solving processes, and procedures in scientific inquiry.

Declarative Knowledge Declarative knowledge in science can be readily assessed through oral interviews, cloze tests, semantic maps, and T-Lists. Teachers can develop probe questions to ask students during oral interviews in order to determine their knowledge of specific topics. Cloze tests in science can be constructed from authentic, grade-level texts by simply deleting occasional words, as described earlier in this chapter. Semantic maps of the kind illustrated in Figure 7.4 are particularly effective for assessing science vocabulary because of the interconnectedness of many terms in science. A simple example would be the use of semantic maps inof hierarchies in the animal kingdom or the classification of different kinds of rocks. T-Lists are also useful in science assessment because science texts often introduce a small number of concepts accompanied by specific examples. What is not so readily assessed in science is procedural knowledge, particularly an understanding of the procedures involved in scientific inquiry.

Scientific Procedures Assessing student knowledge of the procedures for scientific inquiry is important in monitoring student progress and in evaluating preparation for grade-level classrooms. The performance standards for science presented in Figure 7.2 contain considerable emphasis on the procedures of science. These include scientific "habits of mind," taking measurements, making observations and conducting experiments, keeping records, using science materials, and drawing conclusions and making inferences from data. This emphasis is consistent with what grade-level science teachers have indicated are important. As a middle school science teacher once commented to one of us, "When ESL students come into my classroom, I want them to know the procedures of science. Then I have something to build on."

Science teachers encourage students to understand and be able to pursue scientific inquiry through a variety of procedures rather than memorize rigid steps of *the* scientific method (Storey and Carter 1992). The scientific method traditionally has consisted of formal methods that include stating a hypothesis, designing an experiment to test it, collecting data, analyzing the data, and drawing conclusions. Students might be asked to conduct an experiment following these procedures and write or present a report incorporating all of the elements. Students might also be asked to interpret or explain the results relative to a scientific theory.

While aspects of these formal methods may be involved in all scientific inquiry, the actual practices scientists use to answer questions about science can vary depending on the problem. For example, scientists might not state formal hypotheses but could ask questions because insufficient information is available to support a formal prediction. Also, rather than follow specific experimental procedures, scientists might conduct systematic observations of natural phenomena, without any formal intervention. The observations and measurement will vary depending on the nature of the question and the phenomena observed, as in observing the growth of an animal using direct observations or technical instruments. Students following procedures of scientific inquiry should be encouraged to realize the relative nature of

their findings, how the methods of observation can influence the results, how conclusions may differ from one scientist to another or from one time to another, and how any set of findings can stimulate new inquiry. Students construct new knowledge through discovery rather than by rediscovering established facts (Yager 1991). In essence, science teachers are asking students to be aware of the realities and limitations of science, to create meaning from their observations, and to use their knowledge of science to make informed judgments.

Science facts and inquiry procedures are learned most readily through hands-on experiences (Butts and Hofman 1993). Science experiments are basic to many content-ESL instructional approaches because students have multiple opportunities to use language during hands-on learning (e.g., Chamot and O'Malley 1994a; Fathman and Quinn 1989). The students can talk and write about the objects they observe, describe their properties, measure the objects, classify them, and experiment with the consequences of subjecting the objects to various treatments. Teachers conducting science instruction do these kinds of activities with rocks, tree leaves, liquids, magnets, and sometimes with insects or live animals. (Treatments with animals might consist of different feeding schedules.) What students gain from these activities is more than just a grasp of scientific facts. They gain an understanding of the procedures of scientific inquiry and an appreciation for the importance of objectivity and of collaboration with others. In preparing a report, students might state the problem to be investigated, develop a question, make a plan, select materials, follow explicit procedures, make some observations or measurements, construct a table or graph to display the data, and draw conclusions that bear on the original question. These steps may vary depending on the science experiment. For younger students, teachers might ask what students expected, what they saw, heard, or felt, and how they might explain it.

A Scoring Scale for Science Problems or Experiments is presented in Figure 7.9 (adapted from Doran et al. 1993). The scoring scale is differentiated into two major parts, the design and the results, with three numbered components within

Figure 7.9   **Scoring Rubric for Science Problems or Experiments**

Student _____   Date _____

Directions: (1) Identify the numbered components of the report that are applicable to the problem assigned and mark the others NA. (2) Check (√) each applicable element that is present in the report. (3) Circle the total number of checks in each applicable component. (4) Sum the circled numbers to get a Part Score. (5) Mark NR for no response.

Part A: Design   Part A Score: _____

1. Statement of question: 0 1 2 3 4 NR NA
   • is relevant to the problem.   _____
   • is about something that changes (a variable).   _____
   • identifies what makes it change.   _____
   • can be answered by observation.   _____

2. Procedure for investigation: 0 1 2 3 4 NR NA
   • gives replicable sequence and detailed plan.   _____
   • identifies materials needed.   _____
   • indicates uses of equipment/materials.   _____
   • states safety procedures, if needed.   _____

3. Plan to record observations or data: 0 1 2 3 4 NR NA
   • matches data to plan.   _____
   • organizes data clearly.   _____
   • labels units.   _____
   • identifies variables.   _____

Part B: Results   Part B Score: _____

4. Quality of observations   0 1 2 3 4 NR NA
   • has accurate measurements/observations.   _____
   • presents a complete data table.   _____
   • uses correct units of measurement.   _____
   • accompanies data with qualitative description.

5. Graph: 0 1 2 3 4 NR NA
   • plots points accurately.   _____
   • identifies appropriate scale and units.   _____
   • labels axes correctly.   _____
   • has appropriate title.   _____

6. Conclusions   0 1 2 3 4 NR NA
   • are consistent with results.   _____
   • are consistent with scientific principle.   _____
   • state relationships among variables.   _____
   • identify sources of error.   _____

Adapted from Doran et al. (1993).

each. The components of the design include the statement of question, the procedure for investigation, and the plan to record observations. The components for the results are the quality of the observations, the graph or chart, and the conclusions. Each component has a variety of elements that can be rated as present or not present. The scoring is conducted by first marking a check (√) for each element that accurately describes the student's work. Second, add the check marks for each element to obtain a component score, which should be circled (e.g., 0 1 2 ③ 4). Third, add the three circled component scores for a total score on each part. The part scores can be combined for an overall score, if needed. Mark NA (not applicable) for any element not used. Not all teachers will ask students to include each of the components and elements in their science reports, especially at the beginning level of English proficiency. The scoring scale can be simplified depending on the number of components required in the report.

One simple science activity conducted by an ESL teacher[2] we worked with is illustrated in the following example. Students were asked to predict the average temperature during the week and to collect data to test their prediction. The students prepared a written report in which they stated their prediction, the materials (thermometer, paper, pencil), the procedures (the steps in collecting the daily temperatures and averaging them), the data (shown in tabular form and labeled), and their conclusion (Was the prediction accurate?). The students could also have been asked to state the reason for their prediction (past week was cold; looked in the newspaper for five-day weather forecast). Students then made oral presentations based on their written report and explained their findings. The scoring scale in Figure 7.9 could be adapted to score these written or oral presentations.

Self-Assessment in Science Self-assessment is important to encourage responsibility for learning, to promote critical thinking, and to involve students directly in their own learning (Hill and Ruptic 1994). Self-assessment in science is particularly important because students often have preconceived, naive notions about scientific phenomena

that are totally inaccurate and in conflict with new information presented in science lessons. Students have a discouraging tendency to ignore or reject new information that is in conflict with their prior knowledge and to fall back on their previous ways of thinking, especially when the new information is presented only in a text (Bat-Sheva and Linn 1988). Students need an opportunity to reflect on what they knew before the lesson began, what they have learned during the lesson, and how the new and prior information may be compatible or in conflict. Students who sense a discrepancy between what they knew prior to the lesson and what they have learned should be encouraged to reflect on the discrepancy and to integrate the new thinking into their broader conceptual base of knowledge.

Two ways students can begin to analyze their prior knowledge in science is by maintaining learning logs and K-W-L charts (Ogle 1986). In creating a learning log, students answer questions like the following:

- What did I know before the lesson?

- What did I learn?

- What was the same?

- What was different?

A K-W-L chart has similar requirements but is formatted with three columns on a page, one each for the *K, W,* and *L.* Prior to a new lesson, students first list what they *Know* about the topic, and then indicate what they *Want* to know. After the lesson is completed, they indicate what they have *Learned,* which then provides them with an opportunity to make a comparison between the old and the new knowledge. You should give students ample opportunities to review these comparisons and to discuss their findings with each other in order to ensure that the self-assessment actually takes place and is assimilated as part of their thinking. Sometimes an *H* is added to the K-W-L chart (K-W-L-H) to encourage the student to describe *How* the learning took place, what strategies were used, and which ones were successful (C. Ewy, personal communication, 1995). Students can write this information at the bottom of a page containing the three *K, W,* and *L* columns.

MATHEMATICS

As with subjects in science, mathematical knowledge can be differentiated into declarative and procedural knowledge (Hiebert 1986). The simplest forms of declarative or conceptual knowledge in mathematics are represented by number sense, basic mathematical operations, and the meaning of place value. More sophisticated forms of declarative knowledge involve connecting two separate pieces of knowledge. One example is to connect a memorized algorithm for multi-digit subtraction with the place value of the digits. Procedural knowledge is represented by the process of applying an algorithm to a particular problem. Examples are the algorithms to borrow-and-carry in multi-digit addition, to add fractions with unlike denominators, and to solve quadratic equations. Another type of procedural knowledge in math is represented in the syntactic rules for writing number sentences in their correct form, as in $6 \div \square = 2$, but not $6 \div = \square 2$. All of these procedures consist of multi-step actions that are goal-oriented and lead to a solution. It is important to assess this type of procedural knowledge while determining that students have learned basic math facts.

One particularly important type of procedural knowledge is the procedures used in solving word problems. Virtually all students have difficulty with word problems, but ELL students can be expected to have even more difficulty because of the requirements for comprehending the verbal or written message and determining which operation(s) are appropriate, beyond having to execute the calculations correctly. In word problems, you will have an opportunity to rate both declarative and procedural knowledge.

Problem Solving   Students in mathematics classes are regularly given word problems to solve and are often asked to explain their answers. These problems usually have some kind of realistic application in which the student becomes involved in an effort to achieve a goal. For example, students might be asked to purchase items such as food or other goods or to plan a menu for a picnic given limitations on costs and food preferences among those attending. Word problems allow students to exercise their knowledge of computation skills at the same time as they exhibit reasoning, problem-solving, and communication skills. Students can be asked to solve the problems individually or during discussions in small groups.

Recognizing the importance of problem-solving processes, teachers often want to obtain a score for the problem-solving procedures as well as for the correct answer. Students will sometimes obtain an incorrect answer while demonstrating evidence of understanding the problem and of appropriate problem-solving strategies. For example, consider the following problem (adapted from Otis and Offerman 1988):

The product of two consecutive whole numbers is 1,056. Find the sum of these two numbers.

There are a variety of procedures for solving this problem, including the combination of reasoning and guess-and-check used by the following student.

20 x 20 = 400
40 x 40 = 1,600

(The student appeared to know the answer must be between 20 and 40, because of the following:)

32 x 33 = 1,056

This student homed in on the answer rather quickly by using multiples of 10. The student appeared to know that the product of the two numbers in the units digit must be six, and that the numbers 2 and 3 are the most likely candidates because they are sequential, unlike 1 and 6, or 4 and 9. Then the student gave the answer as "32 x 33." Should the student's answer be evaluated as wrong because the answer given does not really answer the question? (Students were asked to *sum* the two numbers.) Should it be considered correct because the correct consecutive numbers were presented? Or is there a way to give the student partial but not full credit?

The standards of performance for mathematics presented in Figure 7.2 provide some guidance on these questions. The mathematics vision statement indicates that students will "use reasoning to explore solutions," and the standards of performance at grade 4 indicate that students should be able to "use arithmetic appropriate to solve a problem" and to "explain solutions." Given that the standards of performance indicate clearly the importance of accurate solutions as well as of being able to explain solutions, scoring of the student's response should take into consideration both accuracy and problem-solving processes.

The general scoring rubric for mathematics shown in Figure 7.10 permits you to rate a student's answers on the accuracy of the solution, the strategies used to obtain the correct answer, and overall understanding of the problem. We have placed this holistic scoring rubric on a scale of 1-4 and defined the levels of performance as Outstanding Achievement, Advanced Achievement, Basic Achievement, and Minimal Achievement. We believe that a scale of 1-4 is effective because you are not forced to make subtle distinctions that take a great deal of time and would be hard for a student to understand. Answers would be assigned a score of zero if the student did not respond to the question, handed in a blank paper, or had responses that fell below the definition of minimal achievement.

In the problem above, the student appeared to understand the question but ignored the aspect of the problem that called for the answer to be presented in terms of the sum of two numbers. The student's strategies were applied effectively but the student reached a subgoal and did not finish. The answer is wrong overall because the student's plan was incomplete. Thus, in the scoring rubric shown in Figure 7.10, the student would receive a rating of 2 for basic achievement. The term *basic achievement* in this case implies that the student had the fundamental skills to obtain the correct answer and might do so with similar problems in the future by redirecting his or her attention to the relevant aspects of the question.

Self-Assessment in Mathematics   Self-assessment is critically important in using problem-solving strategies successfully. As students reflect on the problem-solving approach they have used and their success or difficulty in using it, they gain an awareness of the types of strategies they can bring to similar problems in the future. One simple type of checklist for self-assessment (Stenmark 1991) is shown in Figure 7.11. Students can complete this inventory after finishing a lesson or unit in mathematics. The inventory enables them to reflect back on a particular type of word problem and the suc-

cess of the strategies used. You can encourage students to discuss their strategies with specific tasks in small groups, to share strategies used successfully, and to write about their problem-solving approaches (Burns 1995; Kennedy 1985).

SOCIAL STUDIES

Social studies, like mathematics and science, calls on both declarative and procedural knowledge. Declarative knowledge in social studies includes historical names and dates as well as geographic locations. Declarative knowledge is represented in recalling the names and dates associated with the Presidents of the United States, the capital cities in each of the states, and two differences between the Bill of Rights and the Declaration of Independence. Numerous examples of procedural knowledge are evident in the standards for social studies shown in Figure 7.2. Representative procedural skills include map-reading skills, making time lines, using graphing and statistics to represent population changes, and making comparisons/contrasts between capitalism and socialism. Declarative and procedural knowledge interact and are mutually dependent. Declarative knowledge is often the content to which a multi-step procedure is applied in demonstrating procedural knowledge. For example, the procedural skill of using a map key with icons linked to types of commerce (farming = 🌾, fishing = 🐟 , etc.) could be applied to specific states or countries whose locations are part of declarative memory.

Declarative Knowledge   Declarative knowledge in social studies can be assessed using cloze tests, semantic maps, and T-Lists. We believe that all of these forms of assessment should be used in social studies so that students have an opportunity to demonstrate their knowledge in a variety of ways. Semantic maps are useful in social studies as they are in science because new terminology is often interconnected with other new terms or terms introduced previously. Students can demonstrate a conceptual understanding of these terms by completing semantic maps rather than simply defining terms from a list. T-Lists are useful in social studies because textual materials in social studies often

Figure 7.10 General Scoring Rubric for Mathematics

Level	Description	Definition
4	Outstanding Achievement	• Understanding of the Problem—identifies the question and the components of the problem accurately • Strategies—uses various strategies, as needed, such as making a list, making a table, drawing a picture, finding a pattern, working backwards, and guess and check • Accuracy—correct answer, correctly labeled
3	Advanced Achievement	• Understanding—identifies the question but ignores one component of the problem • Strategies—uses strategies incompletely for the problem or for getting the correct solution • Accuracy—correct answer with incorrect labels or correct labels with minor calculation error
2	Basic Achievement	• Understanding—identifies the question but ignored more than one component of the problem • Strategies—uses inappropriate strategies for the type of problem or reaches a subgoal and does not finish • Accuracy—one or more subcomponents correct but wrong answer overall based on incorrect plan or no evident plan, without correct labels
1	Minimal Achievement	• Understanding—does not identify the question and ignores more than one component of the problem • Strategies—inappropriate strategy started, no attempt to try alternative strategy, numbers simply recopied, subgoals not reached, problem not finished • Accuracy—wrong answer without correct subcomponents or labels

Adapted from Otis and Offerman (1988).

Figure 7.11   Self-Assessment Inventory for Problem-Solving in Mathematics

Name _____ Date _____

What strategies did you use when solving problems? Put a check (√) next to each one you used.

1. I tried the following strategies:

_____ guess and check   _____ solve a simpler problem

_____ make a table   _____ work backward

_____ look for a pattern   _____ draw a picture

_____ make a list   _____ write an equation

_____ other (specify)_____

How successful were your strategies? Answer each question Y for *Yes* or N for *No*.

2. _____ I did not use any strategies at all.

3. _____ I thought about strategies but did not use any.

4. _____ I looked at a list of strategies but did not use any.

5. _____ I tried a strategy and it helped me find a solution.

6. _____ I tried a strategy and it did *not* help me find a solution.

7. I want to try a new strategy with the following task: _____

_____

8. The strategy I plan to use with this task is _____.

Adapted from Stenmark (1991).

give three or so main ideas with a variety of examples or details associated with each (Chamot and O'Malley 1994a). What is not so readily assessed in social studies is the written report.

Report Writing   Students in social studies classes are often called on to produce written responses to one or more prompts or to produce a research paper on a particular topic. The papers are often rated on historical facts and, perhaps, on organization. However, the criteria vary considerably between teachers and are often weighted differently depending on teacher preference. The question we address here is what scoring criteria and weights should be used in judging these papers.

In developing an analytic scoring rubric in social studies for high school students, Baker et al.(1992) asked students to review the Lincoln-Douglas debates of 1858 and write an essay explaining the most important ideas and issues addressed. Baker et al. reviewed essays on this topic produced by high school students, their teachers, and university faculty in order to derive a set of criteria that differentiated experts in the content area from inovices. In their scoring rubric, Baker et al. wanted to resolve the problem of assigning ratings to papers that contained accurate language while missing the major points of the content. The rubric that effectively differentiated experts from novices used five criteria:

1. *General Impression of Content Quality:* overall impression of how well the student understands historical content

2. *Principles/Concepts:* number of principles or concepts introduced in the essay that the student uses with comprehension, (e.g., slavery, social class, North-South politics or traditions)

3. *Prior Knowledge of Facts and Events:* number of facts/events mentioned that are not part of the text of the debates

4. *Proportion of Text Detail:* facts and events drawing directly from the text

5. *Misconceptions:* absence of misconceptions about the debates

A *concept* was defined as an abstract or general notion, such as "inflation," that does not necessarily reference a particular object or event. A *principle* was defined as a rule or belief used to justify an action or judgment. Raters assigned scores ranging from 0-5 on each of these criteria in order to produce a total score. Baker et al. found that the scores on each criterion were acceptably reliable.

We have combined this scoring rubric with a rubric suggested in Herman, Ashbacher, and Winters (1992) to produce a generic holistic rating scale for social studies content, as shown in Figure 7.12. This rating system retains the major components of the scoring system used by Baker et al. (1992) but adds an additional criterion—*argumentation,* or the statement of a clear position supported by evidence—that is appropriate for many social studies essays. This rubric emphasizes many of the components needed to meet standards of performance for history/civics shown in Figure 7.2, such as historical accuracy and understanding of concepts or principles.

A scoring rubric such as the one in Figure 7.12 can be used in combination with a scoring rubric for grammar and mechanics comparable to those introduced in Chapter 6. Separate scores on social studies content and on mechanics/grammar should assist both the teacher and the student in understanding the student's achievement and progress in school.

To use the scoring rubric with ELL students, we recommend selecting textual materials appropriate to the level of English proficiency and grade level of your students. Use any two of the social studies criteria in Figure 7.12 for your scoring rubric at the onset to introduce students to the criteria, such as Proportion of Text Detail (factual information in the text) and Principles/Concepts. Assign an individual rating on each criterion area until students begin to understand what the criteria mean. You should then be able to shift to using the criteria as a guide to deriving an overall, holistic score. Provide opportunities for students to use the criteria to rate their own papers and the papers of other students.

Self-Assessment in Social Studies   In discussing self-assessment in science, we mentioned the use of learning logs and K-W-L charts. Both

Figure 7.12   General Scoring Rubric for Social Studies

Level	Description	Definition
4	Outstanding Achievement	• Principles/Concepts—examines problem from several positions, deals with major issues and identifies relationships of main ideas • Argument—takes a strong, well-defined position with appropriate supporting evidence • Prior Knowledge—uses precise prior historical knowledge to examine issues and relate to past/future situations • Text Details—cites appropriate detail from text in building argument • Misconceptions—has no misconceptions or factual errors
3	Advanced Achievement	• Principles/Concepts—views problems with somewhat limited range but identifies more than one aspect of the problem • Argument—takes a definite but general position with somewhat organized argument • Prior Knowledge—uses general ideas from prior historical knowledge with fair accuracy in discussing issues • Text Details—relates only major text facts to basic issues • Misconceptions—errors in some factual and interpretive information
2	Basic Achievement	• Principles/Concepts—only a general understanding of scope of problem, considers only one aspect of problem or one issue or principle • Argument—presents indefinite position with only generalities and opinion for support • Prior Knowledge—makes limited use of prior historical knowledge • Text Detail—connects few text facts to basic issues • Misconceptions—makes occasional errors in facts and interpretation
1	Minimal Achievement	• Principles/Concepts—little understanding and comprehension of scope of problem or issues • Argument—position is vague, brief, and contains unrelated general statements • Prior Knowledge—barely indicates any prior historical knowledge, relying mainly on facts provided • Text Detail—reiterates only one or two facts unrelated to issues • Misconceptions—makes frequent errors in fact and interpretation

Adapted from Herman, Aschbacher, and Winters (1992).

approaches are also useful in social studies. In using learning logs, students write answers to questions about what they knew before the lesson, what they learned, and what was the same or different between the two. The K-W-L chart is similar but is formatted in a chart with columns identifying what students *Know* about a topic, what they *Want* to know, and what they *Learned*. As we noted, the K-W-L is sometimes expanded by adding an *H* for *How* they learned it, which can be described at the bottom of the chart. Other assessment techniques we have discussed previously in this chapter that can be adapted for self-assessment in social studies are semantic maps, in which students summarize their reading by visually showing causal or inter-dependent relationships; T-Lists, where students divide a page vertically into two parts for the main ideas (on the left) and corresponding details (on the right); and summarizing, where students practice writing the gist of readings in social studies.

Students can also use a self-assessment guide such as the one in Figure 7.13 to assist in thinking about what they have learned in social studies. Students first select a written product from a social studies activity that represents what they consider to be some of their best work. Their decision might be based on the scoring rubric used in Figure 7.12. They then analyze why they like the written product, what was interesting about it, and what they learned. The next step is to choose an area of social studies in which they would like to improve their work and to explain what they will do to learn more effectively. One additional possibility is to write a letter to someone describing their learning goals for the next quarter. The type of self-assessment shown in Figure 7.13 can be used in any subject area, including mathematics.

Using Content Area Assessment in Instruction

• • • • • • • • • • • • • • • •

One of the keys to using authentic assessment lies in the ongoing availability of assessment information and another is the use of multiple measures. With ongoing assessment information, teachers can establish a continuing record of student progress, accomplishments, and educational needs. This type of information can be used to identify which standards of performance are being mastered and to plan instruction that improves learning outcomes and effectiveness. Teachers can assess thinking skills, conceptual knowledge, and writing in content areas in addition to vocabulary and reading.

The use of multiple measures enables teachers to assess declarative and procedural knowledge in the content areas, to assess all language skills, and to encourage student self-assessment. These varied types of information are useful in selecting instructional objectives and planning activities needed to advance learning for individual students. By identifying a student's prior knowledge and strategic approach to learning, teachers can design more effective instruction that builds on student strengths and extends the student's strategic approach to learning. ESL and grade-level teachers can work together to accomplish these ends. The use of varied assessment approaches enables teachers to cross-check and verify independent sources of information to ensure that their evaluations are reliable and their instructional decisions are valid. Assessment results should also be used to provide feedback to students and to communicate information to parents.

Conclusion

• • • • • • • • • • • • • • • •

This chapter has identified a number of ways in which language and content interact in instruction and assessment. The integration of language and content in ESL classrooms demands innovative assessment procedures to monitor student progress and to provide information needed for instructional planning. We began the discussion of assessment in the content areas by identifying two major trends affecting content instruction in ESL and grade-level classrooms: the thinking curriculum and higher standards of performance for all students. We discussed two general guidelines in assessment: you get what you assess, and you do

Figure 7.13 **Guidelines for Self-Assessment in Social Studies**

Name _____ Date _____

1. Choose a paper from social studies that you believe shows your best work.

   Explain why you chose that paper. Be sure to give the topic of the paper in your explanation. Complete the following sentences.

   • I like this paper because _____
   _____.

   • I think this paper is interesting because _____
   _____.

   • What I learned in writing this paper was _____
   _____.

2. Choose an area of social studies in which you need improvement.

   • The area of social studies in which I need improvement is _____
   _____.

   • I will improve in this area by _____
   _____.

3. Write a letter to someone who is not in your class. Explain your feelings and thoughts about social studies this quarter. Explain the following:

   • This quarter I liked _____.

   • A topic that was easy was _____.

   • A topic that was difficult was _____.

   • What helped me learn _____
   _____.

   • My goals for next quarter are _____
   _____.

Adapted from Seago (1993).

not get what you do not assess. We believe that teachers must assess what they want students to know and be able to do. The standards of performance established in the content areas can be used as a guide to setting local standards for ELL students. In discussing specific forms of assessment in the content areas, we mentioned the importance of assessing prior knowledge, thinking skills, and the processes by which students solve problems and reach solutions.

We suggest the following guidelines for teachers conducting assessment in the content areas:

1. Embed assessment in instructional activities to ensure the assessments remain authentic and to facilitate the design and management of assessments.

2. Scaffold assessments to provide contextual supports for meaning by using visuals or cued supports as a way of ensuring that all students will be able to respond to the task.

3. Assess procedural knowledge as well as declarative knowledge, especially thinking skills, problem solving, and strategic approaches to learning.

4. In addition to assessing declarative and procedural knowledge, use assessments that are basic to all content areas, such as the assessment of vocabulary, reading comprehension, and conceptual knowledge.

5. Always assess prior knowledge in specific content areas as a guide to designing instruction that is manageable yet challenging for students.

6. Encourage self-assessment to make students aware of what they have learned, what learning processes are successful for them, and what they can do to become self-directed learners.

7. Use integrated assessments of language and content with authentic tasks, and use differentiated scoring to distinguish between language elements and content elements.

8. Make criteria for assessment visible so students are familiar with the rubrics used in scoring their papers, and involve the students in using the rubrics to rate their own work and the work of their peers.

APPLICATION ACTIVITIES

1. Work with a team of teachers to review the content standards identified in Figure 7.2. Select one or more of the following uses of this table: (a) contrast the standards of performance in this table with grade-level expectations in your local curriculum; (b) use the table to verify that the content and processes you have selected for classroom assessment represent important standards and objectives.

2. Assess what your students know and can do in one or more content areas. Identify their prior education and assess their background knowledge and conceptual knowledge. Rely on scaffolded assessment procedures, such as those in Figures 7.3-7.5 and 7.7.

3. Assess students' reading proficiency in a content area using a cloze test. What do the results tell you about your students' conceptual knowledge?

4. Design your own version of Figure 7.8. Use specific examples of writing prompts drawn from your curriculum. Or, without using prompts, ask students to write a real-life story in which math is used.

5. If you are teaching science content or working with a science teacher, use the scoring rubric in Figure 7.9. Adapt the form to your local science activities and to the type of science assignment students are given.

6. Use a K-W-L chart or learning log to assess knowledge in the content areas. Add to the K-W-L chart information on *How* the learning took place, (i.e., what strategies they used while learning).

EXAMPLES
FROM THE CLASSROOM

• •

This final chapter presents a number of examples from the classroom to illustrate the principles of authentic assessment we have introduced and described throughout this book. Each example is based either on observation of teachers linking assessment with instruction or discussion with teachers who described assessment procedures they had used and found to be effective. Each example is presented as a vignette that describes the purposes of the assessment, the teacher's role during the assessment, what the students do, and a summary comment on the advantages and uses of this type of authentic assessment. Some of these examples involve grade-level classrooms, but because we found them informative for ESL classrooms, we wanted to include them here. All vignettes drawn from grade-level classrooms are accompanied by comments from experienced ESL teachers.[1]

1. Pam Dowdell, ESL teacher, Minnieville Elementary School; Ginette Cain, ESL teacher, Woodbridge Middle School; Kate Dail, ESL teacher, Woodbridge High School; all in Prince William County Schools, Manassas, Virginia.

Figure 8.1   Overview of Authentic Assessment Examples

Title	Subject (Grade Level)	Description
1. Talk Show	ESL-Language Arts (Secondary)	Students simulate a television talk show by presenting themselves as a famous person who is being interviewed.
2. Geoboard	ESL-Mathematics (Middle)	A teacher uses geoboards to assess geometric concepts and applications.
3. Magnet Experiment	ESL-Science (Middle)	A teacher observes and rates students as they identify which magnet is strongest.
4. Interpreting Portfolio Entries	ESL (Secondary)	Two teachers discuss assessment portfolios used in instruction and placement decisions.
5. Reading Response Time	Language Arts (Elementary)	A student presents a personal response to reading to a full class, following which other students give oral feedback as the teacher takes notes for a portfolio.
6. Anecdotal Records	Language Arts (Elementary)	A teacher takes anecdotal notes on an individual reading while managing cooperative learning groups.
7. Book Talks	Language Arts (Elementary)	A teacher tape records an oral presentation in a small group as a student presents a personal response to readings and other students ask questions.

These examples from the classroom, in addition to illustrating the link between assessment and instruction, also illustrate the independence and professionalism of individual teachers in stepping beyond customary forms of assessment. Teachers using authentic assessment sometimes find that other teachers and administrators are not always supportive of their efforts. Developing a team of teachers to work with in your school as we have suggested in this book may become a major challenge and call on leadership qualities. Using authentic assessment may be difficult when, as in many school districts, pressure is placed on principals and teachers to increase scores on standardized tests. Teachers in these districts are often expected to spend time on test-taking strategies and drills on discrete skills. Authentic assessment could be seen as detracting from the time teachers might be spending on these activities. To use authentic assessment often requires teachers to go beyond the college or university course preparation they have received, which most likely did not include coverage of authentic assessment. Moreover, only some school districts are beginning to provide professional development workshops on authentic assessment practices, and few of those focus on authentic assessment with English language learning (ELL) students. Parents also need to be convinced of the value of new forms of assessment, such as portfolios. Thus, while we are hopeful that the examples in this chapter provide you with information on how to integrate assessment with instruction, we also hope that they give you support in knowing that teachers just like you are struggling and succeeding to improve the education of ELL students. We hope these vignettes capture for you the experimental nature of authentic assessment, the ways in which teachers develop and modify their work until it provides them with the feedback they want, and the ways in which students respond to authentic assessment.

The examples we provide cover a range of different types of classrooms, assessment purposes, and grade levels. Most of the examples focus on language arts and include integrated assessment of oral proficiency with reading and writing. There is also one example of science assessment and one of mathematics assessment. The vignettes are presented with the ESL examples first and the grade-level classrooms following. Figure 8.1 shows the sequence and the focus of the assessment for those interested in locating an example of a particular kind of assessment.

1. TALK SHOW

Description

The Talk Show format is used by Kate Dail,[2] a high school ESL teacher, to assess reading comprehension, summarizing, and speaking. Kate begins the activity by describing the major components of the Talk Show. Students select a famous person to role-play in a simulated television talk show. To enable them to play their role, students have prepared a biography of their person. One student can elect to be the interviewer, and several students are interviewed at a time. Students are told that the interviewer will ask them questions, and they are to respond as if they were the person on whom they have prepared the biography. Virtually all students have seen an interview talk show at home but the teacher might videotape one of the more

2. Kate Dail is an ESL Teacher at Woodbridge High School, Prince William County Public Schools, Manassas, Virginia.

popular shows and play it in class to provide an example for discussion. Students have two and a half weeks to prepare their biographies.

Kate has 15 students in a first period class and 11 in a third period class with whom she uses the Talk Show. These students are mostly low intermediate in English proficiency with a few high beginners and high intermediate-level students. Last year Kate had a small number of low beginners who were included in the group and who were able to participate in the Talk Show by the end of the school year.

Students begin by choosing a biography of a famous person whose life they wish to portray in the interview. Kate sometimes provides a list that is tied to Black history, famous women, explorers, scientists, or other topics. Students read a biography about their famous person or any other book

Figure 8.2   Reading Journal: What Do You Think, Feel, and Like?

Name _____ Date _____

Write the number of pages read from your book or the title of the chapter.
Write comments on the right side.

How did you feel about the pages you read? Were they exciting, dull, suspenseful?
Support your comments with details from the story.

Book Title _____

Author _____

Chapter Title/Pages Read	Comments
Title: _____ _____ _____ _____ Pages: _____	
Title: _____ _____ _____ _____ Pages: _____	
Title: _____ _____ _____ _____ Pages: _____	

Figure 8.3   **Talk Show Rating Scale**

Student _____ Date _____

Activity _____

Key: 3 = Usually, 2 = Sometimes, 1 = Rarely

Student:

1. participates in interview/discussion.	3	2	1
2. responds as famous person.	3	2	1
3. uses details from biography.	3	2	1
4. negotiates meaning.	3	2	1
5. invites dialogue from others.	3	2	1
6. agrees/disagrees appropriately.	3	2	1
7. changes topic appropriately.	3	2	1
8. speaks spontaneously.	3	2	1

Comments

Figure 8.4   **Self-Assessment of Speaking**

Name _____

Activity _____ Date _____

How did I do?	Usually	Sometimes	Rarely
1. I spoke loudly enough.	_____	_____	_____
2. I spoke clearly.	_____	_____	_____
3. I responded like my famous person.	_____	_____	_____
4. I organized my thoughts.	_____	_____	_____
5. I agreed/disagreed appropriately.	_____	_____	_____
6. I responded fully to questions.	_____	_____	_____
7. I asked questions of others.	_____	_____	_____
8. I volunteered information.	_____	_____	_____

Comments

Adapted from forms developed by ESL teacher K. Dail.

that will give them insights to the person's character. At least three sources are required. Students use grade-level texts for information but more often rely on books from the public library that are typical of middle school readings. Middle school books are less dense than high school books, contain more illustrations and pictures, and are written at a more comprehensible level for ELL students. These books were not available in the high school library. The teacher assists the students in obtaining a library card and locating reference materials, as needed.

Students keep a daily journal on their reading, as illustrated in Figure 8.2. Students report daily to the teacher on their progress or on any obstacles they encounter, including unfamiliar vocabulary. Students also talk about their character in small groups and brainstorm to select a theme for the Talk Show, such as "What it is like to be famous," "Your native country," etc. The student who has opted to be the interviewer develops a set of questions related to this theme that students can review and prepare to answer. Students talk in small groups about what makes a good talk show host or guest. Students participate in dress rehearsals of the talk show and practice responses to the host's questions as the host practices running the show. Students write suggestions for changes as they watch each other.

On the day of the show, students are expected to become the subject of their chosen biography by dressing as their character. Kate assists with costumes or other supplies, as needed. Students respond to questions extemporaneously during the Talk Show, which the teacher videotapes so students can review and evaluate their performance afterwards. Kate rates each student's performance using the Talk Show Rating Scale, as shown in Figure 8.3, which students have seen in advance so they know the criteria for the rating. Students use a self-evaluation form to rate their own performance, as shown in Figure 8.4. Students participate in the Talk Show and the self-evaluation with enthusiasm and enjoy the opportunity to see themselves on videotape.

Discussion

This teacher integrates assessment and instruction in a way that enables her to assess integrated language skills, including reading, writing, and oral proficiency as well as class participation. She reports having also assessed content such as social studies when students include descriptions of activities and locations from their native countries. In the weeks prior to introducing the Talk Show, the teacher asks students to write biographies so they gain experience in understanding and describing the life of a well-known person. The teacher rates the writing samples produced for these biographies using a holistic rubric developed specifically by ESL teachers in her county (similar to those shown in Chapter 6).

We have made minor changes to the Talk Show Rating Scale by reducing the teacher's original five-point rating scale to a three-point rating scale and by changing some of the descriptors for the levels. We also made minor changes in the Self-Assessment of Speaking to expand coverage of the self-rated items to correspond more closely to the Talk Show Rating Scale.

2. GEOBOARD

Description

The teacher[3] in this middle school ESL classroom uses math geoboards to illustrate and check for understanding of geometric concepts. The geoboard used in this classroom is a square made of plastic about 8″ x 8″, with five rows and five columns of 1″ pegs extending perpendicularly from the surface. Some geoboards have more pegs. The geoboard is used by placing a rubber band over the pegs to make a geometric shape. The teacher has spent prior instructional time introducing and describing various shapes and their characteristics. She has modeled the activity using a clear plastic geoboard and an overhead projector. Students in the classroom where the eoboard was used are from pre-literate backgrounds and have been in a special ESL math program for about six months.

While simple in concept, geoboards have a variety of uses, including showing various shapes, checking for geometric concepts or vocabulary, classifying boards by the shape students place on them, and for more challenging activities. Two examples of challenge activities are to create a figure of a particular shape with the largest perimeter, or to create any figure with the most sides. Teachers also ask students to describe orally or in writing the characteristics of various shapes that make them unique (e.g., a square is a closed figure with four equal sides, four right angles, and so on). Geoboards are used regularly along with other hands-on math manipulatives in this classroom.

3. This example was adapted from a conversation with Mary Helman, former Math/ESL Resource Teacher with the FAST-Math Title VII Program in Fairfax County Public Schools, Virginia. Ms. Helman provided a description of a typical session working with students in the program. The teacher appearing in this photo is Alice Dzanis of Fred Lynn Middle School, Prince William County Public Schools, Virginia.

To begin this session, the teacher distributes one geoboard and one rubber band per student. The teacher asks the students to make any shape on the geoboard with the rubber band. The students spend a few moments completing their activity, after which the

teacher says, "Hold up your geoboards so we all can see them." As she says this, she holds up her own geoboard to illustrate. Then the teacher says, "Lin, look at the geoboards and find the ones that are like yours." Lin has made a triangle on her board, and she responds by pointing to various boards with triangles. The teacher then asks Lin to name the shape and tell what makes the other ones like hers. Lin responds by saying, "Mine is a triangle. The others are like mine because they are also triangles." The teacher pursues this answer by asking how she knows these are triangles. "What makes them triangles?" Then Lin says, "They are all closed figures with three angles and three sides."

The teacher continues with other students in the same manner, asking individual students to find the geoboards like theirs. The students respond by selecting the geoboards, naming the figure, and then providing an explanation of the unique features of each figure. Examples of the figures students identify are squares, rectangles, right triangles, and other polygons.

The teacher then asks students to work in pairs and take turns making a shape on the geoboard for their partner, naming the shape, and providing an explanation of the characteristics of the shape. The student listening draws the shape on a piece of paper, writes the name, and then writes what the other student indicates are the characteristics of the shape. After each pair has made and described four shapes, they turn to the pairs adjacent to them and check the characteristics they identified. As the students work on the activity, the teacher circulates among them, observing and offering suggestions as needed. At the end of the activity, the teacher writes the names of some shapes the students are familiar with but had not worked on and asks the students to finish up by working on these.

Discussion

The teacher combined instruction with assessment in that she was able to verify that students not only could recall the names of the figures but also understood the concepts for various geometric figures. The students had worked on identifying, modeling, labeling, and describing various shapes in a way that enabled the teacher to determine immediately which students were having difficulty and which students would be able to provide support to their peers. If appropriate, the teacher could have taken anecdotal notes to remember which students were having difficulty and needed additional support.

Description

This activity was developed by Elizabeth Varela,[4] an ESL middle school teacher familiar with science content. The activity is an integrated assessment of language and content related to magnetism. Elizabeth tried out the activity with 15 students from a high beginning-level ESL science class in the middle grades. Prior to conducting this activity, Elizabeth had taught lessons on problem-solving steps and had given students prior experiences with mini-experiments.

In this hands-on activity, students work in groups of three to perform an experiment in which they compare the strengths of three magnets. They are

to determine which of the three magnets is strongest. The students had prior experience with hands-on investigations of this kind. Students are given three magnets: a large horseshoe magnet and a medium and small bar magnet. They are also given large paper clips, forceps, and 50 small washers. Students can conduct the experiment any way they choose, but are to reach consensus on the best procedure to follow. At the completion of the experiment, students are required to write a group summary of the procedures they followed, using the format in Figure 8.5. Students are told their experiments will be rated as a group. Students are also asked to write a paragraph about the experiment on their own, using the format shown in Figure 8.6.

Elizabeth observes the students as they are working to capture the processes they are following in

4. Elizabeth Varela is an ESL/Science teacher at Williamsburg Middle School, Arlington Public Schools, Virginia. The program in which she teaches is part of the High Intensity Language Training (HILT) ESL program in the county, and is one of the programs implementing the Cognitive Academic Language Learning Approach (CALLA) in the schools (see Chapter 7).

Figure 8.5　**Group Report Form: Which Magnet is Strongest?**

Name _____ Date _____

1. Draw the three magnets A, B, and C.

A	B	C

2. Talk with your partners. What steps will you take to find out which of the three magnets is strongest?

_____

_____

_____

3. What question do you want to answer? _____

_____

4. Do the experiment. On a separate sheet of paper, draw the steps you followed. Label the steps, if needed.

5. What did you observe? _____

_____

_____

6. What did you conclude? _____

_____

_____

Figure 8.6   **Individual Report Form: Which Magnet is Strongest?**

Name _____ Date _____

1. Draw a picture of the steps you followed in your experiment. Number and label each step.

2. Write about your experiment. Give enough information so that another student could do the experiment the same way. Refer to your drawing above as needed.

_____

_____

_____

_____

_____

_____

_____

_____

solving the problem. After the students complete their work, she interviews them individually (using Spanish as needed) to identify the learning strategies used to solve the problem. She later transcribes these interviews in order to analyze the students' problem-solving procedures. (Elizabeth was doing this for a graduate class. Not all teachers will follow this last step.)

The group summaries of the experiment are scored for following directions appropriately, cooperation, developing an hypothesis, and solving the problem (i.e., coming up with a procedure to determine the strongest magnet). The most effective procedure was one in which students counted washers as they placed them on the magnets. Additional credit is given for clever schemes, such as using paper clips to hang washers so that more washers could be suspended from the magnet. Students who did multiple trials were rated higher than those who did the procedure only once.

The individually written papers were scored holistically by combining science knowledge and language into a single, four-point scale. Four points were awarded to paragraphs that included a clear and accurate explanation of scientific procedures, a logical sequence, correct use of vocabulary, and control of grammatical forms.

Elizabeth found that each group conducted the experiment differently, though all eventually discovered an effective approach to finding the strongest magnet. She observed one group developing the hypothesis retroactively while others developed the hypothesis in the more usual sequence, prior to doing the experiment. Some groups estimated the number of washers a magnet would hold before doing the experiment. Other groups used the forceps to hold the magnets while suspending washers from them. Some students placed the washers in a pile and determined how many hung onto a magnet inserted in the stack. Four of the five groups checked their results.

Discussion

In reviewing the activity, Elizabeth made changes in how she scored students in order to allow for

individual contributions in the group and for creativity in approach, such as suspending washers from a clip. She also felt that a better technique needed to be developed to deal with individually written papers by students who were known to be good problem solvers but were sometimes hindered by lack of English skills. Also, Elizabeth commented that the term *hypothesis* represented a small problem for some students because they seemed focused on "proving" the hypothesis to be accurate or inaccurate. Focusing students on answering a question might be a better approach.

If you choose to try this approach, you might use the group report only to assess the group's project and the individually written paper to assess individual student contributions. To resolve the problem in which English language skills hindered written performance, students could draw and label the steps followed in the experiment in addition to writing the individual paper. The term *question* could be substituted for *hypothesis*. The forms shown in Figures 8.5 and 8.6 have been modified from their original to allow for these suggestions. In scoring, try to provide separate scores in the individually written paper for science knowledge and for language.

4. INTERPRETING PORTFOLIO ENTRIES

Description

Laura McDermott[5] is a high school ESL teacher who uses assessment portfolios to monitor the progress of her beginning ESL students. Secondary teachers in her school system have focused on literacy assessment and have identified required and optional entries for students to make in their portfolios. Among the required entries are: a reading passage with comprehension questions or a reading strategies checklist, a writing sample, a student-selected writing sample, and an example of the student's self-assessment. At the end of each quarter (nine weeks), Laura reviews each portfolio for indications that the student is making progress. At the end of the year, she

reviews them to determine who is ready to go on to a higher level of the ESL program. During this observation, Laura is sitting with the Secondary ESL Resource Specialist, Barbara Fagan,[5] to discuss the end of year status of selected students based on portfolio contents and test scores.

Barbara begins the session by asking Laura to pull the portfolios of students she feels may be ready to move on to the intermediate level of the ESL program. By reviewing the contents of each portfolio, both teachers can confirm individual progress with evidence from the student's work. In the case of one student, Laura expresses concern that he can read much better than he writes. Because he can read so well, Laura recommends him for promotion to the intermediate level. However, Barbara suggests that he should remain at the beginning level because his writing skills do

5. Laura McDermott was an ESL teacher at Washington-Lee High School. Barbara Fagan is an ESL teacher at Kenmore Middle School and a Secondary ESL Resource Specialist. Both teachers work in the High Intensity Language Training (HILT) program of Arlington Public Schools, Virginia.

not meet the criteria for functioning at the intermediate level and because his program test scores reveal minimal ability to use basic syntax and vocabulary. Attending summer school for additional language strengthening will benefit this student.

To help Laura see what an intermediate-level student's work looks like and what portfolio entries should be included, Barbara refers to a sample portfolio she has compiled from one of her own students. By reviewing a sample portfolio, Laura gets a better idea of how to assess students in the future. From this meeting, Laura has learned that to determine reading ability she needs to let students respond to comprehension questions independently rather than as a whole class. Laura can make better informed decisions regarding students' progress by reviewing the student's portfolio, getting feedback from a colleague, examining a relevant portfolio model, and referring to criteria for reading and writing at each program level. The two teachers proceed to review the remaining selected portfolios and to discuss how assessment activities reflect instruction. This session took about 25 minutes and was held after school.

Discussion

This example from a high school ESL program illustrates several principles presented in this book. First, we see how a teacher uses assessment portfolios to monitor student progress in an ESL program. Second, the teacher uses rubrics designed by teachers to help make assessment decisions less subjective and more criterion-referenced. Third, collaborating with a colleague can better inform decisions. Finally, we can infer that teachers receiving student portfolios the following fall will be getting concrete examples of what students could do at the end of their last quarter in school.

Description

Michele Del Gallo,[6] a grade-level teacher of a combined grades 4-5 classroom, devised Reading Response Time to link an instructional activity with authentic assessment. In this activity, students provide peer feedback on integrated language use. Prior to the activity, students prepare a personal response to reading in trade books or other grade-level materials. The personal response is a hand-written report, typically on a single page. Reading Response Time is held at one side of the room where there is a rug for students to sit on, a small table, a few chairs, and a two-person sofa.

Michele begins the session by calling all students to the reading corner, reminding them to bring

their report for "Reading Response Time." When students are all seated on the rug, except for one student seated on the sofa with her, she indicates they are going to select a Manager for the day. Numerous students volunteer, calling "I want to!" and "Me! me!" After selecting one of these students to be Manager, the teacher says, "Okay. Let's review the guidelines for the Manager." Students then volunteer such guidelines as, "Always say something positive," "Be specific about something the student said or wrote," "Speak clearly so the student can understand," and "Say something that will help the student do better next time."

The teacher continues the Reading Response session by asking for a volunteer to read his or her report. Again, a number of students raise their hands. The teacher selects one student, who then takes his report with him to the lone chair facing

6. Michele Del Gallo was a grade 4-5 teacher with the McAuliffe Elementary School, Prince William County Public Schools, Manassas, Virginia. The teacher appearing in this photo is Jennifer Foust of McAuliffe Elementary School.

Figure 8.7 Reading Response Form

Name _____ Date _____

Book Title ____ *The Diary of Anne Frank* _____

The Class Said:	The Teacher Said:

The Class Said:

—I liked how you elaborated on how they found the girl and took her to the concentration camp.

—I agree with Pamela that "evil" exists in the world.

—I could tell she wrote it—she had nice feelings and is very expressive.

—I liked how you projected your voice.

—I like how you elaborated—you painted a picture in my mind.

—Uses good descriptive words

—Clear central idea

The Teacher Said:

—I really like the way you are responding to all of the questions that your classmates are asking.

—I like the way you have such strong opinions about certain issues.

—I like the way you are able to express your thoughts in writing in a clear manner with mature sentences that paint a picture for the audience.

—Nice "feeling tone"

—Excellent elaboration

—Well organized!

—Under style—your "voice" came through.

The Author Responded:

It makes me feel good about my writings. It tells me people really listen to my summary. It makes me feel like I've got good taste in books.

the group. He sits down and proceeds to read his personal response to a book he had recently completed. The report includes what the book was generally about as well as his personal response to the story. When he finishes, the Manager gives her comments, attempting to follow the guidelines for Managers. The teacher prompts other students to give their reactions after the Manager is through, and a few do (see examples in Figure 8.7). When the discussion is completed, the student returns to the group and a new student is selected to read a report. This continues until most students who were ready had an opportunity to read their reports before the group.

While students were reading their papers and the Manager was offering comments, the teacher "scripted," or took notes on what the Manager had said, any additional comments offered by the audience of students, and her personal comments (see Figure 8.7). Michele later placed these scripted comments in each student's portfolio accompanying the written report. This enabled students to have written feedback on their oral presentation and on the organization and message communicated through the written report. There is a space at the bottom of the page on which students write their comments on the feedback they receive from the Manager, their peers, and from the teacher. According to the teacher, the students look forward to these comments and enjoy reading them especially to see the reactions of their peers.

Discussion

This assessment focuses on integrative language activities and mirrors the type of feedback individuals might receive outside the classroom. This teacher has established the notion of a community of learners all working to assist each other in becoming more effective readers and writers. The role of Manager rotates to give each student who expresses interest an opportunity to comment. Students receive feedback on the way in which they analyze the reading, sometimes with comments from others who have read the same work.

The teacher has prepared students during the school year by giving them guidelines for their role as Manager as well as for providing feedback to peers. The teacher also familiarizes students with a rubric to assess their writing that is used for a statewide minimum competency test administered in sixth grade. Each written piece from which the student reads could be scored with this rubric. Early in the school year, the teacher had modeled how to produce a personal response to reading by describing her own personal response to shared readings and by providing constructive feedback as students volunteered and discussed their own responses.

In Reading Response Time, the teacher integrates assessment of reading, writing, and speaking with the students' conceptual understanding of the books on which they have prepared the report. The teacher uses a similar approach in an activity reserved for "Current Events," in which students and the teacher select a current event of significance to discuss in class. The teacher noted that students' discussions during Reading Response Time and Current Events have become more analytical and involve greater use of higher-order thinking skills over the school year.

Comments by ESL Teachers

The assessment could be used with little change in grades two through high school for students at the intermediate/advanced levels of English proficiency. Effective preparation of the students is obviously a key element, since these students were well familiarized with the role of Manager and what was expected in a personal response to reading. One of the great advantages of this approach in an ESL classroom is the assessment of integrated language use. Another advantage would be in using content area readings, as this teacher does with current events. In an ESL setting where the teacher has students for a only short time daily or weekly, Reading Response Time can be spaced over a grading period to ensure every student has a turn.

6. ANECDOTAL RECORDS

Description

In this scene, Becky Patonetz,[7] an elementary grade 1-2 teacher, performs an individual assessment of reading strategies while managing a classroom of students engaged in cooperative learning. The individual assessment could entail an anecdotal record or a running record. However, in this case the teacher is making notes on the strategies each child uses (or does not use) in decoding unknown words. The class has been working on three strategies: sounding out, reading on, and looking at illustrations.

Prior to the individual assessment, Becky gives the class a small group assignment involving being new at school and how to make a new child feel welcome. Students are to read the story *Gila*

Monsters Meet You at the Airport and write a paragraph about making a newcomer welcome. Students are asked to remember the rules of capitalization in their sentences.

When the students are working successfully on this activity, Becky sits in a chair facing the group and calls on one student at a time to sit in the chair beside her. The first student selected picks a trade book from the class library, walks to the chair beside her, and begins to read from the book upon being seated. Becky listens attentively, occasionally taking notes, as in Figure 8.8, while at the same time looking up at the full group.

Becky can see and manage the activities of the larger group of students working on their assignment. As needed, she comments to one or more students to provide encouragement or to remind students how to work in cooperative groups. At

7. Becky Patonetz is a grade 1-2 teacher in the McAuliffe Elementary School, Prince William County Public Schools, Manassas, Virginia.

Figure 8.8 **Anecdotal Records Report Form**

Date __10/10__

Student ____Tori____

Book ____Gila Monsters Meet You at the Airport____

Strategies ____reads ahead, uses context____

Date __10/10__

Student ____Edgar____

Book ____Tonight is Carnaval____

Strategies ____takes notes, makes predictions,____

____makes outlines____

Date _____

Student _____

Book _____

Strategies _____

Date _____

Student _____

Book _____

Strategies _____

one point, a girl walks over, stands directly in front of her, and says, "Look at mine. See what I made?" Becky acknowledges this appeal, silently gives the girl a thumbs up, and the girl continues on to her seat, satisfied with the recognition. The student who is reading is oblivious to this interruption, which takes all of about three seconds. Becky then continues listening to the reading student as she takes notes. After about three to four minutes of reading, Becky thanks the student beside her, congratulates him on his progress, and asks him to return to his seat. She then calls another student to read beside her and the cycle continues again.

Discussion

This entire activity took about 20-25 minutes, during which the teacher was able to conduct an individual assessment with about eight students while keeping other students on task. Later, when asked how she selected the students for the reading, she noted that she performs this individualized assessment with some students who warrant closer monitoring more often than with others. One of these was a bilingual student who read in halting and accented English but had reasonably good fluency with grade-level materials. Students who need more attention read to the teacher at least once each week and also to a parent aide once a week.

Comments by ESL Teachers

This assessment method could be used at all levels of proficiency and grade levels but would be especially helpful with beginning readers. An ESL teaching assistant could help maintain the cooperative learning groups to ensure they are functioning adequately during the assessment. The teacher could focus on any number of classroom objectives in asking questions of the student, including comprehension, but could also complete a Running Record.

7. BOOK TALKS: Integrated Reading Assessment

Description

In this integrated assessment of reading, John Robinson,[8] a grade 4 teacher, engages individual students in conversations that focus on reading comprehension while assessing reading strategies and oral proficiency. This is accomplished through Book Talks, in which students are asked comprehension questions by the teacher and by other students about their individual reading. The student also reads aloud from a paragraph or two in a book the student has selected. Each student's responses to questions and the oral reading are taped to establish a continuing record that is placed in the student's portfolio.

John schedules the participation of individual students for the Book Talk well in advance of the

actual session. Students participate in two sessions during each nine-week grading period. The day of the week in which the sessions are held and the duration over which the sessions are held varies depending on student and teacher preference. John posts a chart of the schedule with the dates and number of students who may attend each session. Students drawn by lottery can indicate their preferred dates for participating in the Book Talk. In preparing for the session, students select any grade-appropriate fiction or non-fiction reading materials and are encouraged to read from a variety of genres. As the school year progresses, John requires specific genres, comparisons of two works by the same author, or comparisons of two works of the same genre.

On the day of the Book Talk, John reviews cooperative learning assignments for the morning with

8. John Robinson is a grade 4 teacher at Henderson Elementary School, Prince William County Public Schools, Manassas, Virginia.

the full class. The assignments vary from week to week but, on the day of the observation, students chose between multiplication practice, individual reading (in preparation for their next Book Talk), and a "Mystery Picture Graph" (practice with graphing x- and y-coordinates). John had these assignments written on the chalkboard and answered questions after reviewing the options.

To begin the Book Talk, John selects five students from the full group and asks them to bring their book and their reading log to the table used for the session. Students had selected the books from the class library, using either fiction or non-fiction. As these students assemble at the table, John asks for a volunteer to go first, second, third, etc. All students respond as he begins to set up the tape recorder. John hands to the first student a 4″ x 6″ card that contains prompts for starting the session. He also hands an 8½″ x 11″ page to each of the other students, containing a series of questions one might ask another student about the reading (see Figure 8.9). John then pulls an audio-tape from a 6″ x 9″ envelope. The envelope has the student's name on it and three columns for the dates on which the student had participated in Book Talks, the names of the books used, and the tape counter reading for each entry. John resets the counter on the tape recorder, inserts the tape, and starts the recorder as he asks the first student to begin.

The first student reads from the 4″ x 6″ card some basic identifying information and fills in with names and dates, as follows:

My name is (student gives name). Today is (date). Other students at the table with me today are (names of students). I am going to read from the book (name of book).

John writes the date and name of the book on the outside of the student's 6″ x 9″ envelope. He starts the tape recorder and begins the session by asking what kind of book the student has read. The student responds by indicating whether it was fiction or nonfiction. In this case, the student had read a work of fiction. John asks if it is realistic fiction and follows up by asking what makes it realistic fiction. He then asks who the main character is

and what kind of person the main character is. After the student responds, John asks what happened in the story, what happened at the end, and whether the student was surprised by the ending. These comprehension questions call for multiple-word responses using complete sentences, not just simple *yes/no* answers.

John continues by asking if any student in the group wants to ask a question. Each student asks one question from his or her 8½″ x 11″ page and waits for the presenting student to respond. Examples of the questions students ask are, "Why did you choose this book?" "Have you read anything by the same author?" "Would you read something by this author again?" "Did you have any difficulty understanding any part of the book?" and "Do you think the story would make a good movie?" The teacher provides these 8½″ x 11″ pages early in the school year in order to model higher-order questions.

In the next phase of the Book Talk, John asks the same student to select a passage to read aloud. John says, "I am going to look for reading fluency, reading with appropriate expression, whether you pause appropriately for punctuation, and how you approach words that are difficult to pronounce or that you don't know." The student reads aloud a few paragraphs as the tape recorder continues running. John rates the student's reading on the form in Figure 8.10. To conclude this student's participation, John compliments the student on his reading, and asks when the student's next reading group is as he withdraws the tape from the recorder, marks the counter position on the outside of the envelope, and places the tape back in the envelope.

John selects the tape for the next student in turn and the session continues as with the first student. From time to time, John will monitor the noise level of the other students, make a management comment to the group or to individual students, or ask a question of one of the students working on the cooperative learning assignments. These diversions are handled without interrupting the flow of activities in the reading group.

Figure 8.9 Sample Questions for Book Talks

1. Why did you choose to read this book?

2. Who tells the story?

3. What are the main problems the character faces?

4. Which of the characters do you admire and why?

5. What was your favorite part of the story and why?

6. Are any of the characters like someone you know? How?

7. Do you think the story would make a good movie? Why might the movie be difficult to make?

8. Did you have any difficulty understanding any part of the story? Which part and why?

9. Did you figure out the story's ending before you finished? Were you happy with the ending? Why or why not?

10. Please read a favorite paragraph from your book.

Other Questions:

_____

_____

_____

_____

_____

_____

_____

Figure 8.10   **Reading Comprehension and Strategies Checklist**

Student _____   Date _____

Title of Book _____

Reading Approach	Comments	Rating
Self-corrects to preserve meaning		
Observes punctuation to enhance meaning		
When confronting unfamiliar words:		
• skips the word and continues to read		
• rereads the sentence		
• uses context clues		
• uses picture clues (when present)		
• attempts to sound out the word		
• asks another person		

Discussion

This integrated assessment of reading and oral proficiency builds a cumulative record for the students' portfolios. The teacher adapts his questions to individual students and the books they have read. He varies the questions from student to student so the questions are not totally predictable. The questions are asked matter-of-factly in a casual conversational way, much as one person would ordinarily do if interested in another person's reading. The students pick up on this casual approach and ask their questions in a very conversational style. The presenting student responds in much the same way. Presumably, the students asking questions would need less to rely on questions on the 8½" x 11" page as the school year progresses. John's use of the tape recorder and the tapes is handled smoothly with a minimum of effort. Each student can review the tape from time-to-time to see progress they have made and to share their progress with parents. John also tapes individual conferences and oral presentations to the class so each student might come close to filling a 90-minute tape by the end of the school year.

Comments by ESL Teachers

This would be an excellent form of assessment to use in an ESL upper elementary, middle school, or high school classroom. Teachers can judge for themselves at what level of proficiency the technique can be used, but the assessment could definitely be used with intermediate and advanced students. The advantage in this type of assessment is that the teacher gets an integrated assessment of reading comprehension, oral reading fluency, word attack skills, and oral reading on five students, all packaged neatly in a 20-minute session. ESL students often welcome the use of a tape recorder. One caution in applying this assessment to ELL students is that the student's pronunciation, if rated at all, should be rated independently of other items shown on the Oral Reading Checklist. Further, if ELL students are asked to read aloud, they should first be given opportunities to hear the teacher model reading the text aloud, practice reading the same passage to a peer a number of times, and develop confidence in their pronunciation and fluency. Most importantly, teachers should not assume comprehension simply because students can read the text fluently but should ask follow-up comprehension questions.

Here are some selected entries from sixth-grader Roxana's first quarter portfolio. Her ESL teacher, Nancy Romeo, and other ESL teachers on Nancy's team have taken steps to provide information to parents in their native language, Spanish. This accounts for the bilingual format of both the cover letter to the parents and the reading checklist. Through the parent letter, the teacher invites Roxana's parents to interact with their child about the portfolio and to note progress in language development.

SPANISH

Dear Parents,

This is your child's ESL portfolio. All Rolling Valley students maintain a Language Arts Portfolio to help the students, their teachers, and their parents evaluate the progress that each student is making in reading, writing and speaking. Students are asked to discuss their progress and future goals with their teachers and their parents. ESL students maintain the same type of portfolio and are, to the best of their ability, also expected to evaluate their own progress.

When your child brings home his or her portfolio, please take the time to look at each section of the portfolio. Ask your child questions about the work and compare each quarter's work with the work of the preceding quarter or quarters.

Sincerely, *Nancy S Romeo*

Estimados padres,

Este es el portafolio de su hijo. En Rolling Valley los alumnos mantienen un Portafolio de Lenguaje para ayudar a los alumnos, sus profesores, y sus padres evaluar el progreso que cada alumno está mostrando en lectura, escritura y al hablar. Se les pide a los alumnos que discutan su progreso y sus metas futuras con sus profesores y sus padres. Los alumnos de ESL (Inglés Como Segunda Langua) mantienen el mismo tipo de portafolio y también se espera que evalúen su propio progreso lo mejor que puedan.

Cuando su hijo lleve a casa su portafolio, por favor tómese el tiempo para mirar cada sección del portafolio. Hágale preguntas a su hijo acerca del trabajo y compare el trabajo de cada trimestre con el trabajo del trimestre o trimestres anteriores.

Atentamente, *Nancy S Romeo*

The reading checklist indicates Roxana's performance on a variety of decoding skills and reading comprehension strategies. From it, we can see that she is an emerging reader who has developed an interest in books, uses picture cues for comprehension, and likes to listen to read-alouds. She is beginning to use sound-symbol and context clues and is learning to summarize a story.

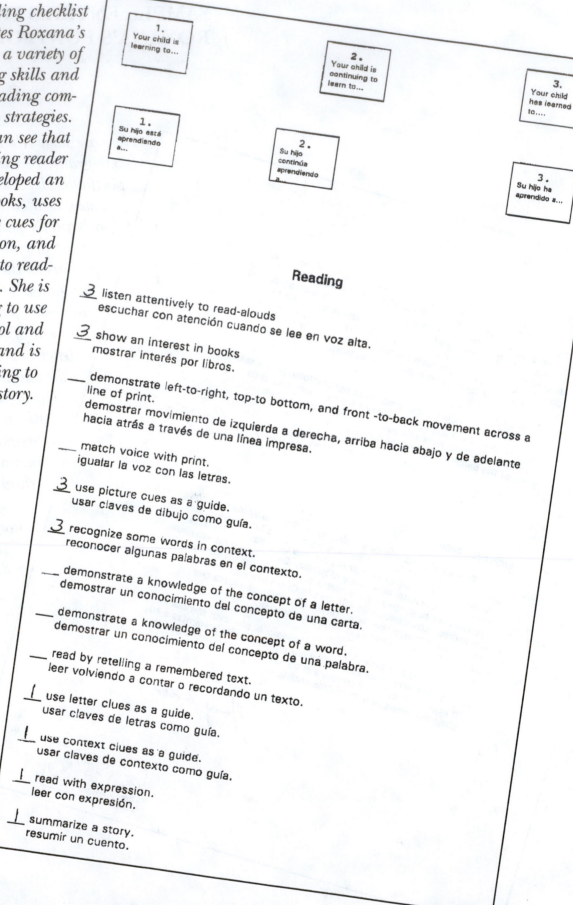

1.
Your child is learning to...

2.
Your child is continuing to learn to...

3.
Your child has learned to....

1.
Su hijo está aprendiendo a...

2.
Su hijo continúa aprendiendo a...

3.
Su hijo ha aprendido a...

Reading

3 listen attentively to read-alouds
escuchar con atención cuando se lee en voz alta.

3 show an interest in books
mostrar interés por libros.

— demonstrate left-to-right, top-to bottom, and front -to-back movement across a line of print.
demostrar movimiento de izquierda a derecha, arriba hacia abajo y de adelante hacia atrás a través de una línea impresa.

— match voice with print.
igualar la voz con las letras.

3 use picture cues as a guide.
usar claves de dibujo como guía.

3 recognize some words in context.
reconocer algunas palabras en el contexto.

— demonstrate a knowledge of the concept of a letter.
demostrar un conocimiento del concepto de una carta.

— demonstrate a knowledge of the concept of a word.
demostrar un conocimiento del concepto de una palabra.

— read by retelling a remembered text.
leer volviendo a contar o recordando un texto.

1 use letter clues as a guide.
usar claves de letras como guía.

1 use context clues as a guide.
usar claves de contexto como guía.

1 read with expression.
leer con expresión.

1 summarize a story.
resumir un cuento.

Roxana's reading response shows comprehension of the Robin Hood story through her drawing, a recommended mode for emerging writers.

Roxana

Reading Response

Who is the main character? Robin Hood Why do you think so? (because) The whole book is about his adventures.

Draw a picture of the character.

ROBIN HOOD

Did you like this book? Yes
Tell why—
Because it's a very good book

Roxana's self-assessment of her reading confirms what the teacher has marked on the checklist with regard to decoding skills and indicates that Roxana has determined to read more fluently next quarter.

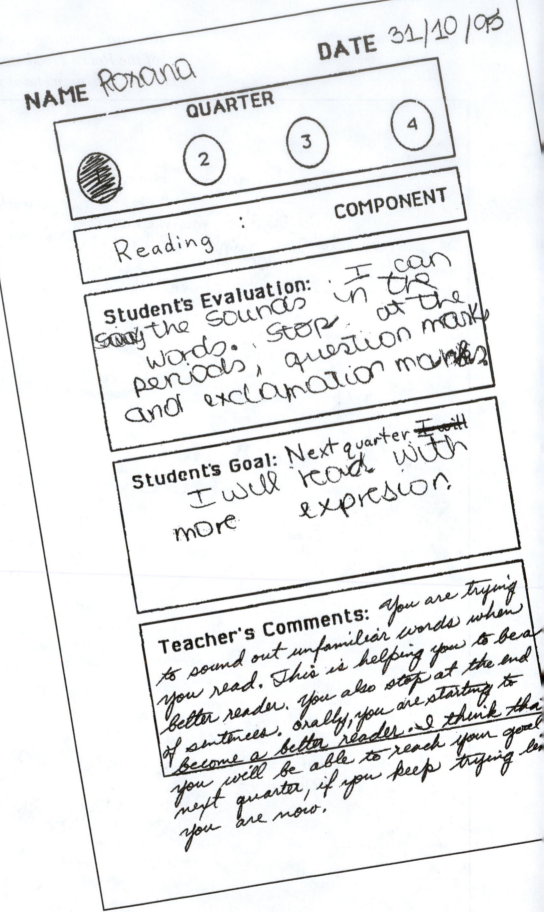

NAME Roxana

DATE 31/10/95

QUARTER

1 ② ③ ④

COMPONENT

Reading :

Student's Evaluation: I can say the sounds in the words. Stop at the periods, question mark and exclamation marks.

Student's Goal: Next quarter ~~I will~~ I will read with more expresion.

Teacher's Comments: You are trying to sound out unfamiliar words when you read. This is helping you to be a better reader. You also stop at the end of sentences. Orally, you are starting to become a better reader. I think tha you will be able to reach your goal next quarter, if you keep trying li you are now.

Roxana's writing sample portrays her mother vividly with many details about her preferred foods and leisure activities. It also shows that Roxana can write a cohesive story, put the final draft on the computer, and dress it up. This sample is a final version of a multi-draft story that was based on a webbing activity.

My Favorite Person
My Mother

My mother is very lovely, she cooks delicious food. She can cook: spaguetti, fish, chicken and more. She has a little cat. He is cute. My mother likes to go to Roy Rogers every Friday. There we eat alot. Her favorite sport is volleyball. She has 32 years old. She like the lobsters and also the crabs. Her favorite color is blue. She has brown eyes and black hair. She likes the steak and the baked potatoes. Her favorite dessert is the cheesecake. She has two best friends Carmella and Joan. She likes walks and she go to the mall. She is the best mother of the whole world.

Roxana
Mrs. Romeo
October 18, 1995

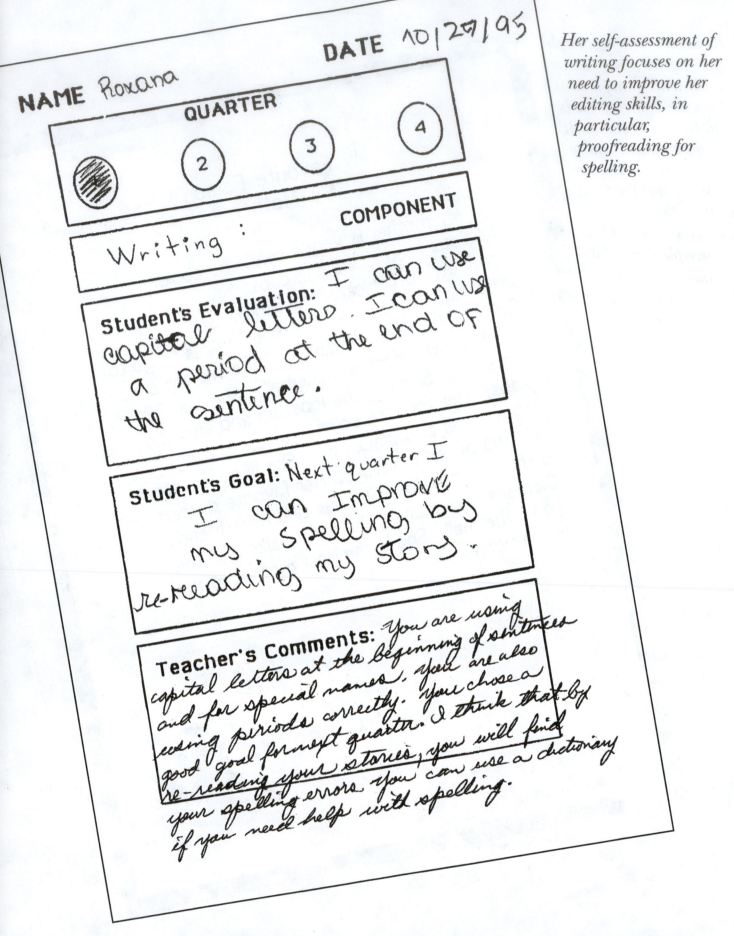

NAME Roxana

DATE 10/27/95

QUARTER
① 2 3 4

COMPONENT

Writing :

Student's Evaluation: I can use capital letters. I can use a period at the end of the sentence.

Student's Goal: Next quarter I can improve my spelling by re-reading my story.

Teacher's Comments: You are using capital letters at the beginning of sentences and for special names. You are also using periods correctly. You chose a good goal for next quarter. I think that by re-reading your stories, you will find your spelling errors. You can use a dictionary if you need help with spelling.

Her self-assessment of writing focuses on her need to improve her editing skills, in particular, proofreading for spelling.

The teacher's listed criteria for assessing writing provide Roxana with feedback on the content and organization of her writing in addition to the mechanics.

Criteria For Assessing Writing

1. Your Story Is Built Around A Central Idea. ✓
2. The Story Makes Sense. ✓
3. Your Sentences Show Some Detail and Description. ✓
4. All Parts Of The Story Belong. You could put everything about "food" together.
5. The Story Is Well-Organized.
6. The Story Has An Interesting Beginning. ✓
7. The Story Has Good Details In The Middle. See number 5
8. The Story Has An Interesting Ending. ✓
9. You Revised And Rewrote. ✓
10. You Used Correct Punctuation. ✓
11. You Used Correct Capitalization. ✓
12. Spelling spaghetti

1 = Poor
2 = Fair
3 = Okay
4 = Good
5 = Great

GLOSSARY[1]

. . . .

alternative assessment: approaches for finding out what students know or can do other than through the use of multiple-choice testing.

analytic scoring: the assignment of separate scores in designated categories on a scoring rubric.

anchor(s): representative products or performances used to characterize each point on a scoring rubric or scale.

anecdotal records: informal written notes on student learning products or processes, usually jotted down from direct observation.

assessment: a systematic approach for collecting information on student learning or performance, usually based on various sources of evidence.

authentic assessment: procedures for evaluating student achievement or performance using activities that represent classroom goals, curricula, and instruction or real-life performance.

benchmark: anchor papers used in defining exemplary performance on the levels of a scoring rubric. May also be a set of objectives, as in *benchmark objectives*, that define what is expected of a student in a particular area at a certain grade level.

cloze test: an assessment of reading comprehension that asks students to infer the missing words in a reading passage.

collection portfolio: a collection of all student work that shows how a student deals with daily classroom assignments.

consequential validity: the extent to which assessments are used to improve classroom instruction, support student learning, and respond to student needs.

1. Some of the terms in this glossary were adapted from the following sources:

Riverside Press. 1994. *Glossary of Terms Related to Performance Assessment.* Chicago, Ill.: Author.

Paris, S. G., and L. R. Ayres. 1994. *Becoming Reflective Students and Teachers with Portfolios and Authentic Assessment.* Washington, D.C.: American Psychological Association.

constructed response item: a type of assessment in which students read or review text materials and then respond to open-ended questions that elicit comprehension and higher-order thinking.

content area: subject matter course or curriculum, such as mathematics, science, history, etc.

content standards: the declarative and procedural knowledge specific to a given content domain.

core entries: required samples of student work or teacher observations entered in a portfolio.

criteria: guidelines, rules, or principles by which student responses, products, or performances are judged.

criteria charts: student-generated characteristics of exemplary work related to a specific classroom task or activity.

critical thinking: using higher-order mental processes, such as analyzing arguments carefully, seeing alternative points of view, evaluating alternatives, and reaching sound conclusions.

curriculum validity: the level of correspondence between assessments and the curriculum presented to students.

declarative knowledge: the type of knowledge that indicates *what* a student knows, as illustrated by memory of facts, names, dates, or knowledge *about* procedures.

dialogue journal: a type of writing in which students make entries in a notebook on topics of their choice, to which the teacher responds, modeling effective language but not overtly correcting the student's language.

differentiated scoring: providing separate scores on a written passage for language conventions and content knowledge.

elaboration: adding detailed explanations, examples, or other relevant information from prior knowledge.

English language learner (ELL): a student who is in the process of acquiring English and whose native language is not English or who comes from a background where a language other than English is spoken.

evaluation: interpretation of assessment data regarding the quality, value, or worth of some response, product, or performance. Evaluations are usually based on multiple sources of information.

fixed ratio cloze: a type of cloze test in which every fifth, seventh, or ninth word is deleted. Sometimes called a *random deletion cloze*, because the words have no systematic relationship to each other.

formative assessment: ongoing diagnostic assessment providing information to guide instruction.

generalizability: the extent to which the performances sampled by a set of assessment items and/or tasks are representative of the broader domain being assessed.

genre: a category or type of writing, such as stories, essays, research papers, letters, journal entries, and newspaper reports.

grade-level classrooms: classrooms designed for native speakers of English and based on local curriculum and standards.

higher-order thinking skills: relatively complex cognitive operations—such as concept formation, analysis, and problem solving—that commonly employ one or more skills.

holistic scoring: the assignment of a single score, based on specific criteria, to a student's performance.

information gap: an oral language activity in which a student is rated on his or her success in describing information that is kept from a partner, such as a picture, map, or object.

integrated assessment: assessment of language and content at the same time (e.g., assessment of an oral report on a science project).

inter-rater reliability: the level of agreement attained between independent raters of student performance. Often expressed as percentage of agreement or as the correlation between the scores of two raters on the same group of students.

language function: the purposes that language serves in oral or written communication, and what an individual is able to do in using language (e.g., describing, evaluating, and persuading).

language minority: in the United States, an individual who comes from an environment where a language other than English is spoken, or whose native language is not English.

learning log: a form of self-assessment in which students write journal entries summarizing what they have learned or commenting on the strategies they used that were successful in aiding their learning.

learning strategies: thoughts or behaviors students use that assist comprehension, learning of new material, or language production.

limited deletion cloze: a form of cloze test in which students are provided with a list of words that have been deleted as options to fill in the blanks.

literature discussion groups: heterogeneous, small group, student-directed, and teacher-guided discussions of a story or book.

literature response log: a record of books or stories read that includes a student's personal response or interpretation. Also called a *reading response log*.

metacognition: self-appraisal and self-regulation processes used in learning, thinking, reasoning, and problem solving.

miscue analysis: a type of reading assessment that provides information on decoding skills, reading strategies, and comprehension while students read aloud.

opportunity to learn: the extent to which students have been provided the information and skills represented in assessments.

optional entries: non-required student work entered into a portfolio that complements the required entries.

outcome: a goal statement specifying desired knowledge, skills, processes, and attitudes to be developed as a result of educational experiences.

peer assessment: assessment of a student's work, products, or learning processes by classmates. Also called *peer evaluation*.

performance assessment: assessment tasks that require students to construct a response, create a product, or demonstrate applications of knowledge.

performance standard: the level of performance required on specific activities represented in content standards.

portfolio: a collection of student work showing student reflection and progress or achievement over time in one or more areas.

portfolio assessment: a selective collection of student work, teacher observations, and self-assessment that is used to show progress over time with regard to specific criteria.

portfolio conference: a meeting between a teacher and a student to discuss student progress and set goals related to the work collected in a portfolio.

primary trait scoring: a type of scoring used to assess writing that focuses on a particular trait or feature emphasized in instruction, such as idea development or language structure.

project: an activity in which students prepare a product to show what they know and can do. Also called *exhibitions* and *demonstrations*.

Process Writing: a form of writing instruction that involves students in the construction of narratives on topics in which they have a personal interest. The process typically includes a prewriting stage, a writing stage, and a postwriting stage.

purposive deletion cloze: a type of cloze test in which specific categories of words are deleted, such as content words or words that have special structural characteristics (like plurals or past tense endings). Also referred to as a *rational deletion cloze*.

reading log: a chart with entries indicating the type and quantity of reading an individual student has completed.

reciprocal teaching: a small group reading activity designed to increase reading comprehension through direct application of reading strategies and peer teaching.

reliability: the degree to which an assessment yields consistent results.

rubric: a measurement scale used to evaluate a student's performance. Rubrics consist of a fixed scale and a list of characteristics that describe criteria at each score point for a particular outcome.

running record: a form of miscue analysis in which teachers record in detail what students do as they read aloud, such as repetitions, substitutions, insertions, hesitations, omissions, and self-corrections.

scaffolding: providing contextual supports for meaning during instruction or assessment, such as visual displays, classified lists, or tables or graphs.

schemata: the structural organization in which knowledge is stored in memory, including background knowledge and cultural meanings.

self-assessment: appraisal by a student of his or her own work or learning processes.

showcase portfolio: a collection of a student's best work, often selected by the student, that highlights what the student is able to do.

standard: an established level of achievement, quality of performance, or degree of proficiency.

standardization: a set of consistent procedures for constructing, administering, and scoring an assessment that ensures all students are assessed under uniform conditions.

summative assessment: culminating assessment for a unit, grade level, or course of study providing a status report on mastery or degree of proficiency according to identified learning outcomes.

task: an activity usually requiring multiple responses to a challenging question or problem.

test: a set of questions or situations designed to permit an inference about what a student knows or can do in an area of interest.

text retelling: a procedure for assessment of comprehension in which students listen to or read a story or text and then retell the main ideas or selected details in their own words.

think-aloud: students describe aloud the thinking processes they are using in reading or in problem solving.

T-List: an activity for reading or listening comprehension in which students mark a large "T" on a page and write main ideas to the left of the vertical bar and corresponding details to the right.

validity: refers to whether or not an assessment is an adequate measure of the curriculum and the objectives it represents.

whole language: an approach to teaching that is meaning-based and learner-centered.

REFERENCES

Abruscato, J. C. 1993. Early results and tentative implications from the Vermont portfolio project. *Phi Delta Kappan* 74 (6):474-477.

Afflerbach, P. 1995. STAIR: A system for recording and using what we observe and know about our students. In P. Afflerbach, ed., *Reading Assessment in Practice: Book of Readings,* 5-10. Newark, Del.: International Reading Association.

Alverman, D. E., and S. F. Phelps. 1994. *Content Reading and Literacy: Succeeding in Today's Diverse Classrooms.* Boston, Mass.: Allyn and Bacon.

Anderson, J. R. 1983. *The Architecture of Cognition.* Cambridge, Mass.: Harvard University Press.

———. 1990. *Cognitive Psychology and Its Implications.* 3rd ed. New York: W. H. Freeman.

Anderson, R. C., and P. D. Pearson. 1988. A schema-theoretic view of basic processes in reading comprehension. In P. L. Carrell, J. Devine, and D. Eskey, eds., *Interactive Approaches to Second Language Reading,* 37-55. Cambridge: Cambridge University Press.

Applebee, A. N., J. A. Langer, and I. V. S. Jullis. 1988. *Who Reads Best?* Princeton, N.J.: Educational Testing Service.

Aschbacher, P. R. 1991. Performance assessment: State activity, interest, and concerns. *Applied Measurement in Education* 4 (4):275-288.

Atwell, N. 1987. *In the Middle: Writing, Reading, and Learning with Adolescents.* Portsmouth, N.H.: Heinemann.

———., ed. 1990. *Coming to Know: Writing to Learn in the Intermediate Grades.* Portsmouth, N.H.: Heinemann.

Au, K. H. 1993. *Literacy Instruction in Multicultural Settings.* Fort Worth, Tex.: Harcourt Brace College Publishers.

Bachman, L. F. 1990. *Fundamental Considerations in Language Testing.* Oxford: Oxford University Press.

Bachman, L. F., and A. S. Palmer. 1989. The construct validation of self-ratings of communicative language ability. *Language Testing* 6 (1):14-29.

Baker, E. L. 1993. Questioning the technical quality of performance assessment. *The School Administrator* 50 (11):12-16.

Baker, E. L., P. R. Aschbacher, D. Niemi, and E. Sato. 1992 *CRESST Performance Assessment Models: Assessing Content Area Explanations.* Los Angeles, Calif.: Center for Research on Evaluation, Standards, and Student Testing, University of California.

Bat-Sheva, E., and M. C. Linn. 1988. Learning and instruction: An examination of four research perspectives in science education. *Review of Educational Research* 58:251-301.

Bloom, B. S., M. B. Engleheart, E. J. Furst, W. H. Hill, and D. R. Krathwohl, eds. 1956. *Taxonomy of Educational Objectives, Handbook I: Cognitive Domain.* New York: David McKay.

Brinton, D., M. A. Snow, and M. Wesche. 1989. *Content-based Second Language Instruction.* New York: Newbury House.

Brodhagen, B. 1994. Assessing and reporting student progress in an integrative curriculum. *Teaching and Change* 1 (3):238-254.

Brown, A. L., and R. A. Ferrara. 1984. Diagnosing zones of proximal development. In J. W. Wertsch, ed., *Culture, Communication, and Cognition: Vygotskian Perspectives,* 273-305. Cambridge: Cambridge University Press.

Brown, G., and G. Yule. 1983. *Teaching the Spoken Language: An Approach Based on the Analysis of Conversational English.* Cambridge: Cambridge University Press.

Burns, M. 1995. Writing in Math Class? Absolutely! *Instructor* 104 (7):40-47.

Butts, D. P., and H. Hofman. 1993. Hands-on, brains-on. *Science and Children* 30 (3):15-16.

Calfee, R. C. and P. Perfumo. 1993. Student portfolios: Opportunities for revolution in assessment. *Journal of Reading* 36 (7):532-537.

California Assessment Program (CAP). 1990. *Writing Assessment: Thinking through Writing.* Sacramento, Calif.: Author.

Calkins, L. M. 1994. *The Art of Teaching Writing.* Portsmouth, N.H.: Heinemann.

Cantoni-Harvey, G. 1987. *Content Area Language Instruction: Approaches and Strategies.* Reading, Mass.: Addison-Wesley.

Carrell, P. L. 1988. Some causes of text-boundedness and schema interference in ESL reading. In P. L. Carrell, J. Devine, and D. Eskey, eds., *Interactive Approaches to Second Language Reading,* 101-113. Cambridge: Cambridge University Press.

Carrell, P. L., J. Devine, and D. Eskey, eds. 1988. *Interactive Approaches to Second Language Reading.* Cambridge: Cambridge University Press.

Carruthers, R. 1987. Teaching pronunciation. In M. H. Long and J. C. Richards, eds., *Methodology in TESOL,* 191-199. New York: Newbury House.

Casazza, M. E. 1992. Teaching summary writing to enhance comprehension. *Reading Today* 9 (4):28.

Case, S. H. 1994. Will mandating portfolios undermine their value? *Educational Leadership* 52 (2):46-47.

Cazden, C. B. 1992. *Whole Language Plus.* New York: Teachers College Press.

Center for Applied Linguistics. 1993. *A Descriptive Study of Content-ESL Practices.* Final data analysis report, Contract No. T291004001. Washington, D.C.: U.S. Department of Education.

Chamot, A. U. 1987. *Language Development through Content: Social Studies—American History.* Reading, Mass.: Addison-Wesley.

Chamot, A. U., and J. M. O'Malley. 1986. *A Cognitive Academic Language Learning Approach: An ESL Content-based Curriculum.* Rosslyn, Va.: National Clearinghouse for Bilingual Education.

———. 1988. *Language Development through Content: Mathematics Book A.* Reading, Mass.: Addison-Wesley.

———. 1994a. *The CALLA Handbook: Implementing the Cognitive Academic Language Learning Approach.* Reading, Mass.: Addison-Wesley.

———. 1994b. Instructional approaches and teaching procedures. In K. Spangenberg-Urbschat and R. Pritchard, eds., *Kids Come in All Languages: Reading Instruction for ESL Students,* 82-107. Newark, Del.: International Reading Association.

Chamot, A. U., J. M. O'Malley, and L. Küpper. 1992. *Building Bridges: Content and Learning*

Strategies for ESL, Teacher's Manual and Tests. Books 1-3. Boston, Mass.: Heinle and Heinle.

Church, C. J. 1993. Record keeping in whole language programs. In B. Harp, ed., *Assessment and Evaluation in Whole Language Classrooms*, 187-210. Norwood, Mass.: Christopher-Gordon.

Clarke, M. A. 1988. The short circuit hypothesis of ESL reading—or when language competence interferes with reading performance. In P. L. Carrell, J. Devine, and D. Eskey, eds., *Interactive Approaches to Second Language Reading*, 114-124. Cambridge: Cambridge University Press.

Clay, M. 1993a. *An Observation Survey of Early Literacy Achievement.* Portsmouth, N.H.: Heinemann.

————. 1993b. *Reading Recovery: A Guidebook for Teachers in Training.* Portsmouth, N.H.: Heinemann.

Clemmons, J., L. Laase, D. Cooper, N. Areglado, and M. Dill. 1993. *Portfolios in the Classroom, Grades 1-6.* New York: Scholastic Professional Books.

Cohen, A. D. 1994. *Assessing Language Ability in the Classroom.* 2nd ed. Boston, Mass.: Heinle and Heinle.

Collier, V. P. 1987. Age and rate of acquisition of second language for academic purposes. *TESOL Quarterly* 21 (4):617-641.

————. 1989. How long? A synthesis of research on academic achievement in a second language. *TESOL Quarterly* 23 (3):509-531.

Collier, V. P., and W. P. Thomas. April 1988. Acquisition of cognitive-academic second language proficiency: A six-year study. Paper presented at the annual meeting of the American Educational Research Association, New Orleans.

Council for Basic Education. 1994. A standards primer. *Perspective* 6 (2).

Council of Chief State School Officers. 1991. *Summary of State Practices Concerning the Assessment of and the Data Collection about Limited English Proficient Students.* Washington, D.C.: Author

Cramer, R. L. 1982. Informal approaches to evaluating children's writing. In J. J. Pikulski and T. Shanahan, eds., *Approaches to the Informal Evaluation of Reading*, 80-93. Newark, Del.: International Reading Association.

Crandall, J. A., ed. 1987. *ESL in Content Area Instruction.* Englewood Cliffs, N.J.: Prentice Hall Regents.

Crandall, J. A., T. C. Dale, N. Rhodes, and G. Spanos. 1989. *English Skills for Algebra.* Washington, D.C./Englewood Cliffs, N.J.: Center for Applied Linguistics/Prentice Hall Regents.

Crawford, J. 1989. *Bilingual Education: History, Politics, Theory, and Practice.* Trenton, N.J.: Crane.

Cummins, J. 1980. The construct of proficiency in bilingual education. In J. E. Alatis, ed., *Georgetown University Round Table on Languages and Linguistics*, 81-103. Washington, D.C.: Georgetown University Press.

————. 1981. Age on arrival and immigrant second language learning in Canada: A reassessment. *Applied Linguistics* 2 (2):131-149.

————. 1982. *Tests, Achievement, and Bilingual Students.* Wheaton, Md.: National Clearinghouse for Bilingual Education.

————. 1983. Conceptual and linguistic foundations of language assessment. In S. S. Seidner, ed., *Issues of Language Assessment: Language Assessment and Curriculum Planning.* Wheaton, Md.: National Clearinghouse for Bilingual Education.

————. 1984. *Bilingualism and Special Education: Issues in Assessment and Pedagogy.* San Diego, Calif.: College-Hill.

————. 1989. *Empowering Minority Students.* Sacramento, Calif.: California Association for Bilingual Education.

Cunningham, P. 1982. Diagnosis by observation. In J. J. Pikulski and T. Shanahan, eds., *Approaches to the Informal Evaluation of Reading*, 12-22. Newark, Del.: International Reading Association.

Darling-Hammond, L. 1994. Performance-based assessment and educational equity. *Harvard Educational Review* 53 (1):5-30.

De Fina, A. A. 1992. *Portfolio Assessment: Getting Started.* New York: Scholastic Professional Books.

Dellinger, D. 1993. Portfolios: A personal history. In M. A. Smith and M. Ylvsikes, eds., *Teachers' Voices: Portfolios in the Classroom*, 11-24. Berkeley, Calif.: National Writing Project.

Devine, J. 1988. The relationship between general language competence and second language reading proficiency: Implications for teaching. In P. L. Carrell, J. Devine, and D. Eskey, eds., *Interactive Approaches to Second Language Reading,* 260-277. Cambridge: Cambridge University Press.

Donahue, M., and A. H. Parsons. 1982. The use of roleplay to overcome cultural fatigue. *TESOL Quarterly* 16 (3):359-365.

Doran, R. L., J. Boorman, F. Chan, and N. Hejaily. 1993. Authentic assessment. *The Science Teacher* 60 (6):37-40.

EAC-West. 1992. How to determine student grades. Workshop handout. Albuquerque, N.Mex.: Author.

Ennis, R. H. 1993. Critical thinking assessment. *Theory Into Practice* 32 (3):179-186.

Enright, D. S., and M. L. McCloskey. 1989. *Integrating English: Developing English Language and Literacy in the Multilingual Classroom.* Reading, Mass.: Addison-Wesley.

Eskey, D. E. 1988. Holding in the bottom: An interactive approach to the language problems of second language readers. In P. L. Carrell, J. Devine, and D. Eskey, eds., *Interactive Approaches to Second Language Reading,* 93-100. Cambridge: Cambridge University Press.

Eskey, D. E., and W. Grabe. 1988. Interactive models for second language reading: Perspectives on instruction. In P. L. Carrell, J. Devine, and D. Eskey, eds., *Interactive Approaches to Second Language Reading,* 223-238. Cambridge: Cambridge University Press.

Fairfax County, Virginia, Public Schools. 1989. *Suggestions for Assessment/Evaluation in the Integrated Language Arts Classroom.* Fairfax, Va.: Author.

Farnan, N., J. Flood, and D. Lapp. 1994. Comprehending through reading and writing. In K. Spangenberg-Urbschat and R. Pritchard, eds., *Kids Come in All Languages: Reading Instruction for ESL Students,* 135-157. Newark, Del.: International Reading Association.

Fathman, A., and M. E. Quinn. 1989. *Science for Language Learners.* Englewood Cliffs, N.J.: Prentice Hall Regents.

Feuer, M. J., and K. Fulton. 1993. The many faces of performance assessment. *Phi Delta Kappan* 74 (6):478.

Fielding, L. G., and P. D. Pearson. 1994. Reading comprehension: What works. *Educational Leadership* 51 (5):62-68.

Flower, L. S., and J. Hayes. 1981. A cognitive process theory of writing. *College Composition and Communication* 32:365-387.

Forrest, T. 1992. Shooting your class: The video-drama approach to language acquisition. In S. Stempleski and P. Arcario, eds., *Video in Second Language Teaching,* 79-92. Alexandria, Va.: Teachers of English to Speakers of Other Languages.

Fradd, S. H., P. L. McGee, and D. K. Wilen. 1994. *Instructional Assessment: An Integrative Approach to Evaluating Student Performance.* Reading, Mass.: Addison-Wesley.

Freed, C. S. 1993. The standard-setting process for the interim assessment period: A white paper. Draft. Dover, Del.: Delaware Department of Public Instruction.

Freeman, Y. S., and D. E. Freeman. 1992. *Whole Language for Second Language Learners.* Portsmouth, N.H.: Heinemann.

Gagné, E. D., C. W. Yekovich, and F. R. Yekovich. 1993. *The Cognitive Psychology of School Learning.* 2nd ed. New York: Harper Collins.

Garcia, G. E. 1994. Assessing the literacy development of second language students. In K. Spangenberg-Urbschat and R. Pritchard, eds., *Kids Come in All Languages: Reading Instruction for ESL Students,* 180-205. Newark, Del.: International Reading Association.

Garcia, S. B., and A. A. Ortiz. 1988. Preventing inappropriate referrals of language minority students to special education. Wheaton, Md.: National Clearinghouse for Bilingual Education.

Gebhard, A. O. 1983. Teaching writing and reading in the content areas. *Journal of Reading* 27 (3):207-211.

Genesee, F. 1994. TESOL's role in setting standards. *TESOL Matters* 4 (4):3.

Genishi, C. 1985. Observing communicative performance in young children. In A. Jaggar and M. T. Smith-Burke, eds. *Observing the Language*

Learner, 131-142. Newark, Del.: International Reading Association.

Glazer, S. M., and C. S. Brown. 1993. *Portfolios and Beyond: Collaborative Assessment in Reading and Writing.* Norwood, Mass.: Christopher-Gordon.

Gonzalez Pino, B. September 1988. Testing second language speaking: Practical approaches to oral testing in large classes. Paper presented at the Northeast Conference of Teachers of Foreign Languages, New York.

Goodman, K. 1986. *What's Whole in Whole Language?* Portsmouth, N.H.: Heinemann.

Goodman, Y. M., D. J. Watson, and C. L. Burke. 1987. *Reading Miscue Inventory: Alternative Procedures.* New York: Richard C. Owen.

Gottlieb, M. April 1993. Portfolios as instructional and assessment alternatives for language minority (and majority) students. Paper presented at the annual meeting of the American Educational Research Association, Atlanta, Ga.

Gottlieb, M. 1995. Nurturing student learning through portfolios. *TESOL Journal* 5 (1):12-14.

Grabe, W. 1988. Reassessing the term "interactive." In P. L. Carrell, J. Devine, and D. Eskey, eds., *Interactive Approaches to Second Language Reading,* 56-70. Cambridge: Cambridge University Press.

Graves, D. 1983. *Writing: Teachers and Children at Work.* Portsmouth, N.H.: Heinemann.

Hakuta, K., D. August, and D. Pompa. 1994. Limited English proficient students and systemic reform. Manuscript. Stanford, Calif.: Stanford University.

Halliday, M. A. K. 1975. *Learning How to Mean: Explorations in the Development of Language.* London: Edward Arnold.

Hamayan, E. V. 1989. *Teaching Writing to Potentially English Proficient Students Using Whole Language Approaches.* Silver Spring, Md.: National Clearinghouse for Bilingual Education.

Hamayan, E. V., and R. Perlman. 1990. *Helping Language Minority Students after They Exit from Bilingual/ESL Programs: A Handbook for Teachers.* Washington, D.C.: National Clearinghouse for Bilingual Education.

Hamp-Lyons, L. 1983. Survey materials for teaching advanced listening and note-taking. *TESOL Quarterly* 17 (1):109-122.

————. 1990. Second language writing: Assessment issues. In B. Kroll, ed., *Second Language Writing: Research Insights for the Classroom,* 69-87. Cambridge: Cambridge University Press.

————. 1991. Scoring procedures for ESL contexts. In L. Hamp-Lyons, ed., *Assessing Second Language Writing in Academic Contexts,* 241-276. Norwood, N.J.: Ablex.

Harris, K. R., and S. Graham. 1992. Self-regulated strategy development: A part of the writing process. In M. Pressley, K. Harris, and J. T. Guthrie, eds., *Promoting Academic Competence and Literacy in Schools,* 277-309. San Diego, Calif.: Academic Press.

Hayward, V. 1993. Assessing students' writing: A hands-on guide from the Northern Territory. In C. Bouffle, ed., *Literacy Evaluation: Issues and Practicalities,* 63-76. Portsmouth, N.H.: Heinemann.

Hedgecock, J., and S. Pucci. Winter 1993/94. Whole language applications to ESL in secondary and higher education. *TESOL Journal* 3 (2):22-26.

Herman, J. L. 1991. Research in cognition and learning: Implications for achievement testing practice. In M. C. Wittrock and E. L. Baker, eds., *Testing and Cognition,* 154-165. Englewood Cliffs, N.J.: Prentice Hall.

Herman, J. L., P. R. Aschbacher, and L. Winters. 1992. *A Practical Guide to Alternative Assessment.* Alexandria, Va.: Association for Supervision and Curriculum Development.

Herman, J. L., and L. Winters. 1994. Portfolio research: A slim collection. *Educational Leadership* 52 (2):48-55.

Hiebert, J., ed. 1986. *Conceptual and Procedural Knowledge: The Case of Mathematics.* Hillsdale, N.J.: Lawrence Erlbaum.

Hill, B. C., and C. Ruptic. 1994. *Practical Aspects of Authentic Assessment: Putting the Pieces Together.* Norwood, Mass.: Christopher-Gordon.

Hillocks, G., Jr. 1987. Synthesis of research on teaching writing. *Educational Leadership* 44 (8):71-82.

Holmes, B. C., and N. L Roser. 1987. Five ways to assess readers' prior knowledge. *The Reading Teacher* 40:646-649.

Hoover, H. D. May 1995. Remarks presented at the meetings of the Virginia Association of Test Directors, Richmond, Va.

Hudelson, S. 1989. *Write On: Children Writing in ESL.* Englewood Cliffs, N.J.: Prentice Hall.

Hughes, A. 1989. *Testing for Language Teachers.* Cambridge: Cambridge University Press.

Jan, L. W. 1992. Think about it! One approach to reflective learning. In K. S. Goodman, L. B. Bird, and Y. M. Goodman, eds., *The Whole Language Catalog Supplement on Authentic Assessment,* 117. New York: SRA Macmillan McGraw-Hill.

Johns, J. L. 1982. The dimensions and uses of informal reading assessment. In J. J. Pikulski and T. Shanahan, eds., *Approaches to the Informal Evaluation of Reading,* 1-11. Newark, Del.: International Reading Association.

Johnston, J., and M. Johnston. 1990. *Content Points.* Books A-C. Reading, Mass.: Addison-Wesley.

Jones, B. F., A. S. Palincsar, D. S. Ogle, and E. G. Carr. 1987. *Strategic Teaching and Learning: Cognitive Instruction in the Content Areas.* Alexandria, Va.: Association for Supervision and Curriculum Development.

Joyce, B. R., and B. Showers. 1987. *Student Achievement through Staff Development.* White Plains, N.Y.: Longman.

Kagan, S. 1993. *Cooperative Learning.* San Juan Capistrano, Calif.: Resources for Teachers, Inc.

———. 1995. Group grades miss the mark. *Educational Leadership* 52 (8):68-71.

Kennedy, B. 1985. Writing letters to learn math. *Learning* 13 (6):59-60.

Kessler, C., L. Lee, M. L. McCloskey, M. E. Quinn, and L. Stack. 1994. *Making Connections.* Boston, Mass.: Heinle and Heinle.

Kessler, C., and M. E. Quinn. 1980. Positive effects of bilingualism on science problem-solving ability. In J. E. Alatis, ed., *Georgetown University Round Table on Languages and Linguistics 1980,* 295-308. Washington, D.C.: Georgetown University.

Khattri, N., M. B. Kane, and A. L. Reeve. 1995. How performance assessments affect teaching and learning. *Educational Leadership* 53 (3):80-83.

Kohn, A. 1994. Grading: The issue is not how but why. *Educational Leadership* 52 (2):38-41.

Kolls, M. R. March 1992. Portfolio assessment: A feasibility study. Paper presented at the annual meetings of Teachers of English to Speakers of Other Languages, Vancouver, B.C., Canada.

Koretz, D. September 1993. Consequences and equity: The challenge of making it happen. Presentation as part of a symposium at CRESST, University of California, Los Angeles, Calif.

Kramsch, C. 1986. From language proficiency to interactional competence. *The Modern Language Journal* 70 (4):366-372.

Krashen, S. D. 1991. *Bilingual Education: A Focus on Current Research.* Washington, D.C.: National Clearinghouse for Bilingual Education.

Kritt, D. 1993. Authenticity, reflection, and self-evaluation in alternative assessment. *Middle School Journal* 25 (2):43-45.

Lamme, L. L. and C. Hysmith. 1991. One school's adventure into portfolio assessment. *Language Arts* 68 (8):629-640.

Lapp, D., J. Flood, and N. Farnan. 1989. *Content Area Reading and Learning: Instructional Strategies.* Englewood Cliffs, N.J.: Prentice Hall.

Littlewood, W. 1981. *Communicative Language Teaching.* Cambridge: Cambridge University Press.

Maryland State Department of Education. (n.d.). *Questions for Quality Thinking.* Baltimore, Md.: Author.

———. *Writing Assessment Program.* Baltimore, Md.: Author.

Marzano, R., R. S. Brandt, C. S. Hughes, B. F. Jones, B. Z. Presseisen, S. C. Rankin, and C. Suhor. 1988. *Dimensions of Thinking: A Framework for Curriculum and Instruction.* Alexandria, Va.: Association for Supervision and Curriculum Development.

Marzano, R.J., and J. S. Kendall. 1993. The systematic identification and articulation of content standards and benchmarks: An illustration using mathematics. Draft. Aurora, Colo.: Mid-continent Regional Educational Laboratory.

Marzano, R., D. Pickering, and J. McTighe. 1993. *Assessing Student Outcomes: Performance Assessment Using the Dimensions of Learning Model.* Alexandria, Va.: Association for Supervision in Curriculum Development.

McLeod, B. and B. McLaughlin. 1986. Restructuring or automatization? Reading in a second language. *Language Learning* 36 (2):109-126.

Meloni, C. F., and S. E. Thompson. 1980. Oral reports in the intermediate ESL classroom. *TESOL Quarterly* 14 (4): 503-510.

Misencik, K., J. Briggs, and the DMES Alternative Assessment Committee. 1993. Developmental descriptors. Manuscript. Dumfries, Va.: Dumfries Model Effective Elementary School.

Mohan, B. A. 1986. *Language and Content.* Reading, Mass.: Addison-Wesley.

Mundahl, J. 1993. *Tales of Courage, Tales of Dreams: A Multicultural Reader.* Reading, Mass.: Addison-Wesley.

Murphy, J. M. 1991. Oral communication in TESOL: Integrating speaking, listening, and pronunciation. *TESOL Quarterly* 25 (1):51-75.

National Assessment of Educational Progress (NAEP). 1987. *Writing Objectives: 1988 Assessment.* Princeton, N.J.: Educational Testing Service.

National Council of Teachers of Mathematics (NCTM). 1989. *Curriculum and Evaluation Standards for School Mathematics.* Reston, Va.: Author.

National Council on Education Standards and Testing. 1992. *Raising Standards for American Education.* Washington, D.C.: U.S. Government Printing Office.

National Education Association (NEA). 1993. *Student Portfolios.*West Haven, Conn.: NEA Professional Library.

Navarrette, C., J. Wilde, C. Nelson, R. Martinez, and G. Hargett. 1990. *Informal Assessment in Educational Evaluation: Implications for Bilingual Education Programs.* Washington, D.C.: National Clearinghouse for Bilingual Education.

Newell, G. 1989. Why writing? *Resource Bulletin* (6). Madison, Wis. National Center on Effective Secondary Schools, University of Wisconsin.

Newmann, F. R. 1989. Writing across the curriculum. *Resource Bulletin* (6):1. Madison, Wis.: National Center on Effective Secondary Schools, University of Wisconsin.

Noddings, N., K. Gilbert-MacMillan, and S. Leitz. April 1983. What do individuals gain in small group mathematical problem solving? Paper presented at the annual meetings of the American Educational Research Association, Montreal, Que., Canada.

Nourse, J., E. Wilson, and S. Andrien. March 1994. Expanding our notions of oral competence: Developing benchmarks. Paper presented at the annual meeting of the Teachers of English to Speakers of Other Languages. Baltimore, Md.

Ogle, D. 1986. K-W-L group instruction strategy. In A. S. Palincsar, D. S. Ogle, B. F. Jones, and E. G. Carr, eds., *Teaching Reading as Thinking.* Alexandria, Va.: Association for Supervision and Curriculum Development.

Oller, J. W. 1979. *Language Tests at School.* London: Longman.

Omaggio Hadley, A. 1993. *Teaching Language in Context.* Boston, Mass.: Heinle and Heinle.

O'Malley, J. M. 1992. Looking for academic language proficiency. In Office of Bilingual Education and Minority Language Affairs, ed., *Proceedings of the Second Research Symposium on Limited English Proficient Students' Issues,* 173-182. Washington, D.C.: U.S. Government Printing Office.

O'Malley, J. M., and A. U. Chamot. 1990. *Learning Strategies in Second Language Acquisition.* Cambridge: Cambridge University Press.

O'Malley, J. M., A. U. Chamot, and L. Küpper. 1989. Listening comprehension strategies in second language acquisition. *Applied Linguistics* 10 (4):418-437.

O'Malley, J. M., and L. Valdez Pierce. 1991. Portfolio assessment: Using portfolio and alternative assessment with limited English proficient students. *FORUM* 15 (1):1-2.

O'Malley, J. M., and L. Valdez Pierce. 1994. State assessment policies, practices, and language minority students. *Educational Assessment* 2 (3):213-255.

O'Malley, J. M., L. Valdez Pierce, M. Gottlieb, and M. Kolls. March 1992. Portfolio development: Experiences from the field. Papers presented at a colloquium of the annual meeting of the Teachers of English to Speakers of Other Languages, Vancouver, B.C., Canada.

O'Neil, J. 1993. Can national standards make a difference? *Educational Leadership* 50 (5):4-8.

Oscarson, M. 1989. Self-assessment of language proficiency: Rationale and applications. *Language Testing* 6 (1):1-13.

Otis, M. J., and T. R. Offerman. 1988. How do you evaluate problem solving? *Arithmetic Teacher* 35 (8):49-51.

Palincsar, A. S., and A. L. Brown. 1984. Reciprocal teaching of comprehension-fostering and comprehension-monitoring activities. *Cognition and Instruction* 1 (2):117-175.

Palmer, A. S., T. S. Rodgers, and J. Winn-Bell Olsen. 1985. *Back and Forth: Pair Activities for Language Development.* Englewood Cliffs, N.J.: Alemany Press.

Paris, S. G., and L. R. Ayers. 1994. *Becoming Reflective Students and Teachers with Portfolios and Authentic Assessment.* Washington, D.C.: American Psychological Association.

Paulson, F.L., and P. R. Paulson. 1992. The varieties of self-reflection. *Portfolio News* 4 (1):1, 10-13.

Paulson, F. L., P. R. Paulson, and C. A. Meyer. 1991. What makes a portfolio a portfolio? *Educational Leadership* 48 (5):60-63.

Pearce, D. L. 1983. Guidelines for the use and evaluation of writing in content classrooms. *Journal of Reading* 27:212-218.

Pearson, P. D. 1993. Teaching and learning reading: A research perspective. *Language Arts* 70 (6):502-511.

Peregoy, S. F., and O. F. Boyle. 1993. *Reading, Writing, and Learning in ESL: A Resource Book for K-8 Teachers.* New York: Longman.

Perkins, K. 1983. On the use of composition scoring techniques, objective measures, and objective tests to evaluate ESL writing ability. *TESOL Quarterly* 17:651-671.

Peyton, J. K., and L. Reed. 1990. *Dialogue Journal Writing with Non-Native English Speakers: A Handbook for Teachers.* Alexandria, Va.: Teachers of English to Speakers of Other Languages.

Pikulski, J. J., and T. Shanahan, eds. 1982. *Approaches to the Informal Evaluation of Reading.* Newark, Del.: International Reading Association.

Pikulski, J. J., and A. W. Tobin. 1982. The cloze procedure as an informal assessment. In J. J. Pikulski and T. Shanahan, eds., *Approaches to the Informal Evaluation of Reading,* 42-62. Newark, Del.: International Reading Association.

Porter, D. and J. Roberts. 1987. Authentic listening activities. In M. H. Long and J. C. Richards, eds., *Methodology in TESOL,* 177-187. New York: Newbury House.

Pradl, G. M., and J. S. Mayher. 1985. Reinvigorating learning through writing. *Educational Leadership* 42 (5):4-8.

Pressley, M., and Associates. 1990. *Cognitive Strategy Instruction That Really Improves Children's Academic Performance.* Cambridge, Mass.: Brookline Books.

Ramirez, J. D., S. D. Yuen, and D. R. Ramey. 1991. Longitudinal study of structured English immersion strategy, early-exit and late-exit transitional bilingual education programs for language-minority children. Final report to the U.S. Department of Education. San Mateo, Calif.: Aguire International.

Resnick, L. B. 1987. *Education and Learning to Think.* Washington, D.C.: National Academy Press.

Resnick, L. B., and L. E. Klopfer. 1989. Toward the thinking curriculum: An overview. In L. B. Resnick and L. E. Klopfer, eds., *Toward the Thinking Curriculum: Current Cognitive Research,* 1-18. Alexandria, Va.: Association for Supervision and Curriculum Development.

Resnick, L. B., and D. Resnick. 1991. Assessing the thinking curriculum: New tools for educational reform. In B. R. Gifford and M. C. O'Connor, eds., *Changing Assessments: Alternative Views of Aptitude, Achievement and Instruction,* 37-75. Boston, Mass.: Kluwer.

Rhodes, L. K. 1993. *Literacy Assessment: A Handbook of Instruments.* Portsmouth, N.H.: Heinemann.

Rhodes, L. K., and S. Nathenson-Mejia. 1992. Anecdotal records: A powerful tool for ongoing literacy assessment. *The Reading Teacher* 45 (7):502-509.

Richard-Amato, P. A. 1988. *Making It Happen: Interaction in the Second Language Classroom.* New York: Longman.

Richards, J. C. 1983. Listening comprehension: Approach, design, procedure. *TESOL Quarterly* 17 (2):219-240.

Richards, J. C., and T. S. Rodgers. 1986. *Approaches and Methods in Language Teaching: A Description and Analysis.* Cambridge: Cambridge University Press.

Rief, L. 1990. Finding the value in evaluation: Self-assessment in a middle school classroom. *Educational Leadership* 47 (6):24-29.

Rigg, P. 1988. The miscue-ESL project. In P. L. Carrell, J. Devine, and D. Eskey, eds., *Interactive Approaches to Second Language Reading,* 206-219. Cambridge: Cambridge University Press.

Romberg, T.A., and L. D. Wilson. 1992. Alignment of tests with the standards. *Arithmetic Teacher* 40 (1):18-22.

Routman, R. 1994. *Invitations: Changing as Teachers and Learners K-12.* Portsmouth, N.H.: Heinemann.

Samuels, S. J., and M. L. Kamil. 1988. Models of the reading process. In P. L. Carrell, J. Devine, and D. Eskey, eds., *Interactive Approaches to Second Language Reading,* 22-36. Cambridge: Cambridge University Press.

Samway, K. D. 1992. *Writers' Workshop and Children Acquiring English as a Non-Native Language.* Washington, D.C.: National Clearinghouse for Bilingual Education.

Scarcella, R. C. 1987. Sociodrama for social interaction. In M. H. Long and J. C. Richards, eds., *Methodology in TESOL,* 208-213. New York: Newbury House.

Schmidt, M. B. 1986. The shape of content: Four semantic map structures for expository paragraphs. *The Reading Teacher* 40 (1):19-23.

Scott, K. 1989. Writing to learn. *Resource Bulletin* (6):6-7. Madison, Wis.: National Center for Effective Secondary Schools, University of Wisconsin.

Seago, N. 1993. *Portfolio Selections with Reflections.* Pittsburgh, Pa.: Arts Propel.

Self, J. (n.d.). *Virginia's Literacy Passport Test (LPT) for Writing: A Performance Assessment. A Resource Notebook for Teachers.* Radford, Va.: Virginia Department of Education, Regional Field Services, Radford University.

Sharp, Q. Q. 1989. *Evaluation: Whole Language Checklists for Evaluating Your Children.* New York: Scholastic.

Shepard, L. 1989. Why we need better assessments. *Educational Leadership* 46 (7):4-9.

Shepard, L. 1993. Evaluating test validity. In L. Darling-Hammond, ed., *Review of Research in Education* 19:405-450. Washington, D.C.: American Educational Research Association.

Short, D. J. 1991. *How to Integrate Language and Content Instruction: A Training Manual.* 2nd ed. Washington, D.C.: Center for Applied Linguistics.

———. 1993. Assessing integrated language and content instruction. *TESOL Quarterly* 27 (4):627-656.

Short, D. J., M. Seufert-Bosco, and A. G. Grognet. 1991. *Of the People: U.S. History.* Washington, D.C./Englewood Cliffs, N.J.: Center for Applied Linguistics/Prentice Hall Regents.

Shuman, R. B. 1984. School-wide writing instruction. *English Journal* 73 (2):54-57.

Simmons, W., and L. Resnick. 1993. Assessment as the catalyst of school reform. *Educational Leadership* 50 (5):11-15.

Simpson, M. L. 1987. Alternative formats for evaluating content area vocabulary understanding. *Journal of Reading* 30 (1):20-27.

Siu-Runyan, Y. 1993. Holistic Assessment in intermediate classes: Techniques for informing our teaching. In B. Harp, ed., *Assessment and Evaluation in Whole Language Programs,* 117-145. Norwood, Mass.: Christopher Gordon.

Sperling, D. 1993. What's worth an 'A'? Setting standards together. *Educational Leadership* 50 (5):73-75.

Stanovich, K. E. 1980. Toward an interactive compensatory model of individual differences in the development of reading fluency. *Reading Research Quarterly* 16 (1):32-71.

Stempleski, S., and P. Arcario, eds. 1992. *Video in Second Language Teaching: Using, Selecting, and Producing Video for the Classroom.* Alexandria, Va.: Teachers of English to Speakers of Other Languages.

Stenmark, J. K., ed. 1991. *Mathematics Assessment.* Reston, Va.: National Council of Teachers of Mathematics.

Stevenson, H. W. 1993. Why Asian students still outdistance Americans. *Educational Leadership* 50 (5):63-65.

Stiggins, R. J. 1988. Revitalizing classroom assessment: The highest instructional priority. *Phi Delta Kappan* 69 (5): 363-368.

———. 1988. *Strategies for Developing Sound Grading Practices.* Portland, Ore.: Northwest Regional Educational Laboratory.

———. 1991. Facing the challenges of a new era of educational assessment. *Applied Measurement in Education* 4 (4):263-272.

———. 1992. *In Teachers' Hands: Investigating the Practices of Classroom Assessment.* Albany, N.Y.: State University of New York Press.

Stiggins, R. J., D. A. Frisbie, and P. A. Griswald. 1989. Inside high school grading practices: Building a research agenda. *Educational Measurement: Issues and Practices* 7 (summer):5-14.

Stiggins, R. J., E. Rubel, and E. Quellmalz. 1986. *Measuring Thinking Skills in the Classroom.* Washington, D.C.: National Education Association.

Storey, R. D., and J. Carter. 1992. Why THE scientific method? *The Science Teacher* 59 (9):18-21.

Sweet, D. 1993. Student portfolios: Administrative uses. *Education Research Consumer Guide* 9. Washington, D.C.: Office of Educational Research and Improvement (OERI).

Taylor, W. L. 1953. "Cloze procedure": A new tool for measuring readability. *Journalism Quarterly* 30 (4):415-433.

Tchudi, S. 1991. *Planning and Assessing the Curriculum in English Language Arts.* Alexandria, Va.: Association for Supervision in Curriculum Development.

Thorndike, R. L., and E. P. Hagen. 1977. *Measurement and Evaluation in Psychology and Education.* 4th ed. New York: John Wiley and Sons.

Tierney, R. J., M. A. Carter, and L. E. Desai. 1991. *Portfolio Assessment in the Reading-Writing Classroom.* Norwood, Mass.: Christopher-Gordon.

Tomalin, B. 1992. Teaching young children with video. In S. Stempleski and P. Arcario, eds., *Video in Second Language Teaching,* 47-55. Alexandria, Va.: Teachers of English to Speakers of Other Languages.

Underhill, N. 1987. *Testing Spoken Language.* Cambridge: Cambridge University Press.

Ur, P. 1984. *Teaching Listening Comprehension.* Cambridge: Cambridge University Press.

Vacca, R. T., and J. L. Vacca. 1993. *Content Area Reading.* New York: Harper Collins.

Valdez Pierce, L., and M. Gottlieb. March 1994. Portfolios: Matching purpose to practice. Paper presented at the annual meeting of the Teachers of English to Speakers of Other Languages, Baltimore, Md.

Valdez Pierce, L., and J. M. O'Malley. 1992. *Performance and Portfolio Assessment for Language Minority Students.* Washington, D.C.: National Clearinghouse for Bilingual Education.

———. April 1993. Teacher concerns and strategies in the implementation of language minority student portfolio assessment. Paper presented at the annual meeting of the American Educational Research Association, Atlanta, Ga.

Valencia, S. 1990. A portfolio approach to classroom reading assessment: The whys, whats, and hows. *The Reading Teacher* 43 (4):338-340.

Valencia, S. W. 1991. Portfolios: Panacea or Pandora's Box? In F. L. Finch, ed., *Educational Performance Assessment,* 33-46. Chicago, Ill.: Riverside Publishing Co.

Vermont Department of Education. 1990. *This is My Best: Vermont's Writing Assessment Program.* Montpelier, Vt.: Author.

Watson, D., and J. Henson. 1993. Reading evaluation-miscue analysis. In B. Harp, ed., *Assessment and Evaluation in Whole Language Programs,* 53-75. Norwood, Mass.: Christopher-Gordon.

Weinstein, C. E., and R. E. Mayer. 1986. The teaching of learning strategies. In M. C. Wittrock, ed., *Handbook of Research on Teaching,* 3rd ed., 315-27. New York: Macmillan.

Wiggins, G. 1989. Teaching to the (authentic) test. *Educational Leadership* 46 (7):41-47.

———. 1992. Creating tests worth taking. *Educational Leadership* 49 (8):26-33.

———. 1993. *Assessing Student Performance: Exploring the Purpose and Limits of Testing.* San Francisco, Calif.: Jossey-Bass.

Wilder, L. I. 1991. *Little House in the Big Woods.* New York: Harper Collins.

Wilkins, D. A. 1976. *Notional Syllabuses.* Oxford: Oxford University Press.

Winn-Bell Olsen, J. 1984. *Look Again Pictures for Language Development and Lifeskills.* Englewood Cliffs, N.J.: Alemany Press.

Winograd, K., and K. M. Higgins. 1994/95. Writing, reading, and talking mathematics: One interdisiplinary possibility. *The Reading Teacher* 48 (4):310-318.

Wolf, D. 1989. Portfolio assessment: Sampling student work. *Educational Leadership* 46 (7):35-39.

Wolf, K.P. 1993. From informal to informed assessment: Recognizing the role of the classroom teacher. In E. Jongsma and R. Farr, eds., *Literacy Assessment,* 6-11. Newark, Del.: International Reading Association.

Yager, R. E. 1991. The constructivist learning model: Towards real reform in science education. *The Science Teacher* 58 (6):52-57.

Yancey, K. B. 1992. *Portfolios in the Writing Classroom.* Urbana, Ill.: National Council of Teachers of English.

INDEX OF CLASSROOM-BASED ASSESSMENT TECHNIQUES

· · · · · · · · · · · · · ·

Throughout this book we have focused on the importance of embedding assessment in instruction. This index identifies headings that describe classroom-based instructional activities we have used as assessment techniques.

INDEX
Subject

· · · · · · · · · · · · ·

INDEX
Author

• • • • • • • • • • • • • • •

Quinn, M.E., 164, 165, 188
Ramey, D.R., 164
Ramirez, J.D., 164
Reed, L., 151
Reeve, A.L., 7, 8
Resnick, D., 168, 174, 181
Resnick, L., 169
Resnick, L.B., 2, 4, 10, 25, 168, 174, 181
Rhodes, L.K., 89, 90, 105, 115, 124, 125
Rhodes, N., 164
Richard-Amato, P.A., 85, 89
Richards, J.C., 34n, 58, 59, 63
Rief, L., 38
Rigg, P., 125
Roberts, J., 59–60, 62, 80
Rodgers, T.S., 34n, 83
Romberg, T.A., 174
Roser, N.L., 175, 176
Routman, R., 96, 97, 99, 100, 105, 111, 112, 113, 114, 120, 124, 125, 127
Rubel, E., 181
Ruptic, C., 75, 90, 102, 106, 107, 111, 112, 115, 116, 124, 144, 153, 190
Samuels, S.J., 94
Samway, K.D., 39
Scarcella, R.C., 85
Schmidt, M.B., 175, 178
Scott, K., 185, 186
Seago, N., 198
Self, J., 144, 145
Seufert-Bosco, M., 164
Shanahan, T., 105
Sharp, Q.Q., 104
Shepard, L., 25, 168
Short, D.J., 164, 165, 166, 183
Showers, B., 25
Shuman, R.B., 139
Simmons, W., 169
Simpson, M.L., 180, 181
Siu-Runyan, Y., 132
Snow, M.A., 164
Spanos, G., 164
Sperling, D., 38
Stanovich, K.E., 94
Stempleski, S., 81
Stenmark, J.K., 192, 194
Stevenson, H.W., 168

Stiggins, R.J., 1, 6, 15, 29, 30, 181
Storey, R.D., 188
Sweet, D., 49
Taylor, W.L., 114
Tchudi, S., 138
Thomas, W.P., 60
Thompson, S.E., 87
Thorndike, R.L., 90, 125
Tierney, R.J., 34, 35, 36, 38, 39, 42, 49, 102, 112, 127
Tobin, A.W., 114, 118, 180
Tomalin, B., 81
Underhill, N., 62, 64, 66, 69, 76, 78, 81, 83, 85, 86, 89
Ur, P., 69
Vacca, J.L., 96, 97
Vacca, R.T., 96, 97
Valdez Pierce, L., 3, 4, 34, 46, 53, 71, 82, 126, 127, 164, 205, 206
Valencia, S., 36, 54
Valencia, S.W., 5
Vermont Department of Education, 137
Vygotsky, L.S., 183
Waller, C., 157, 158
Watson, D., 124
Watson, D.J., 124
Weinstein, C.E., 10
Wesche, M., 164
Wiggins, G., 2, 29, 62
Wilder, L.I., 119
Wilen, D.K., 4
Wilkins, D.A., 61
Wilson, E., 74
Wilson, L.D., 174
Winn-Bell Olsen, J., 83
Winograd, K., 185
Winters, L., 1, 4, 5, 7, 16, 17, 20, 21, 25, 36, 37, 38, 42, 51, 65, 76, 99, 120, 142, 195, 196
Wolf, D., 36, 38
Wolf, K.P., 132
Yager, R.E., 188
Yancey, K.B., 44
Yekovich, C.W., 10, 175, 187
Yekovich, F.R., 10, 175, 187
Yuen, S.C., 164
Yule, G., 58, 59, 60, 64, 65, 69, 76, 79, 81, 83, 85